IN HARD TIMES

IN HARD TIMES

Security in a Time of Insecurity

Edited by
Manoj Joshi
Praveen Swami
Nishtha Gautam

BLOOMSBURY
NEW DELHI • LONDON • OXFORD • NEW YORK • SYDNEY

BLOOMSBURY INDIA
Bloomsbury Publishing India Pvt. Ltd
Second Floor, LSC Building No. 4, DDA Complex, Pocket C – 6 & 7,
Vasant Kunj, New Delhi 110070

BLOOMSBURY, BLOOMSBURY INDIA and the Diana logo
are trademarks of Bloomsbury Publishing Plc

First published in India 2022
This edition published 2022

ISBN: PB: 978-93-54359-76-7; e-ISBN: 978-93-54359-82-8
2 4 6 8 10 9 7 5 3 1

Typeset in Fournier MT Std by Manipal Technologies Limited
Printed and bound in India by Thomson Press India Ltd.

FSC MIX Paper FSC® C010615

To find out more about our authors and books, visit www.bloomsbury.com and sign up for our newsletters

Dedicated to our daughters:

Saba, Manya, Tarsha and Nyasa

With love, affection and the hope that they will live in a much, much more secure and serene world.

CONTENTS

FIGURES

TABLES

INTRODUCTION

The Age of the Battle Pig

MANOJ JOSHI AND PRAVEEN SWAMI

'At the siege of Megara', so recorded the Macedonian historian Polyaenus in a masterwork authored around 161 CE, 'Antigonus brought his elephants into the attack; but the Megarians daubed some swine with pitch, set fire to it, and let them loose among the elephants. The pigs grunted and shrieked under the torture of the fire, and sprang forwards as hard as they could among the elephants, who broke their ranks in confusion and fright, and ran off in different directions.'[1]

The story of how the humble pig was used to defeat the highly trained Indian battle elephants of the King of Macedonia, Antigonus II Gonatas, has a simple lesson: in war, it's often the smarter not the stronger side that wins.

Faced with an epoch-changing pandemic, an economy that had begun slowing even before this catastrophic event and the distinct shifts in global power equations, the time has come to revisit the foundational assumptions on which Indian national security strategy has been built.

Ever since the mid-1990s, Indian thinking on national security has been influenced by the assumption that the country would progress on a growth trajectory adequate to fund the thoroughgoing modernisation of its national security capacities. This, most in India's strategic community expected, would enable some form of strategic parity with the superpower next door, China, by the middle of this century, if not earlier.[2]

The events leading up to the 2020 pandemic, though, give a reason for a radical revisiting of these assumptions.

First, defence spending has been under pressure for several years. Successive budgets have committed less than 2 per cent of GDP, the lowest levels since the war of 1962. This budgetary pressure has manifested itself not only in spending on the military but also in police forces and intelligence services. Second, rising pensions and salary commitments have left ever-less money available for modernising India's national security capabilities. Third, demands for social sector spending—education, health and public welfare—are likely to be intense for some years to come, given the devastation the pandemic has inflicted on India's social and economic fabric.

Even if defence spending rises to 3 per cent of GDP—a figure advocated by many military and civilian experts as well as members of parliament—studies conducted for this volume show little funding will be available for defence modernisation, except in the most roseate growth scenarios.

Put simply, India needs a national security strategy for hard times: a strategy that embraces the battle pig, as it were, rather than the battle elephant.

Any national security strategy must, of course, have its feet planted firmly on the ground. China can set an objective of becoming a 'fully developed, rich and powerful nation', and the US's target is that it remains the world's foremost technological and military power for the foreseeable future.

But India's strategy must also aim to remove the abject poverty that afflicts hundreds of millions of its citizens.

Shaping a Strategy

Lawrence Freedman, in his magisterial survey of strategy, said a strategy involves 'identifying objectives ... [and working out] the resources and methods for meeting such objectives'.[3] Put simply, a strategy is a point at which means and ends converge.

Freedman's pithy observation ought to serve as a compass to guide the Indian discourse on national security. Governments have, for many years, conflated strategy with aspiration. Too often, an outsize ambition has been followed by anaemic, ill-conceived or simply chaotic processes that have undermined any prospect of these ends ever being achieved.

In the new world that has begun in the wake of the pandemic, there is no more room for the dubious pleasures of spending without aiming or aiming without spending. The essays in this volume, thus, are fundamentally efforts to introduce rigour to India's national security debate.

The process of marrying means and ends, though, is not a simple one. First, the threats to India have not diminished. The growth of China has seen the asymmetry of national power between it and India rise to historically unprecedented levels. Along their borders, on the oceans and across India's near-neighbourhood, China projects an evermore muscular strength. The crisis along the Line of Actual Control, in the summer of 2020, underlined the risk that the two powers could—by misjudgment or wilfully—end up at war. India continues to face multiple threats, moreover, from Pakistan.

Inside India, fissures of religion, ethnicity, caste and class—all of which have sharpened through recent years—hold the risk of aggravating the small wars that have scarred the country since Independence.

It needs no great imagination to realise that no nation-state can be prepared to fight every conceivable kind of conflict at all times. Even the US found itself bleeding by being involved in multiple global insurgencies, regional security commitments and securing overmatch against possible adversaries.[4] The notion that India ought to be prepared to fight a simultaneous two-and-a-half-front war—against China, Pakistan and insurgents in Kashmir—was, in some key sense, an evasion of the problem of defining means and ends.

Evasion of this kind is no longer possible. Instead of preparing to fight all possible wars, India will now have to focus on the core capacities it needs to deter aggression along its borders and contain threats within. This needs a clear-eyed look at what India's most pressing threats are, the country's real capacities to address them and what is needed to most efficiently plug the gaps.

The Geography of Security

At the heart of any national security strategy, there will have to be India's geography. The stretch of land from Central Asia to the equator is often not captured by the projections used by the everyday maps in use around the world.

The salience of the US in world affairs cannot be understood without a reference to its geography, just like the power of Russia or the dilemmas of China trapped by two island chains. But geography only defines your potential; what you do with it is what matters. Geopolitics is about people: how they take their geography, maximise its advantages, minimise its difficulties and generate their hopes, aspirations and fears.

Geographies are meant to be static, but geopolitics is mobile—and among the elements that make it up are education, economics, trade, science and technology and so on. Geopolitics also help focus our attention on issues. Thus, till recently, the US described the vast region between its Pacific coast and Southeast Asia as the Asia Pacific. South Asia, in this reckoning, was an extension of the Middle East, another focus area for the US.

Now, the US has redefined the region as the Indo-Pacific, which extends by its nomenclature from the western shores of the Pacific to the western shores of India. In the Asia-Pacific, China began to loom larger and larger. By stretching the region to include India, the US has shifted geopolitical gears, which ensures that because of India, China doesn't look as large as it did earlier.

For its part though, China seeks to overcome its geographical limitations through its connectivity schemes embedded in the Belt and Road Initiative.

India, on the other hand, extends from the latitude of southern Japan down nearly to the equator. It juts out 2,000 km into the Indian Ocean, and so its geopolitical perspective has elements of the continental and the maritime.

India's continental geopolitical outlook was rudely disrupted by Partition, which cut off its connection to the Asian heartland and made it, in effect, an island (70 per cent by value and 95 per cent by volume of its trade going through the sea). In its dealings with Pakistan and Bangladesh, India is still trying to overcome that geopolitical trauma.

Any national strategy will give primacy to the neighbourhood. In India's case, it does not mean just its neighbours across its land borders but those separated by a sea as well. The count then goes well beyond South Asia to Southeast Asia, the Indian Ocean Region (IOR), East Africa, the Saudi peninsula, Iran and Afghanistan. In their human manifestation, geographies are not static but also depend on connectivity. Links between India and Dubai or Singapore have financial, economic, political and cultural repercussions, which, in turn, have geopolitical implications.

South Asia and the Indian Ocean Region

At the core of any Indian policy, there has to be a mix of geography and geopolitics. In India's case, this is also suffused by history, cultural links, trade, security, investment and economic development. India has been lucky till now because of geography—not quite in politics though. The reason for this is that while all of the South Asian states border India, none border each other. They all have, in some measure or the other, cultural connections with India, either in terms of language, history or ethnicity.

Nepal is India-locked, as is Bhutan, and their geography, specifically the Himalayan range that forms their border with Tibet, makes access to India degrees of magnitude easier than to the north. Bangladesh is almost completely surrounded by Indian territory.

Regional geography and geopolitics play both ways. If India has geographical equities, so do its neighbours.

Pakistan blocks our overland access to Eurasia. The onus is on us to find ways of dealing with it. So far, we have not done too well. Nepal juts out into the Indian heartland and is the upper riparian for many Indian rivers. Indian diplomacy with Kathmandu has tended to be heavy-handed and abrupt. Bangladesh may be surrounded by India, but its existence, whether as East Pakistan or as Bangladesh, has significantly disrupted India's ability to integrate its North Eastern Region (NER) into the country. A friendly Bangladesh is vital for our security precisely because of its location.

In the Indian Ocean, too, India has geographic advantages. Sri Lanka is less than 100 km from the shores of India and far away from everyone else. The Maldives is about equidistant from Colombo and Kochi, but again, far from everyone else. Both are important for India's maritime security given their locations. A major volume of global maritime traffic goes past Mangaluru and Kochi, and to the Maldives and around Sri Lanka and past the Nicobar Islands to the Strait of Malacca.

There is a different kind of connection with distant Mauritius; it is the people-to-people connection arising from the diaspora there. Links with Seychelles are not shaped to that extent by the diaspora but by contemporary politics. Madagascar, too, does not have a diaspora connection with India, even though India has developed important relations with it.

The Middle East

One of the major problems that South Asia suffers from is the lack of hydrocarbon sources of energy. India does have a lot of coal, but it is of inferior quality. The closest country to India with exportable oil and gas is Iran. The Persian Gulf region, primarily Iran, is also a means for India to beat the Pakistani blockade of Eurasia. The Chabahar Port project and the International North–South Transport Corridor (INSTC)) are important in the longer-term geopolitical perspective of the country.

India has age-old ties with countries of the Middle East, with connectivity built over land as well as the seas. Today, it is also airborne, with over 120 flights a day between Indian airports and those of the Gulf.

Southeast Asia

India's geographic connection with the region comes through its overland border with Myanmar as well as maritime boundaries of its Andaman and Nicobar Islands territories with Myanmar, Indonesia, Malaysia and Thailand. Given its location, proximate to key Southeast Asian countries as well as the Malacca Straits, the Andaman and Nicobar Islands have the potential of offering India a great geopolitical dividend.

Historically, Indic culture provided a connection with several countries, and even now, the Indian diaspora is significant in Malaysia and Singapore.

East Africa

Across the Indian Ocean from the peninsula, India's links with East Africa date back to antiquity. Colonialism only deepened the contact as Indians were physically shipped out as indentured labour to East Africa and South Africa. Many other Indians went to these lands as traders and entrepreneurs.

Africa is not just the continent of the world's future but India's future as well. With its vast expanse, resources and markets, it is very much a part of India's strategic neighbourhood. The key binder for Indian interests is the two-million-strong diaspora spread across the Indian Ocean islands of Seychelles, Reunion and Mauritius as well as the littoral states, such as Kenya, Tanzania and South Africa, which were part of the British Empire.

Politics and Economics

The priority for India is to be able to establish its economic and political primacy over the South Asian region as its starting point. India may be one of the world's great economies, but it has not translated this into even regional hegemony.[5] India must have the key attribute of a regional leader: the ability to shape the policies of its neighbours whether through economic enticement, cultural attraction or diplomatic and military coercion.

Pakistan has been an irritant for India. Let us be clear about one thing, there is no getting away from it. It may be a failing state, but it is unlikely to fail, leaving us with the challenge of coping with it. That is what we have been doing for the past 70 years, and not doing very well at it.

China remains a major neighbour. Its economic prowess has brought its politics to the South Asia–Indian Ocean Region where it is a direct challenge to India and Indian interests. India has the capacity to take on China on all fronts—economic, technological and cultural. But India has not been able to get its act together. As a result, there is a growing gap in what the Chinese call the 'comprehensive national power' of the two countries. This is a gap we must reduce, if not eliminate, in the coming decades.

India needs to always be aware of the sensitivities of its smaller neighbours who are, in some cases, extremely small. New Delhi needs to go out of its way to accommodate them on the economic front and remain mindful of the need to focus on overcoming the delivery deficit in its aid projects. The challenge is to convince them that their security and ours are intertwined.

Since non-engagement is not an option, India's relationships must be shaped through bilateral mechanisms as well as through regional and subregional groupings such as the South Asian Association for Regional Cooperation (SAARC), the Bay of Bengal Initiative for Multi-Sectoral Technical and Economic Cooperation (BIMSTEC) or the Bangladesh, Bhutan, India, Nepal (BBIN) Initiative. In recent years, frustrated by the Pakistani relationship, India has sought to focus on BIMSTEC and BBIN. But New Delhi should not forget that unless it can also rope in Pakistan, its goal of regional primacy, or for that matter security, will remain distant.

In the past, India has seen itself as being endowed by history and geography as the pre-eminent force in the Indian Ocean. For this reason, its policy in the 1970s was to call for all foreign navies to leave the Indian Ocean. However, given the importance of the region, especially the north-western part for its oil resources, this was not likely to occur—and it did not. Even though the Soviet Union left, the US remained strongly entrenched, and its forces have fought three wars in the region using the Indian Ocean as an important staging area. From a practical point of view, New Delhi cannot ignore the fact that in the region of its immediate interest—the Indian

Ocean—the US will remain the dominant power for the foreseeable future.

The Chinese have already developed important interests in the Indian Ocean Region. But it is highly unlikely that they will challenge India and the US in the Indian Ocean for another two decades. Their interest will be the protection of their sea lanes of communications and their economic and trading interests by systematically cultivating the states of the region and expanding their naval presence.

West Asia is arguably the most important external geography for India. The Persian Gulf region accounts for 60 per cent of Indian oil imports. The seven to eight million-strong Indian diaspora sends back $35–$40 billion per annum, one of the largest remittances that any diaspora sends home. Peace and stability in the region are of paramount concern to India because any disruption of oil or remittances, or the physical security of its diaspora, can have serious consequences for the country.

India's policy has to balance carefully, given the tangled politics of the region. So far, we haven't done too badly. India has sound ties with Israel, Saudi Arabia, Iran and the US, the four pillars of geopolitics in the region. Under Prime Minister Narendra Modi, it has been uncommonly vigorous, seeking investment from the Arab states and technology from Israel. However, in recent years, ties with Iran have stumbled on account of US pressure. This has negative implications for India's connectivity schemes and larger ties with Eurasia.

India has good relations with Mauritius, shaped in considerable measure by the political coming of age of its diaspora. New Delhi plays a role in aiding the security and stability of Indian Ocean countries like Seychelles and Madagascar as well.

In East Africa, India has significant economic relations with all four countries—Kenya, Tanzania, Mozambique and South Africa—in terms of investment of Indian private and public sector companies, such as ONGC, Tata, Bharti, Mahindra, Essar and almost all Indian pharma majors. Indian companies and groups are also involved in the oil and gas industry, automobiles, textiles, telecommunications, engineering products and medicine.

One of the lesser-known areas of Indian interest is in the floriculture and agriculture sector. Many African nations have an investment-friendly attitude towards agriculture. For example, Karuturi Global, originally a floriculture company from Bengaluru, now owns a vast land bank in Ethiopia and Kenya, where it is involved in floriculture as well as commercial farming of sugarcane, palm oil and coffee.

The Cold War era saw some stagnation in India's ties with Southeast Asia and East Africa as our attention was focused closer home. New Delhi has had ambitious plans for its relations with Southeast Asia, encapsulated in the 'Look East' and, later, 'Act East' policies. But these have not worked as well as expected. In the meantime, China has made major inroads into the South Asia–Indian Ocean Region. With the emergence of the new Indo-Pacific concept and the revitalisation of the Quadrilateral Grouping (Quad), India has another chance, this time to work with countries like the US, Singapore, Australia, Vietnam, Indonesia and Japan, to enhance its imprint in the region.

This Book's Structure

Each essay in this volume seeks to approach the problem from a different perspective. Some of the essays are granular, ranging from proposing new, more efficient, means of war-fighting and reforms in India's intelligence and counter-insurgency architecture. Others focus on the wider strategic picture, examining how India could better manage its strategic environment. The overall idea is to engender an informed public debate on the crisis that confronts India's national security in the hope that such discussion will propel policymakers to begin serious discussions on the way forward.

In the first chapter, Sanjaya Baru surveys India's strategic landscape as it emerges from the Covid-19 pandemic and argues for a medium-term reappraisal of India's strategic ambitions. Although the world is being ordered into what he describes as a 'bi-multipolar' system, with many countries orbiting either the US or China, this offers India opportunities it can use to its advantage.

Pranay Kotasthane, in the next chapter, provides granular analysis of the pressures on India's defence expenditure and the impacts these have on military modernisation—the foundation, as it were—on which the country's response to its strategic environment will rest.

The six subsequent chapters—five of them written by former military officers who have played an important role in Indian discussions on national strategy—debate how the armed forces might evolve and grow in a resource-constrained environment. Arun Prakash makes the case for looking beyond naval power alone and paying greater attention to India's overall maritime capabilities. D.S.

Hooda argues for deep human resource reforms to free up resources for modernisation. Manmohan Bahadur reflects on the doctrinal changes needed to rethink how India's airpower capabilities might best be grown in challenging times. Vivek Chadha and Kishore Kumar Khera offer alternative perspectives on the military challenge. In the final chapter on Indian military power, Nishtha Gautam makes the case for gender to be placed at the centre of Indian military debates, pointing to the advantages greater representation of women in the armed forces could bring.

In the next two chapters, Praveen Swami and a senior intelligence officer who has, because of legal constraints, chosen to write anonymously, consider how India's way of counter-insurgency and intelligence could be rethought to address the challenges. Both chapters point to deep deficits of capacity and make the case for thoroughgoing reforms.

Finally, in the afterword, Manoj Joshi sums up the debates raised in the course of this book and reviews the challenges that lie ahead.

Conclusions

There can be no such thing as absolute security. Neither can there be 'security' in the abstract. What we seek is a stable, democratic, peaceful environment in which India and the region can undertake what it desperately needs—an economic transformation that will eliminate poverty for hundreds of millions and place India in the ranks of developed economies.

There are things going for us: the shift of power eastwards, the diffusion of power arising out of technology, our demographics, etc. But some of these factors could work the other way. The diffusion of power arising out of technology also empowers the bad non-state actors like extremists. Likewise, demographics minus education and employment can become a nightmare.

To deal with them, we need an optimum combination of internal self-strengthening and purposefulness as well as a benign external environment. In both these areas, there has been erosion. Internally and externally, the polity is becoming more divisive, creating conditions for instability both at home and abroad. Many of these trends have been accelerated by the pandemic whose end state we cannot forecast even at this point.

1

India's World

SANJAYA BARU

Many epithets have been used to describe India's global status in the first two decades of the 21st century. She has been called an 'emerging power', a 'major power', a 'rising power', a 'premature power', a 'leading power' and so on.[1] The reassessment of India, a post-colonial developing economy, as a regional and global power, has taken place against the background of the end of the Cold War and India's economic performance and reintegration into the global economy after half a century of inward-oriented development. India's geopolitical rise has, however, been contingent upon her economic performance. The recent medium-term economic slowdown accentuated by the Covid-19 lockdown and the growing power differential between India and China prompt a re-evaluation of India's power aspirations and medium-term status within an altered global balance of power system.

Assessments of India's rise and power made between 1991, at the end of the Cold War, and 2015, early after Narendra Modi took charge as prime minister, based on India's improving economic performance and global economic integration, are being reassessed against renewed concerns about India's economic capability and performance, further impacted by the Covid-19 pandemic. Addressing the Asian Leadership Conference in November 2020, India's External Affairs Minister S. Jaishankar placed India among the ranks of middle powers, such as Russia, Germany, France, Japan and Australia.[2] The journey forward to a global power status requires India to become a bigger, more domestically capable, more globally competitive economy with the required human capital, technological and defence capability.

We characterise the emerging global balance of power system, deploying a variant of historian Samuel Huntington's 'uni-multipolar' formulation of the post-Cold War period, as being 'bi-multipolar'.[3] If the US, as the sole superpower in the immediate post-Cold War period, had dealt with a range of middle powers in a uni-multipolar world, today the US and China do so in a bi-multipolar system. Being a middle power, India may be able to play a 'leading' rather than a merely 'balancing' role as it did like a leader of the non-aligned nations during the Cold War.[4] However, it will have to regain its economic momentum and build better capability to be able to do so.

Foundations of India's Rise

An influential historical study that contributed to increased global awareness of India's potential as a major power was Angus Maddison's statistical inquiry into the global distribution of income and productive resources that showed how China and India accounted for close to half of world income for close to a millennium till the advent of European colonialism. India's share of world income went down from 22.6 per cent in 1700 to 3.8 per cent by 1950 (China's was down from 23.1 per cent to 5.2 per cent during the same time).[5] For several decades after India's independence, the world continued to view the country as a laggard, incapable of regaining its global economic weight. India, too, was satisfied being a leader of the developing economies and opted for non-alignment between global power blocs through the Cold War period. Her global aspirations were articulated in ideological and political terms—non-alignment, anti-imperialism, new international economic order, Concert of Democracies—and not in terms of economic power and geopolitical reach and influence. It was against the background of the end of the Cold War and the new phase in India's economic policy and performance in the early 1990s that the strategic thinker and diplomatic historian Henry Kissinger referred to India as a potential major power of the 21st Century. Writing in 1994, he said:

> The international system of the 21st century will be marked by a seeming contradiction—on the one hand, fragmentation; on the other hand, growing globalisation. On the level of the relations among states, the new order will be more like the European State system of the 18th and 19th centuries than the rigid patterns of the Cold War. It will contain at least six major powers—the US, Europe, China, Japan, Russia, and probably India—as well as a multiplicity of medium-sized and smaller countries.[6]

The 1990s were a turning point for India. After recording an annual average rate of growth of national income of 3.5 per cent between 1950 to 1980, the annual average growth rate accelerated to 5.5 per cent after 1980. Beginning with Indira Gandhi's second term (1980–1984) and through the tenures of Rajiv Gandhi, P.V. Narasimha Rao and Atal Bihari Vajpayee, the economy continued to grow, with the growth rate touching an all-time high of over 9 per cent per annum in 2005–2007, when Dr Manmohan Singh was prime minister. It was against the background of a more open economy, rising at higher rates of growth, that Kissinger wrote his futuristic assessment of world powers of the 21st century.

India's industrial economy, which was growing at less than 2 per cent per year in the first half of the 20th century, recorded a growth rate of around 6 per cent per year in the 1950s; this went up close to 7 per cent in the 1980s and 1990s after a dip in the 1960s and 1970s. The pessimism of the 1960s and 1970s was erased by the optimism of the 1990s. By the end of the 1990s, there was so much confidence in India's economic capability and potential that the country chose to conduct nuclear weapons tests in the summer of 1998 and declared itself a nuclear power. India also stepped up its campaign for permanent membership in the United Nations Security Council.

After Kissinger's 1994 essay, the next intellectual intervention by an American strategist that altered global perceptions about India was former US national security advisor and secretary of state Condoleeza Rice's 2000 essay in *Foreign Affairs,* in which she drew attention to India's potential as a major power.[7] Written in the wake of India's contribution to the global Y2K challenge and the emerging challenge of a rising China and global jihad, Rice's effort was to convince the US that India ought to be viewed as being more than just a neighbour of Pakistan. Rice's essay was followed by the publication in 2001 of a book by Brookings Institution scholar Stephen Cohen entitled *India: Emerging Power*. While Cohen was sceptical about India's capabilities and attitudes, he gave the benefit of doubt to her potential. It was in this context that I wrote a paper in 2001 on the strategic consequences of India's economic performance,[8] drawing attention to the required economic homework India had to do to be able to emerge as a regional and global power. To quote:

> It is not economic growth in itself that holds the key to India's global profile and power, its strategic role and relevance and its national security, but the nature of that growth process and the manner in which the economic challenges it faces today are addressed. By 'nature' we mean the distributional aspects of growth, the impact of growth on global competitiveness and integration with the global economy and the sectoral distribution of that growth, that is the extent of industrialisation, and its fiscal sustainability.[9]

The paper underscored the strategic importance of economic growth and industrialisation both in dealing with internal and external security threats and challenges and, more specifically, in the context of China's 'comprehensive national power' and global presence:

> The strategic consequences of the economic competition with China are, therefore, fundamental to India's future role within Asia and the global system. If India can sustain above-average growth (of over 7.0 per cent per annum in the next decade) and if China experiences a deceleration of growth, coupled with domestic political uncertainty, the widening gap between the two civilisational neighbours can be reversed to an extent. If not, China will emerge as the pre-eminent Asian power and force India into accepting its leadership in Asia. The key to this strategic rivalry will be the relative economic performance of the two countries.[10]

India's improved economic performance in the first decade of the century, with the economy growing at around 7.5 per cent per annum in the period 2000–2010 (Table 1.1), unleashed a flood of theorising on India's economic rise and its implications for Asian and global power balances. Beyond theorising, it also had institutional consequences. The Russian initiative to convert a Goldman Sachs investment concept dubbed BRIC—the four 'emerging markets' of Brazil, Russia, India and China—into a political grouping, which then became BRICS with China's invitation to South Africa, created a new plurilateral grouping of fast-growing economies. While the developed market economies (DMEs) used the opportunity provided by the transatlantic financial crisis of 2008–2009 to create a larger group—the G-20, which included the G-7 and BRICS—these two groups functioned separately with agendas of their own.

TABLE 1.1 India: Real GDP Growth Rates (Factor Cost)

Year	*Growth Rate (%)*
1999–2000	8.00
2000–2001	4.15
2001–2002	5.39
2002–2003	3.88
2003–2004	7.97
2004–2005	7.05
2005–2006	9.48
2006–2007	9.57
2007–2008	9.32
2008–2009	6.72
2009–2010	8.59
2010–2011	8.91
2011–2012	6.69
2011–2020	6.40

Source: Planning Commission/NITI Aayog, Government of India

National income growth had an important consequence on national power and standing. It improved the fiscal balances of the state and yielded increased revenues that were available both for development and defence.[11] An important policy dilemma of the 1970s and even the 1980s—defence vs development—was resolved to an extent with more revenues available for both. While there was no perceptible increase in the tax-to-GDP ratio, the growth in national income after 2000 yielded increased revenues. An important change in the structure of the economy was the increase in the share of trade in national income, which more than doubled from around 20 per cent before trade liberalisation in 1991 to over 50 per cent in the 2010s, with the share of exports to GDP also doubling from around 10 per cent in the 1990s to around 20 per cent by 2015. India's share of world merchandise trade trebled from around 0.5 per cent in 1990 to 1.7 per cent by 2018. A sustained improvement in India's economic size and its integration into the Asian growth process altered regional and global perceptions about India. India had the third-fastest rate of export growth, behind China and Vietnam, between 1995 and 2018 (at an annual rate of 13.4 per cent).[12]

Apart from these macroeconomic trends, optimistic forecasts about India's rise have also been based on assumptions about demographic dividend from a young population, assuming there would be an adequate investment in human capital formation. The optimism about India's rise, reflected in a range of economic forecasts, is well echoed in this projection of a London-based multinational bank Standard Chartered. It forecasts India's nominal GDP, using purchasing power parity exchange rates, to be $46.3 trillion in 2030, compared to $64.2 trillion for China and $31 trillion for the US (Table 1.2). By 2050, various forecasts have suggested that India would be the second-largest economy in US dollar terms as well.

TABLE 1.2 Country Ranking on Nominal GDP to 2030

Country	*PPP (trillion $)*
China	64.2
India	46.3
United States	31
Indonesia	10.1
Turkey	9.1
Brazil	8.6
Egypt	8.2
Russia	7.9
Japan	7.2
Germany	6.9

Source: *Opportunity 2030: The Standard Chartered SDG Investment Map*[13]

To be sure, these forecasts predate the Covid-19 pandemic. No one knows for sure how individual countries and their economies will emerge from this crisis, nor can we accurately predict the level of economic disruption that will eventually be caused by the post-outbreak lockdown of economic activities. What we do know is that India has been among the worst-hit economies on account of the Covid-19 pandemic and the economic lockdowns imposed to contain it. This economic slowdown is bound to impact not just the fiscal capacity of the state, an important determinant of national power, but also India's global standing as a rising power.[14]

A Slowdown and Retreat

In the financial year 2020–2021, the economy has been estimated to have contracted by -7.3 per cent, according to official statistics. This negative growth comes on top of a medium-term decline in national income growth on account of a decline in investment and savings rates. Since 2016, the rate of growth of the economy in each subsequent year has been lower than in the previous year (Table 1.3). The economic slowdown has, in turn, reduced the fiscal capacity of the state, constraining its ability to intervene through public investment and spending.

TABLE 1.3 India: National Income Growth

Year	*Growth Rate %*
2016–2017	8.0
2017–2018	6.6
2018–2019	6.0
2019–2020	3.9
2020–2021	-7.3

Source: Economic Survey (Various Years), Ministry of Finance, Government of India

Industrial growth and exports have stagnated, raising fresh concerns about the competitiveness of the industrial economy. These have induced the government to raise import duties, reassess foreign trade policy and reinvigorate the 'Make in India' policy by launching a new import-substituting economic strategy called Atmanirbhar Bharat. Trade liberalisation in the post-1991 'Rising India' phase had contributed to a reduction in the average tariff rate from 125 per cent to 13 per cent by 2014. However, since 2014, tariff rates have been increased for 3,200 of the 5,300 product categories, accounting for 70 per cent of India's imports, from the average rate of 13 per cent to 18 per cent. For some product categories, especially items imported from China, the rates have been increased by 10 to 15 percentage points.[15]

While this policy shift has been a response to the medium-term deceleration of growth, especially industrial growth, it has since been shaped by the sharp economic downturn caused by the Covid-19 pandemic and the consequent lockdowns. In the first quarter of fiscal 2020–2021 (April–June 2020), the economy shrunk by -23.9 per cent, and in the second quarter (July–Sept), the degrowth was -7.5 per cent. India experienced the severest growth decline for any major economy, with the Euro area recording degrowth of -14.8 per cent and -5.3 per cent in the two respective quarters. China, on the other hand, had positive rates of growth during the two quarters (3.2 per cent and 4.9 per cent respectively).

In response to the economic slowdown, the Narendra Modi government has been proactive in introducing a slew of economic policy reforms and initiatives aimed at increasing investment—domestic, foreign, private and public—further facilitating the ease of doing business and raising the rate of growth. After the sharp downturn of 2020, the economy is expected to regain momentum. However, several medium-term forecasts suggest that India's annual average rate of growth over the next five years is likely to remain far below the last two-decade average of 7.5 per cent.[16] Gulzar Natarajan, a serious analyst of the Indian economy, has suggested that the medium-term growth outlook for India is not very encouraging and that the economy could remain in a low-growth phase of around 4 per cent to 5 per cent per annum in the near term.[17] The global economics forecasting firm Oxford Economics has also forecasted a medium-term growth rate of 4.5 per cent (Table 1.4). A 6 per cent rate of growth over the next five years will not allow India to attain Prime Minister Modi's aim of making it a $5 trillion economy by 2024 or 2025. The medium-term slowdown will keep India within the World Bank's category of 'low-income developing countries', delaying its transition to the status of a 'middle-income country'. This would be a major setback for India's power aspirations.

TABLE 1.4 Real GDP Growth Rates, 1951–2030

Year	1951–52 to 1960–61	1961–62 to 1970–71	1971–72 to 1980–81	1981–82 to 1990–91	1991–92 to 2000–01	2001–02 to 2010–11	2011–12 to 2019–20	2020–21* to 2024–25
CAGR	4.1%	3.9%	3.1%	5.4%	5.9%	6.7%	6.4%	4.50%

Source: Economic Survey, Ministry of Finance, Government of India (Various Issues)

The government's response to this challenge has been a combination of increased protectionism and an 'industrial policy' aimed at promoting domestic industrialisation. Critics see in this policy package a return to a pre-1991 mindset, if not a regime, of import-substituting industrialisation coupled with a 'Control Raj'.[18] It is against this background that many have viewed India's decision to opt out of the Regional Comprehensive Economic Partnership (RCEP) agreement as a sign of economic and strategic weakness. The ratification of RCEP by all the Indo-Pacific economies, except India, has been a geopolitical and geoeconomic gain for China.[19]

Even though India's tariff increases and the emphasis on import substitution is specifically targeted against China, and so has been projected as a geo-economic response by India to China's geopolitical moves in Asia, the decision has nevertheless brought into question the Modi government's approach to a three-decade-old 'Look East' policy and to his own 'Act East' policy. India's RCEP decision has also been viewed as a setback to the development of the Indo-Pacific as a geopolitical and geoeconomic space.[20] India's inhibitions in participating more energetically in a deepening and widening Asian regional economic integration process draw attention to domestic weaknesses at a time when an assertive and aggressive China is able to rope in all the Indo-Pacific nations, including Japan and Australia. This brings into question the very basis of the 'Rising India' narrative.

Indeed, the optimism about India's economic growth and its emergence as a major power has always been accompanied by scepticism. In an early comment, Zorawar Daulat Singh argued in a 2007 paper that India's limited economic engagement with its immediate neighbourhood, its dependence on both imported energy and defence equipment, low share of world trade and so on, impose hard constraints on its power capabilities.[21] However, the impressive performance of the economy through the first decade of the century, when India recorded the highest annual rates of economic growth, made such scepticism seem misplaced. India's ability to initially withstand and subsequently manage the impact of the Asian and the transatlantic financial crises reinforced confidence in the 'Rising India' narrative.

India's economic slowdown since 2016, the growing power differential vis-a-vis China and global economic challenges—including the US trade policy action by the Donald Trump administration and India's inability to cope with external competition with East and Southeast Asian economies—combined to raise questions about India's standing in the ranks of rising powers. In an assessment of post-Covid global power rankings, the Lowy Institute has observed that 'Covid-19 has triggered a race to the bottom between Asian powers. 18 states in the Indo-Pacific experienced significant downward shifts in their relative power in 2020, outcompeting each other only by degrees of underperformance.'[22]

While most OECD economies are expected to contract or experience slower growth, the US and China are the two major economies likely to register positive rates of growth in 2020–2021. Other BRICS countries too will see their economies contracting (Brazil -5.8 per cent; Russia -4.2 per cent; South Africa -8.0 per cent). The upshot of this would be that the US and China will come out of the Covid-19 pandemic relatively stronger than most other major economies.

It appears that, as a consequence and at least in the medium term, India has opted to be cautious about its rise and will work with middle powers, including Russia, France, Germany, Japan and Australia, to protect its strategic interests. In his address to the Asian Leadership Conference 2020, Jaishankar said as much when he observed thus:

> If the old order erodes and a new one is yet to emerge, we are probably headed for a long transition. It will be one characterised by convergences among powers and working arrangements to give that practical shape. Middle powers are likely to have a greater role and regional solutions perhaps more space to unfold.[23]

By placing India in the ranks of middle powers, such as Russia, Japan, Germany, France, the UK and Brazil, the Modi government has taken a realistic view of the economic impact of Covid-19—and other challenges the Indian economy faces—on India's national power potential. In the foreseeable future, the global balance of power system will be characterised by two dominant powers—the US and China—and a clutch of middle powers with whom India will have to work cooperatively, taking advantage of the space for policy action provided by the rivalry between the top two.

This is an inversion of the old G-2 idea that hypothesised US-China cooperation aimed at bipolar management of the global security and economic system.[24] In the aftermath of the 2008–2009 transatlantic financial crisis, Zbigniew Brzezinski and Fred Bergsten suggested that the US and China ought to work together to take on the responsibility of addressing global challenges and providing global public goods. If the Brzezinski-Bergsten G-2 hypothesised 'cooperation', the 'New Cold War' between the US and China posits a G-2 defined more by conflict than cooperation.

The competition, if not conflict, between the two biggest powers of the West and the East, has put at risk multilateralism and the functioning of multilateral institutions. It has become incumbent upon middle powers to defend multilateralism and secure space for their growth and development. It is not surprising that even European powers are in search of 'strategic autonomy', a principle dear to India and other middle powers, such as Russia and Japan.[25]

A Bi-multipolar World

By viewing itself as a middle power, working with other middle powers and not getting drawn into a G-2 conflict or rivalry, India can widen its strategic space, preserve its strategic autonomy and address its near-term economic challenges. While the US and China focus on their larger global power struggle, it would be advisable for India to strengthen economic and strategic relations with middle-power economies, seeking market access, investment and technology flow. India's critical partners would be the European Union, Japan, Russia, South Korea, Israel and Saudi Arabia. The global balance of power system may well move in the direction of witnessing superpower conflict or cooperation, while middle powers secure their interests by working together. This is a variation on the theme of the Cold War bipolar system in which countries such as India chose not to align with the two poles. In the emerging context, India may align with the US but will also simultaneously pursue a strategy of 'multi-alignment' with middle powers, seeking to preserve its national interest if not strategic autonomy.

In a 1999 paper, Huntington suggested that the post-Cold War balance of power system was only briefly unipolar and that it had quickly evolved into a uni-multipolar system. While the US is the biggest military, economic, technological and cultural power, many other major powers have the capacity to stand up to the US. Huntington named Russia, China, Germany, France, Japan, India, Iran, Brazil, South Africa and Nigeria as the nine 'other powers' of the uni-multipolar world.[26] To quote Huntington:

> The superpower or hegemon in a unipolar system, lacking any major powers challenging it, is normally able to maintain its dominance over minor states for a long time until it is weakened by internal decay or by forces from outside the system, both of which happened to fifth-century Rome and nineteenth-century China. In a multipolar system, each state might prefer a unipolar system with itself as the single dominant power but the other major states will act to prevent that from happening, as was often the case in European politics.

The post-Cold War global system was bound to be uni-multipolar, suggested Huntington, because the group of regional major powers would come together to prevent any single nation from becoming the hegemon of a unipolar power system.

> The superpower's efforts to create a unipolar system stimulate greater effort by the major powers to move toward a multipolar one. Virtually all major regional powers are increasingly asserting themselves to promote their own distinct interests, which often conflict with those of the United States. Global politics has thus moved from the bipolar system of the Cold War through a unipolar moment—highlighted by the Gulf War—and is now passing through one or two uni-multipolar decades before it enters a truly multipolar 21st century.[27]

Between 1999, when Huntington wrote his essay, and the present, the one major change that has taken place has been the rise of China. Indeed, not just its rise but also its emergence as the second-most powerful country and economy, a trading superpower and a pre-eminent competitor to the US. China has increased its distance from Europe, Russia, Japan and India and hopes to challenge US dominance. The impact of Covid-19 has further widened this gap between China and the rest in favour of China. While the US remains the pre-eminent superpower, given its military, technological, economic, ideological and cultural power, China has emerged as a second superpower.

This suggests that the global balance of power system is no longer uni-multipolar, as Huntington claimed in 1999, but has become bi-multipolar. In the medium term, it will be a G-2–plus system in which, on the one hand, there is conflict and competition rather than cooperation between the G-2 and, on the other hand, there is space for alliance building among middle powers such that neither of the two superpowers nor the two together can dominate the global system. A bi-multipolar system offers opportunities for middle powers, but it also poses challenges, especially because it will not entail a stable equilibrium as the two big powers as well as the aspiring middle powers will constantly jostle for power.

In recent years, India has claimed that the global system is evolving into a multipolar balance of power system. Jaishankar echoed this to an audience in Washington DC: 'The world will be increasingly multipolar as distribution of power broadens and alliance discipline dilutes.'[28] While dilution of alliance discipline and the German, French and Japanese search for strategic autonomy, along with Russia and India, would create a multipolar power system, the dominant position of the US in the western hemisphere and China in the eastern hemisphere, would create what is better described as a bi-multipolar system by Huntington. Given India's priority to accelerate economic growth and ensure rapid economic development and a stable neighbourhood, the bi-multipolar balance of power offers opportunities that India can gainfully utilise.

Postscript: This essay was written in 2021, long before the Russian invasion of Ukraine and the consequent shifts in global power balances. Given the course of events till mid-2022, it is easy to predict that the medium-term impact of the war and the West's response to it could well be a consolidation of the bi-multipolar system. The United States has sought to consolidate its power by bringing all its allies closer within the framework of NATO. Russia has become more dependent on China, further enhancing China's status as a rival pole. Interestingly, a range of 'middle powers', including India, Indonesia, South Africa and perhaps Brazil (if Lula returns to power) have positioned themselves in between. With time, France, and even Germany, may opt for a more nuanced policy. Taken together, these developments may well contribute to the consolidation of the bi-multipolar balance of power system.

2

Neither Guns nor Butter: The Inconvenient Truth of India's Defence Financing

PRANAY KOTASTHANE

At the heart of all defence planning is an economic story: wealth underpins military power. Resources needed for financing defence are directly related to economic growth as China's dual rise has shown yet again. When an economy is growing steadily, this link between wealth and defence is taken for granted. During such happy times, policy debates focus on more comfortable problems such as 'What portion of the growing economy should be reserved for defence expenditure?', 'How should the growing defence kitty be allocated among the three armed forces?', 'What proportion of this defence expenditure must be allocated for acquiring new defence platforms?' and so on.

This chapter argues that such happier times are behind us and getting back on the growth path will take time and purposeful effort. A decade of lacklustre economic performance, bracketed towards the end by an unprecedented economic shock (detailed in the previous chapter), means that resources funding both defence and development are set to decline. This situation is not an ordinary financial challenge requiring incremental adjustments such as symbolic salary cuts or fewer uniforms. Nor will the routine blame games that civilian and military stakeholders frequently indulge in serve any purpose.

If this feels unnecessarily alarmist, think again. India's economy in FY 2020–2021 was smaller than it was in FY 2019–2020. Moreover, an economic contraction of this kind last happened in India nearly forty years ago in FY 1979–1980; more than half of all adult Indians have never experienced a recession. Thus, even if an economic turnaround is assumed as soon as the pandemic is contained, India's GDP in real terms would reach the pre-pandemic level only by the end of the current financial year.

Not to forget, India's economic situation was weak even before the pandemic. FY 2019–2020 marked the end of an entire decade of economic slowdown, which saw a meagre 3.1 per cent decadal growth in per capita GDP, way below the robust growth of 11.9 per cent in the 2000–2010 period.[1] Consequently, income levels of Indians over the last decade have risen far slower than those of Bangladeshis, Vietnamese and, sure enough, the Chinese.

This slowing economy, combined with a sudden economic shock, has begun to show its impact on India's defence spending. This chapter argues that even if the defence expenditure is increased to 2.5 per cent of GDP for the next 10 years, up from the current allocation of 2.1 per cent of GDP,[2] resources for defence modernisation will remain severely constrained. This is the truth that India's strategic establishment needs to confront.

Hitherto, any such discussion on resource allocation for India's armed forces usually ended in formulaic blame games. For instance, when the issue of rising defence pensions is raised, the armed forces community finds a punching bag in defence civilians. Or, when the subpar performance of India's defence public sector units is brought up, the defence production bureaucracy blames the private sector's incapability in developing and producing weapons systems.

All policy changes begin with an acknowledgement that a problem *exists* in the first place. By laying bare our current predicament, the hope is that India's strategic establishment will be forced to come together as one team to design creative solutions.

To make a case for why incremental changes are no longer an option, I begin by narrating the story of India's defence financing over the last decade in the next section. After that, I construct scenarios to visualise the economic impact of Covid-19 on India's defence expenditure profile over the next decade. In the final section, I discuss four approaches to solve this challenge.

Story of the Decade Gone By

Guns versus butter describes the unavoidable trade-off between two critical priorities of a State—defence (guns) and development (butter). The trade-off exists because a common pool of money finances both development and defence. Spending more on one implies less money for the other. Finding an optimal balance between guns and butter under resource constraints is a choice that every government needs to make. In this section, I look at what the budgetary choices made by the Union governments over the last ten years reveal about the guns versus butter question.

Defence Expenditure: How Much Is Enough?

The first five items in the Union List of the Constitution's seventh schedule relate directly to India's defence. This is because defence functions are unambiguously the most important constitutional function of the Union government. Consequently, the budgetary allocation to the Ministry of Defence (MoD) is the highest among all Union ministries.[3] For instance, in FY 2019–2020, the Union government's total expenditure accounted for 13.2 per cent of GDP of which MoD alone accounted for 2.2 per cent of GDP.[4] Moreover, MoD's spending in nominal terms has increased at a compounded annual rate of 9.2 per cent over the last decade.[5]

At first glance, this defence expenditure scene doesn't look all that bad. But under the hood, the situation is quite different. At the start of the decade, defence expenditure made up 2.8 per cent of GDP and 17.6 per cent of Union government expenditure. By FY 2021–2022, this has declined to 2.1 per cent of GDP and 14 per cent of Union government expenditure.[6] In other words, when a slowing economy forced its hand, the Union government chose butter over guns at the margin. Defence has declined in priority relative to non-defence functions.[7]

While the supply of funds declined, the demand for higher defence expenditure became louder. Citing the unavailability of funds for modernisation, the Parliamentary Standing Committee on Defence (2017–2018) noted that a defence spending of at least 3 per cent of GDP is 'considered to be optimal and necessary for ensuring the operational preparedness of the Forces'.[8]

The Ministry of Finance expressed its inability to commit to such a benchmark, citing the guns versus butter paradox in response: 'Since government resources come with a definite cost, resource allocation is made among various competing priorities. Thus, defence expenditure as a definite percentage of total government expenditure/GDP cannot be ensured considering the fact that resource allocations are made on need basis.'[9] With the economic shock of Covid-19 to recover from, increasing defence expenditure to the 3 per cent benchmark is unlikely.

Meanwhile, the other important reason for increasing India's defence expenditure comes because of changing threat perceptions. China's hostile actions along India's northern borders have underscored the point that China, and not Pakistan, should be the focus of India's defence planning for the next decade. India needs to manage a much bigger and richer adversary in the backdrop of an economic slowdown.

Defence Expenditure: What to Spend On?

Even as the debate on how much to spend on defence continues, the qualitative nature of this spending has undergone a significant change over the last decade, as illustrated in Figure 2.1, which gives the percentage-wise composition of India's defence expenditure components. The significant components are salaries, defence pensions, capital outlay, stores (maintenance expenditure) and others.

FIGURE 2.1 India's Defence Expenditure Profile over the Last Decade in Percentage Terms[10]

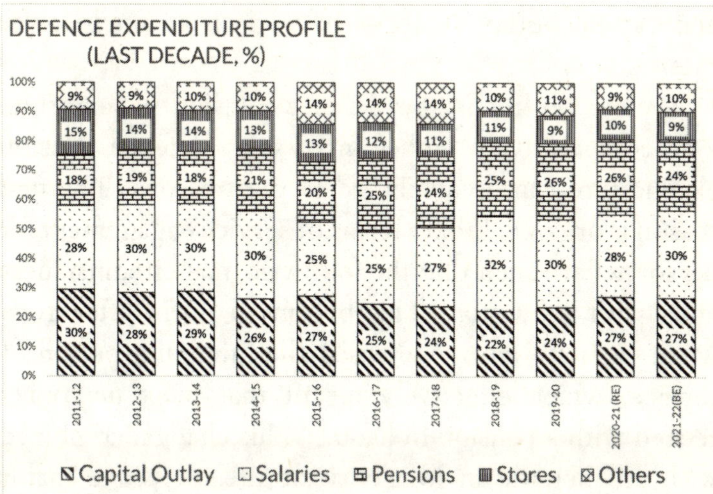

While pensions as a percentage of the overall defence budget increased from 18 per cent in 2011–2012 to 26 per cent in 2020–2021, the proportion of capital outlay dropped from 30 per cent to 27 per cent in the same period. This drop was much sharper until 2018–2019, when it hit a low of 22 per cent. Since then, the capital outlay has increased incrementally. Moreover, these capital outlay numbers are an overestimate as they include some revenue expenditure items under the Capital Budget Revenue Procedure (CBRP) since 2007–2008.[11] Quite clearly, the expenditure profile has skewed towards higher personnel costs, such as salaries and pensions. This has come at the cost of an equivalent drop in capital outlay and stores (operational and maintenance expenditure).[12]

Numerically, while the overall defence expenditure has increased at a nominal annual rate of 9.5 per cent, salaries expenditure increased by 9.3 per cent and pension expenditure by 14 per cent. On the other hand, the non-personnel costs—stores (4.8%), others (8.9%) and capital outlay (8.4%)—have risen at much lower rates.

A clear outlier is the defence pension expenditure. The comparatively higher increase in defence pension expenditure can be attributed to two reasons. The first reason is organic. India's terms of service engagement for personnel are such that the job in normal circumstances ends with a pension. This became a norm after 1976 when the new terms increased the minimum period of service, which effectively meant that most personnel retired with a pension in hand.[13] This change, combined with an increase in longevity of life, played a major role in increasing the defence pension budget from 2.28 billion rupees in 1980–1981 to 1.25 trillion rupees in 2020–2021.[14]

The second reason is the implementation of the One Rank One Pension (OROP) scheme. Since it came into effect, the pension expenditure has risen even faster than before, which is at a compound annual growth rate of 15 per cent.[15] Moreover, OROP being a defined benefit scheme that updates outgoing pension periodically based on current employee compensation, the Union government committed itself to a liability that will keep growing at even higher rates. The OROP scheme order was issued in November 2015, and it came into effect retrospectively on 1 July 2014. Since then, the Union government has disbursed nearly 100 billion rupees on account of arrears in addition to a yearly recurring expenditure of about 70 billion rupees.[16] Even so, the controversy over pensions hasn't gone away. The Supreme Court of India is examining a plea filed by the Indian ex-servicemen's movement demanding an annual revision of pension under OROP instead of the proposed five-year periodic revision.[17] If this is carried out, the defence pension expenditure will rise faster.

On the other hand, a clear casualty in the defence expenditure story over the last decade has been capital acquisition. Given the military dimension of the China challenge, modernising India's forces is of immediate importance. Strengthening India's maritime power also requires substantial capital investment. However, the rise in the pension bill seems to have crowded out the expenditure on capital acquisition and stores.[18] Such has been the decline that the budget for modernisation does not even cover the liabilities on past purchases.[19] This has been the case every year since 2016–2017, forcing the standing committee on defence (2019–2020) to observe that inadequate allocation for committed liabilities could lead to India defaulting on contractual obligations.[20] This situation has meant that there is virtually no fiscal space for new schemes of modernising the armed forces. Even the financing of existing schemes is not guaranteed.

Taken together, the dual supply-side challenge due to an economic slowdown, plus the Covid-19 economic shock and the demand-side challenge posed by China mandate major changes in India's defence planning.

Peering into the Future

How is India's defence-expenditure profile likely to look over the next decade given the dual impact of a slowing economy and an economic shock? This section attempts a tentative answer to this important question by first imagining two economic recovery paths and interplaying them with two likely defence expenditure trends.

Even making simple defence projections over the next decade is no longer easy because the economic impact of Covid-19 is still not fully known. Given this constraint, I rely on models that imagine possible recovery pathways out of the crisis. Figure 2.2 shows two such pathways for India's economic recovery over the next decade, compiled using multiple economic reports.

FIGURE 2.2 Possible Economic Pathways for India over the Next Decade[21]

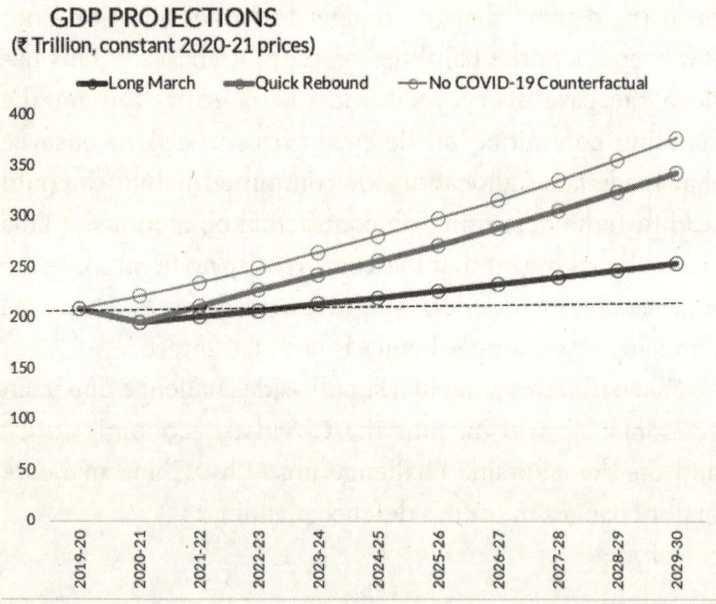

Both the pathways are realistically optimistic to varying degrees. In the first pathway, labelled 'quick rebound', the economy rebounds to FY 2019–2020 levels by FY 2022–2023. In the second pathway, labelled the 'long march', the economy recovers to FY 2019–2020 levels only by

FY 2023–2024 due to a slow annual recovery rate of 3 per cent. The 'no Covid-19 counterfactual' pathway serves as a reference to show what the economy was projected to be before the pandemic. For this analysis, the more pessimistic economic pathways have intentionally been omitted as they tend to divert the discussion towards cynicism and inaction instead of cogitation and reform.

The actual recovery is most certainly going to be quite different from these simplified projections. Nevertheless, the two pathways are useful for our purpose of defence planning.

The defence expenditure itself can be imagined following two separate trend lines. At the lower end, we have a 'chalta hai' (it's OK as it is) trend where the Union government continues to allocate 2.1 per cent of GDP to defence over the next ten years. The implicit assumption here is that the Union government does not see a need to accord a higher relative priority to defence than it currently does. At the higher end is an 'achche din' trend in which the Union government increases defence expenditure to 2.5 per cent of GDP starting FY 2022–2023, taking cognisance of the challenge posed by China's military power and the resulting need to rapidly modernise. Though the demand has been to set 3 per cent of GDP aside for defence expenditure, discussing this target seems unhelpful given the economic shock of Covid-19, which has increased the need for immediate spending on developmental heads, such as infrastructure and health, on the one hand, and decreased the taxable capacity of the economy, on the other.

Interplaying the two economic pathways with the two defence expenditure trends creates these four useful analytical scenarios.

TABLE 2.1 Analytical Scenarios at the Intersection of Defence Trends and Economic Pathways

	Long March	*Quick Rebound*
Chalta Hai (it's OK as it is)	2.1% GDP allocated to defence in a slowly recovering economy	2.1% GDP allocated to defence in a fast-recovering economy
Achche Din (good days)	Defence expenditure raised to 2.5% GDP in a slowly recovering economy	Defence expenditure raised to 2.5% of GDP in a fast-recovering economy

These scenarios give a peek into the defence expenditure profile of the future. This helps us visualise if there is any fiscal space available for capital acquisition and modernisation of the armed forces.

In order to do that, two more assumptions are needed. First, assume that all components of defence expenditure, except capital acquisition, continue to grow at their current rates. This is a reasonable assumption because expenditure on the two biggest components, pensions and salaries, are existing commitments that need to be honoured.[22] Second, the space for capital acquisition in each year is derived by subtracting all other components from the projected defence budget of that year.

Table 2.1 shows the defence expenditure profile in the two 'chalta hai' scenarios. Assuming that all other components grow at current rates, the fiscal space for capital outlay will become zero by the end of FY 2027–2028 in case of slower economic recovery. This is because of the economic contraction initially, and later, because of the higher rate of increase in defence pensions. The negative numbers indicate that even components other than capital outlay growing at their current pace become unsustainable. In practice, the Union government is likely to borrow to avoid defaulting on contractual payments for committed capital acquisition liabilities in the short term. In case of a quick economic recovery, capital outlay expenditure continues to remain in the current range of 1.2 trillion rupees per year until the end of the decade. In short, any significant modernisation can be ruled out in these two scenarios (Figure 2.3).

FIGURE 2.3 The Two 'Chalta Hai' Defence Expenditure Scenarios (Inflation Assumption: 4 Per Cent)

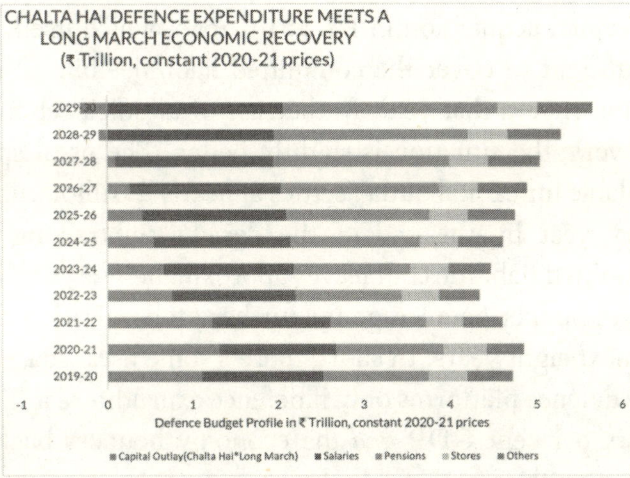

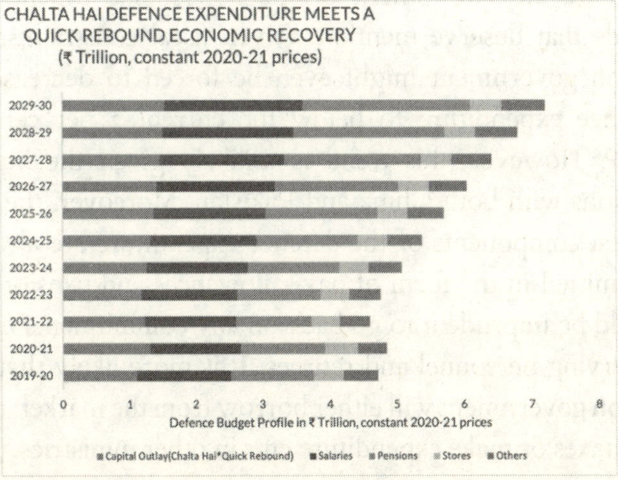

In contrast, Figure 2. 4 shows the defence expenditure profile in the two 'achche din' scenarios. If the Union government were to ramp up its defence expenditure to 2.5 per cent GDP starting next financial year, the fiscal space for modernisation opens up but only just. In case of a 'long march' recovery, the funds available for acquisition decline to an insignificant number, barely covering the existing committed liabilities for a couple of years. This is not very different from the 0.89 trillion rupees that were allocated for capital acquisition in FY 2019–2020, which itself was insufficient to cover the committed liabilities bill of 1.13 trillion rupees that year. In the case of a 'quick rebound' recovery, the situation is slightly better. The fiscal space available for capital outlay settles at nearly 2 trillion rupees every year by the end of the decade. Subtracting the committed liabilities bill leaves approximately 1.38 trillion rupees budget on average for further modernisation over the next eight years. In short, there's some fiscal space for new defence platforms only if defence expenditure is hiked to 2.5 per cent GDP *and* the economy bounces back to high growth rates.

There are two other, less likely, defence expenditure trends that deserve mention. Given fiscal constraints, the Union government might even be forced to decrease its defence expenditure to below the current 2 per cent of GDP. However, this trend is unlikely given the border tensions with both China and Pakistan. Moreover, the two largest components of the defence expenditure are already committed in the form of pay/allowances and pensions. It would be imprudent to go back on any commitments made to serving personnel and retirees. It is more likely that the Union government will either borrow from the market, raise new taxes or make expenditure cuts in other ministries.

FIGURE 2.4 The Two 'Hopes Fulfilled' Defence Expenditure Scenarios (Inflation Assumption: 4 Per Cent)

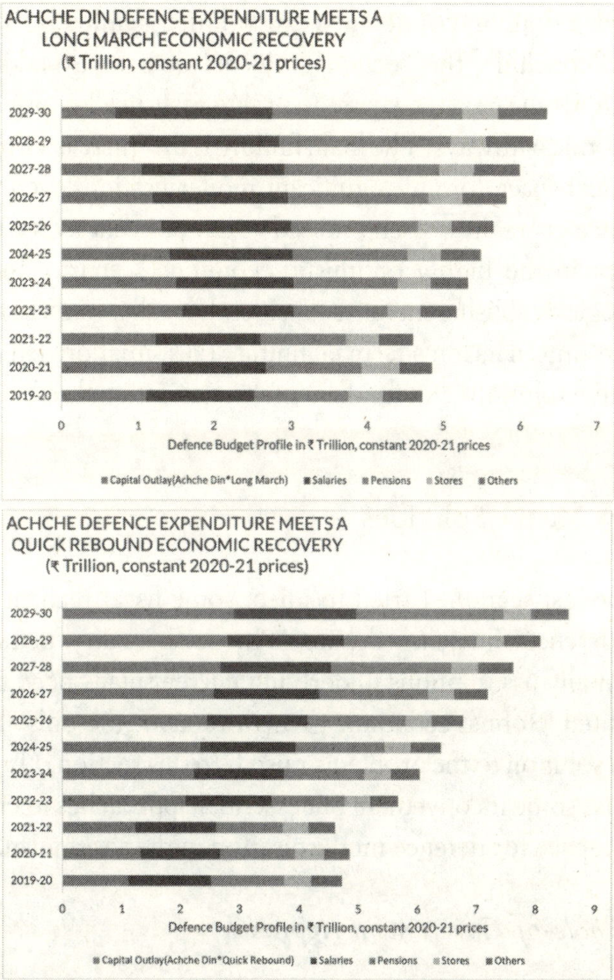

The second less-likely trend is the one proposed by the standing committee on defence in 2017, arguing that defence spending, after excluding pension and other non-services expenditure, should be at 3 per cent of GDP. This looks impractical given that this translates to nearly 4.4 per cent of GDP, including pension expenditure, which is more than double the current 2.1 per cent of GDP. With government revenues set to decline and the developmental challenges ahead, a doubling of defence expenditure is unlikely.

To conclude, this section projected defence expenditure trends for the next ten years, assuming realistically optimistic economic pathways. The main finding is that there is virtually no fiscal space for any significant modernisation, even with defence expenditure being raised to 2.5 per cent every year, except in the highly optimistic economic scenario. India's strategic establishment must consider the reality of these fiscal constraints in its long-term planning. This situation demands creative solutions and fundamental organisational reforms.

Show Me the Solutions

In the last section, I tried to inject some fiscal realism into the defence financing debate. The stark reality demands that many assumptions underlying current plans need to be revisited. Robust economic growth remains the only long-term solution to the problems raised. In this section, I briefly discuss some inconvenient but essential approaches to create fiscal space for defence modernisation in the short term.

A Whole-of-Government Approach

India's strategic establishment needs to acknowledge that the defence finance crunch cannot be solved by the MoD alone. The solution lies in a whole-of-government approach[23] where the Union government must commit to prioritising defence expenditure in line with future threat projections, even if it means borrowing from the market or reducing expenditure elsewhere. The good news is that there is enough slack in government expenditure, which, if reduced, can permit defence modernisation without affecting key developmental priorities like health, education, food and water. Here's a quick look at some of the areas where expenditure can be curtailed:

- Cut non-merit subsidies: One estimate suggests that in 2015–2016, unwarranted non-merit subsidies of the Union and all state governments combined amounted to over 5.7 per cent of GDP.[24] Nearly a fourth of this is doled out by the Union government. Even halving this subsidy bill can free up a fiscal space of nearly 0.8 per cent of GDP.
- Rationalise centrally-sponsored and central-sector schemes: Currently totalling 116, many of the Union government schemes encroach on the domain of state governments. Rationalising them will create fiscal space for defence.
- Disinvest from non-strategic firms: There are currently 249 operating Central Public Sector Enterprises (CPSEs). The Union government should divest its stake from all CPSEs except a select few of core strategic importance. It is unconscionable for the government to cut defence expenditure while injecting taxpayers' money into failing airline companies and banks.

A Non-lapsable Fund for Capital Acquisition

Multiple parliamentary standing committees on defence have repeatedly highlighted the need for a non-lapsable defence capital fund account as a budgetary mechanism for handling the multi-year capital acquisition processes. The Fifteenth Finance Commission, too, has recommended the creation of such a fund. Since capital acquisition is a complex process spanning multiple years, a non-lapsable capital account would be useful in the seamless carry-over of surplus funds from one year to the next instead of the normal budgetary procedure of handing over unutilised funds back to the Consolidated Fund of India.

Money can be drawn out of this non-lapsable fund as and when a capital acquisition deal fructifies. Crucially, such a fund can be initially seeded by the MoD itself using two revenue streams. One stream is monetising of non-essential defence land. The MoD is the biggest landholder of the Union government, a lot of which is now prime real estate in India's major urban centres. Back in 2015, we estimated that the value of army land in Bengaluru city alone was around 3 trillion rupees.[25] Selling some of this land can generate the resources to build bigger and better defence facilities away from city centres, while the surplus can be parked in the capital account fund. It would be unconscionable for the MoD to hold on to this land while compromising on defence modernisation.

The second potential source for seeding the capital acquisition fund is to divest stake in underperforming defence public sector enterprises. There are nine defence public sector undertakings and 39 ordnance factories under the MoD operating at widely varying performance levels. Privatising some of these can help populate the capital acquisition fund.

Reduce Defence Pension Expenditure over Time

Reducing defence pension expenditure is a wicked problem. The reduction in pension outgo must be made without violating the terms of employment of the entire current set of retirees and serving personnel. This can be done by applying pension reforms to future personnel without any change in the arrangements for the current beneficiaries. For example, starting in 2004, the Union government transitioned all civilian employees joining after 1 January 2004 to a new scheme called the National Pension System (NPS), a defined contribution scheme where the pension is paid out of a corpus the employee creates using their own wages. All employees and pensioners before this date continue to remain on the older defined benefit scheme in which the pension liability rests solely with the government. The budgetary savings because of the NPS reform will start showing up once the first cohort of employees who joined in 2004 start retiring.

The armed forces were left out of the NPS in the first phase. They continued to be on a defined benefit scheme that was further improved after the OROP came into effect. It is now time to create an NPS customised to the armed forces personnel and apply it to incoming personnel going ahead so that savings start accruing once they retire after 15 years of service. There are no good short-term solutions to the defence pension problem.

Execute Shifts in Operational Doctrine

A significant part of India's military might is focused on countering the threat posed by Pakistan, even though the bigger strategic challenge comes from China. Given the fiscal constraints, India's operational military doctrine needs to rebalance this military weight. This would mean breaking up the Pakistan-focused strike corps into smaller formations that can deliver punitive strikes without posturing. These smaller formations would require firepower assets like airpower, long-range missiles and artillery coupled with special forces capabilities. At the upper limit, there's a need for division- or brigade-sized formations for executing shallow thrusts.[26]

Resources freed up by breaking up of the strike corps could then be used to strengthen the capability to execute quid pro quo operations in response to China's salami-slicing on the northern borders. Such an approach would also obviate the need for a separate mountain strike corps.[27]

These then are a non-exhaustive set of solutions that can help tide over India's defence financing problems. None of them is convenient. Executing any of them will require a fundamental shift in attitude, positive leadership and lots of luck.

Conclusion

In this chapter, I presented a forward-looking analysis of India's defence financing over the next decade. The important takeaway was that even if the defence expenditure were to be increased to 2.5 per cent of GDP, there is little scope for modernising India's defence forces to face the China challenge. The gravity of the situation needs the political and defence leadership to come together as a team instead of indulging in blame games. Continuing with a zero-sum guns versus butter approach will only result in a situation where we have neither of them in sufficient measure.

Postscript: The Union cabinet approved the Agnipath Scheme for recruiting youngsters for a service term of four years. Couched as a scheme to reduce the age profile of India's armed forces, the government steered clear of the fiscal reasons behind this move. But to any observer of India's defence, it is clear that the government is trying to reduce India's pension bill over time. The purported pension savings of Agniveers recruited today would start accruing only after a decade and a half. The impact of this scheme on military effectiveness, the careers of outgoing Agniveers and the society at large need deeper reflection. To the extent that the government is considering significant reforms to reshape India's military instrument rather than find comfort in incremental budget rises, the purpose of this chapter has been served.

3

India's Neglected Maritime Domain: A Missed Opportunity

ADMIRAL ARUN PRAKASH (RETD)[1]

> It is a fact that in the transport sector, most of the funding in our country has been towards the railways, roads and highways sectors. While the importance of roads and railways in the economy is undeniable, there is also a greater need to encourage the maritime sector to enable it to achieve its full potential.
>
> —*Annual Report 2019–2020* (para 5.10), Inland Waterways Authority of India, Ministry of Ports, Shipping and Waterways

July 2021 witnessed two significant developments that should have had a positive impact on India's maritime sector. The first was the designation of Sarbananda Sonowal as a minister to head the Ministry of Ports, Shipping and Waterways. This ministry, known till November 2020 as the Ministry of Shipping, had, so far, been headed by a minister of state.

The second development was the government's decision to appoint a National Maritime Security Coordinator to be the government's principal advisor on maritime security issues. This functionary will bring a synergistic approach to addressing diverse, but critical, maritime issues currently dealt with by over a dozen ministries and departments that have a stake in the maritime domain.

These were seen as reassuring indicators that India's maritime sector, in its multiple dimensions, was about to receive the attention that is required and it has long deserved. This would have also been the redemption of a promise made in the BJP's 2014 election manifesto to 'set up the National Maritime Authority which will be equipped with the best of infrastructure, and will focus on coastal security'.[2] In February 2022, Vice Admiral Ashok Kumar was appointed to the post of National Maritime Security Coordinator.

Maritime Security and the Maritime Sector

A November 2019 news report quoted the CEO of the Indian National Shipowners Association (INSA) as saying, 'INSA has requested the Modi 2.0 government to finalise a comprehensive shipping development policy that would enable India to triple its national fleet and recapture its position as one of the leading sea powers in the world.'[3]

This sentiment highlighted the fact that the maritime sector has a critical bearing not only on a nation's economy but equally on its holistic maritime security. It echoed what US strategist Admiral Mahan said in 1890: 'The necessity of a navy springs from the existence of peaceful (merchant) shipping and disappears with it....'[4] Just as a country's merchant fleet is the raison d'etre of its 'fighting navy', a sound shipbuilding industry, too, forms the bedrock on which such a navy is built and sustained.

Thus, India's failure to bring a sharp focus on maritime capacity-building represents a huge missed opportunity in two ways. The maritime sector, apart from boosting the nation's ocean or 'blue economy', could have provided an impetus to heavy industry, spawned a complex of ancillaries, helped in skilling our youth and created job opportunities by the thousands. At the same time, it could also have established an indigenous supporting industrial base for the Indian Navy, which is currently forced to rely largely on imported weapons and systems. India's approach to the maritime sector, inextricably linked to its maritime security, has, however, lacked vision as well as coherence and consistency.

Russia's March 2014 annexation of the Crimean Peninsula, home to its Black Sea Fleet, was a declaration of its intent to uphold its maritime security interests. This enabled Russia, after its February 2022 invasion, to blockade Ukraine's Black Sea ports, threatening not only to strangulate the Ukrainian economy but also to spark a global food crisis by preventing Ukraine's agricultural exports from reaching international markets. These are ominous portents in the maritime domain that India needs to take note of.

Against this backdrop, Prime Minister Narendra Modi's latest exhortation to his countrymen to strive for an 'atmanirbhar Bharat', or self-reliant India, is certainly a step in the right direction if implemented judiciously and with earnestness. This essay suggests that nowhere will *atmanirbharta* have more relevance than in the revival of India's declining maritime sector.

The Missing 'Whole-of-Government' Approach

The term 'maritime sector' is officially described by the ministry of shipping as comprising 'ports, merchant shipping, shipbuilding, ship repairs and inland waterways'.

Many other components that are integral to the maritime sector do not find a mention here because in the organisation of the Government of India, they are farmed out to different ministries. For example, seabed exploration comes under the Ministry of Earth Sciences and Fisheries within the purview of the agriculture ministry; offshore exploration comes under the Ministry of Petroleum and Natural Gas, coastal security is looked after by the home ministry and the Indian Navy and the Indian Coast Guard come under the Ministry of Defence (MoD).

The question then arises: who will synergise endeavours in the maritime domain? Today, there is no single government agency that has either the span of responsibility or the authority to act as the focal point for India's maritime policies and interests. Nor is there an organisation that has the physical means to exercise control over the myriad activities that take place on and under the oceans. Apart from the navy and the coast guard, as many as sixteen different ministries, departments or organisations, some of which were mentioned before, are involved in ocean-related matters.

A pragmatic proposal for the constitution of a multidisciplinary maritime commission or oceanic administration to coordinate activities, conceptualise plans, fast-track projects and exercise oversight in the maritime domain has been mooted by the navy on many occasions in the past twenty years. But each time it ran into rough weather and finally foundered on the rocks of inter-ministerial rivalry and bureaucratic turf battles.

The government's latest decision to appoint a National Maritime Security Coordinator is a welcome move, but it is not clear whether this functionary will be empowered to engender a 'whole-of-government' approach towards the maritime sector.

Components of Maritime Power

The statement of the CEO of INSA comes as a surprise because 'sea power' is a phrase rarely heard in India. Even in western discourse, sea power (or maritime power, as some call it) has lacked a precise definition, and it was Soviet Admiral Sergei Gorshkov who provided an expansive view of this concept, pointing out that 'sea power emerges as one of the most important factors for accelerating the nation's technical and industrial development and consolidating the economy'. Among the components of the maritime domain that Gorshkov identified as critical for sea power are 'a strong merchant navy and efficient ports, a ship-building industry, an ocean-going fishing fleet, the ability to exploit seabed resources, and finally, the presence of a navy to safeguard the interests of the state'.[5]

In India's case, it is ironic that it took the June 2020 Sino-Indian border confrontation on the Himalayan heights to bring focus to India's maritime domain. The stark reality is that, given the huge asymmetry—economic, military and technological—between the two Asian giants and the active China–Pakistan nexus, the best that India can hope for in a land conflict is a stalemate on its northern and western fronts. All eyes are, therefore, turning to the maritime domain, where, it is believed, India may have some cards to play against China.

So, what are these cards? In the Indian Ocean, naval forces operating from the dominant Indian peninsula can pose a threat to China's shipping traffic. Vessels carrying vital cargoes of energy, raw materials and finished goods are vulnerable to interdiction as they traverse 3,000 nautical miles between the Straits of Hormuz and Malacca.

The Indo-Pacific, on the other hand, offers fertile avenues for like-minded democracies to strike accords and form maritime partnerships that can, collectively, act as a deterrent or bulwark against Chinese hegemony.

The basic assumption in both cases is that India's maritime power, either on its own or certainly in partnership with others, packs a credible punch vis-à-vis China. The validity of this notion needs to be examined.

Even as India derives considerable satisfaction from its robust and competent navy, most decision-makers have failed to realise that a 'fighting navy' is just one component of maritime power. In early September 2020, alarm bells rang all over when a US Department of Defence (DoD)[6] report declared that China has overtaken the US in the number of ships in its navy's inventory. But that was not all. The report went on to narrate that China has also created the biggest coast guard, the biggest merchant navy and the biggest fishing fleet in the world. China's shipbuilding yards are the most productive and many of the best ports in the world are China's.

Clearly, China's political leadership, heeding Admiral Gorshkov's advice, had acknowledged the salience of comprehensive maritime power and accorded it the highest priority in its grand strategic vision. In China's deliberate and calibrated rise as a maritime power, there are lessons for India, which we need to examine at the outset.

China's Dramatic Maritime Rise

While successive Communist party leaders have advocated modernisation and enhancement in the capabilities of the People's Liberations Army Navy—also known as PLA

Navy or PLAN—'for the new century', it was in 2012 that General Secretary Hu Jintao startled Western analysts by declaring to the 18th National Congress of the Chinese Communist Party that China aimed to become not just a maritime power but 'a maritime great power'.[7] It is now clear that this was a well-considered and strategic objective, driven as much by China's growing dependence on the seas for trade-led economic growth as by its ambitions for influence and territorial aggrandisement.

Surprises at this ambitious declaration arose because China's shipbuilding industry, which was being run on the socialist model till the late 1990s, was still technologically backward and had shown abysmally low productivity. Taking note of how Japan and South Korea had used shipbuilding as a means of enhancing industrial capability and energising their economies, China's leadership embarked on modernisation and corporatisation of this sector as a major step towards attaining the status of maritime great power.

Having designated shipbuilding a 'strategic industry', the Chinese government lent it strong support via tax benefits as well as loans and subsidies. All this, combined with the availability of cheap labour, helped make China the world leader in shipbuilding by 2010. Today, almost 40 per cent of the world's ocean-going merchant ships are Chinese built. China's emphasis on 'civil–military integration' in its industry has ensured that the boom in merchant shipbuilding and the availability of large shipyards with modern infrastructure and skilled manpower have directly benefitted its warship and submarine building programmes.

Tangible examples of China's shipbuilding prowess are the commissioning of its first homebuilt aircraft carrier, the Shandong, in four years flat and the 'assembly line' delivery of thirty Type 054A frigates within weeks of each other. Such demonstrations of industrial skill and dexterity are reassuring for the PLA Navy, which can expect early replacements of combat losses and quick battle-damage repairs.

While the exact number of shipyards in China is not known, studies have identified over 1,200 shipbuilding, ship-repair and ship-conversion yards under China State Shipbuilding Corporation and China Shipbuilding Industry Corporation. In 2019, these two giant corporations were merged to create the world's biggest shipbuilding entity, the China Shipbuilding Group.

By way of contrast, India's indigenous aircraft carrier was under construction for fourteen years, and a frigate/destroyer takes, on an average, seven to nine years to build. This is the backdrop against which we need to examine the state of affairs in India's maritime domain. But before that, it is useful to cast a glance at the kind of 'maritime leverage' India hopes to exert and the limitations associated with it.

India's Maritime Leverage?

Given the current Chinese intransigence and our misreading of their imperialist-expansionist intent, Sino-Indian tensions are likely to persist. Keeping tensions confined to the Himalayan arena is, therefore, not only militarily advantageous to China but a continental focus also helps to keep India contained in a 'South Asia box'. If India is to not cede ground physically or diplomatically, it must muster all elements of its 'comprehensive national power', including maritime, and create a strong negotiating position.

India's favourable maritime geography enables the peninsula to dominate both the Bay of Bengal and the Arabian Sea, with the Andaman and Nicobar Islands sitting astride the entry/exit of the Strait of Malacca. Given these advantages, there is a school of thought that since Indian Ocean sea lines of communication (SLOC) constitute China's 'jugular vein', India must threaten China to exert pressure. 'Commerce raiding' is a potent strategy, and once hostilities commence, India could declare certain areas as 'exclusion zones' subject to 'contraband control', thereby dictating or denying the flow of food, energy and trade to China.

However, while contemplating a proactive maritime strategy, it must be borne in mind that such actions not only invite retaliation but are escalatory in nature and could lead to a geographically dispersed maritime conflict. While in the Indian Ocean the Indian Navy would have the distinct advantage of nearby bases and 'interior lines', to the east of the Strait of Malacca, the situation would be favourable to the PLA Navy. In both cases, a question mark hangs over the ability of India's defence-industrial base (DIB) to provide timely material and logistic support to our naval task forces for extended periods.

Today, even as India faces two revisionist and aggressive neighbours, the weakness of its huge DIB (consisting of the Defence Research and Development Organisation, or DRDO, defence PSUs and the ordnance factories) has rendered it import-dependent and eroded the combat capability of its armed forces. In 2014, it seemed that India's comatose DIB would be jolted awake by Prime Minister Modi's inspiring exhortation to 'Make in India', but eight years later, an indifferent politico-bureaucratic system seems to have reduced it to a sterile slogan. We now have to see whether the latest *atmanirbharta* slogan will prove to be more productive.

The roots of this conundrum lie in two factors. At the political level, successive defence ministers, oblivious of the critical importance of self-sufficiency in defence production, have neglected to draw up a long-term vision or plan for the DIB. At the same time, the MoD bureaucracy, which controls the DIB, lacks comprehension of defence technology and has shown an apathetic approach. From this, it emerges that, in the current system, since electoral politics occupy most of a minister's time and attention, the management of ministerial portfolios is increasingly left to the bureaucracy. This is a widespread malaise in India's governance and needs a closer look because a similar syndrome prevails in the maritime sector too.

India's Maritime Sector: Organising Principles

At the outset, it is instructive to note the lack of comprehension that has prevailed in the minds of the bureaucracy about maritime and nautical affairs. Although tedious to recount, a brief resume of the department/ministry of shipping shows the absence of any organising principle, in the government, to guide the destiny of 'shipping' and the reason for its neglect over seven decades.

In 1957, when the Department of War Transport was renamed as Ministry of Transport and Communications, shipping was placed under its Department of Transport and Shipping. In 1966, this department was shifted to the Ministry of Transport and Aviation, and a year later, this ministry was bifurcated into the Ministry of Transport and Shipping and Ministry of Tourism and Civil Aviation. In 1985, the Ministry of Transport and Shipping became the Department of Surface Transport, and in 1986, this department was upgraded to the Ministry of Surface Transport, organised into a Department of Shipping and a Department of Road Transport and Highways.

In 2000, the Ministry of Surface Transport was bifurcated into two, namely the Ministry of Road Transport and Highways and the Ministry of Shipping. Four years later, these two ministries were again merged and renamed as Ministry of Shipping and Road Transport and Highways, with two departments under it: Department of Shipping and Department of Road Transport and Highways. A separate Ministry of Shipping was, at long last, created in 2009 but survived only till November 2020, when it was renamed, yet again, as the Ministry of Ports, Shipping and Waterways!

In the midst of this confused state of affairs, a dim consciousness has persisted in New Delhi of the unexploited potential of the maritime sector because successive governments have issued ambitious 'maritime perspective plans' that bear critical examination.

A Review of Project Sagarmala

Background

The less time a ship spends in port, the more efficient and competitive the port. Ports with shorter turnaround times are more attractive to shippers and carriers; therefore, the number of port calls tends to be higher in such ports compared with ports that have longer turnaround times. By this yardstick, China with 206,000 port calls is rated No. 1

out of the 25 top nations, while India, with 39,000 port calls, ranks No. 15. In the list of the top fifty container ports worldwide, fourteen are Chinese (including seven out of the top ten), while India has only two, at Nos. 33 and 38.

Given these discouraging indicators, the development of the port sector assumes importance and urgency for the health of India's economy. According to the Ministry of Shipping's annual report for 2019, 'The main vision of the Sagarmala Programme is to reduce logistics cost for export-import (EXIM) and domestic trade with minimal infrastructure investment.' While reduction of logistics costs will certainly benefit businesses as well as consumers, it is not clear whether it will have similarly beneficial spin-offs for port efficiency and attract more traffic.

The first version of the Sagarmala project was announced in August 2003 by the Atal Bihari Vajpayee-led National Democratic Alliance (NDA) government. The stated objective of this plan was to ensure that all major ports are connected to the then proposed grid of highways—the Golden Quadrilateral—through a network of expressways. This would facilitate a seamless flow of goods from ports to different parts of the country and vice versa.

The 2003 Sagarmala project was, however, abandoned within months, even before Cabinet clearances could be obtained, due to unforeseen events that led to the dissolution of Parliament in February 2004, which necessitated a fresh general election. It is educative to follow the subsequent trajectory of this project.

National Maritime Development Plan–2005

The United Progressive Alliance (UPA) government, which came into power in 2004, replaced Sagarmala with the National Maritime Development Plan (NMDP) in 2005. While the stated aim of NMDP–2005, much like that of Sagarmala, was to 'develop India's maritime sector', it was confined only to the modernisation of port infrastructure and enhancement of rail-road connectivity to these ports. To fulfil these goals, the NMDP included 276 projects at an investment of over 1 trillion rupees.[8]

The progress of the plan, however, remained tardy, and seven years after its commencement, Lok Sabha was informed that only 82 of the 276 (or 29 per cent) projects had been completed, while 30 had been dropped and 66 were still in the planning stage.

Maritime Agenda 2010–2020

In 2011, the UPA government abandoned the NMDP–2005 and replaced it with a new ten-year plan titled Maritime Agenda 2010–2020 (MA–2020). While Sagarmala–2003 and NMDP–2005 were focused mainly on port modernisation and enhancing rail-road connectivity, MA–2020, ostensibly, had a much broader scope. It envisaged an outlay of 5 trillion rupees to achieve quantum jumps in shipping tonnage, shipbuilding and coastal trade, apart from ports, cargo handling and other capacities.

However, a reading of the MA–2020 document serves to seriously undermine its credibility on two counts. First, it had set extremely unrealistic and overambitious targets: aiming to increase, in just seven-eight years, shipbuilding capacity by five times and enhance cargo throughput in Indian ports by four times. Second, it showed clear signs of confusion in the ministry. Whereas the minister of shipping said, in the foreword to the document, that the 'agenda' was a perspective plan that 'will form a roadmap to guide this ministry', the secretary to the shipping ministry, in the preface, cautioned that the MA–2020 'does not reflect the position of the GoI ... it is more an agenda for consideration, rather than agenda for action'. Predictably, therefore, MA–2020 failed to achieve anything of substance before it was overtaken by the next plan.

Sagarmala–2015

The NDA government that came to power in 2014 followed the earlier practice and, having terminated MA–2020, revived the Sagarmala project. Like all its predecessors, Sagarmala–2015 also focuses on modernising ports and enhancing connectivity in the country to transform the maritime sector.[9] The four pillars of 'port-led development' envisaged by Sagarmala–2015 are port modernisation, port connectivity, port-led industrialisation and coastal community development. By enhancing connectivity and strengthening port capacities, the government hopes that Sagarmala–2015 will boost trade by facilitating the smooth flow of cargo from manufacturing centres to ports and vice versa.

This version of Sagarmala held out much hope because it had a structured, progress monitoring framework. However, data from the ministry of shipping's Sagarmala Project Tracker, updated till September 2019, shows a project completion rate no better than past trends. Out of a total of 574 listed projects, only 125, or 22 per cent, have been completed since the Cabinet approval in 2015. Similarly, while the plan aimed to create four million direct jobs and six million indirect jobs, the government admitted in 2019 that only 10,000 jobs had been created.[10]

Four Different Plans—Same Problems

The stop-start process of abandoning projects and starting them afresh has not only caused disruptions but also prevented a long-term, coherent vision from emerging. While experts have been retained from the commercial world to draw up the plans, the validity and feasibility of these plans/agendas have, apparently, not been subjected to verification by professionals. Consequently, projects with unrealistic and overambitious targets, left to the bureaucracy to implement, have largely fallen flat.

Shipbuilding

While the basic driver of shipbuilding is global seaborne trade, it is a strategic industry that an emerging power like India has been gravely remiss in not nurturing. Apart from constituting the foundation and support of a nation's naval power, the shipbuilding industry generates huge secondary and tertiary benefits in terms of ancillary industries, skilled manpower and employment creation, which have the potential to transform India's economy.

Of all the Indian-flagged merchant vessels, just over 10 per cent have been built in Indian shipyards because of higher costs, lengthy delivery periods and, sometimes, due to indifferent quality. Countries like China, South Korea, Japan and even Vietnam and the Philippines, have marshalled their strengths to create a shipbuilding industry that produces quality ships at competitive prices. While these nations have monopolised the world's shipbuilding market, it is a measure of India's myopic vision that we have failed to capitalise on our many natural advantages and create dynamic shipbuilding and ship-repair industry.

Unlike port development and connectivity, which have formed the essential focus of programmes like Sagarmala–2003, NMDP–2005 and Sagarmala–2015, shipbuilding, despite its enormous potential, has not attracted the attention it deserves. An overview of this industry will help us comprehend its problems.

Overview of India's Shipbuilding Industry

Despite an ancient tradition of shipbuilding, which saw a brief revival post-Independence, today, this industry is debt-ridden and heavily reliant on government contracts and accounts for a negligible share of global shipbuilding capacity. Some statistics will provide an idea of the dismal state of affairs. In 2019, India ranked 16th among ship-owning nations, with 1,019 merchant ships, of which only 10 per cent had been built in domestic shipyards. While China accounts for 40 per cent of the world's shipbuilding capacity, Japan and South Korea account for 25 per cent each. Production of Indian shipyards accounts for only 0.045 per cent of global shipbuilding capacity.[11]

According to the 2019–2020 annual report of the shipping ministry, India has twenty-eight shipyards. Of these, six are in the public sector—two are owned by the shipping ministry and four by the defence ministry—two by state governments and the remaining twenty are in the private sector.[12] Not counted among these is a government-owned shipyard that builds nuclear submarines in partnership with the privately-owned Larsen and Toubro Shipbuilding.

Statistics show that an overwhelming majority of government orders (nearly 90 per cent), consisting of warships and submarines for the Indian Navy and patrol vessels for the Indian Coast Guard, are placed with the public sector shipyards. This clear monopoly over government contracts has ensured the well-being of public sector shipyards at the cost of the private ones.

The factors that have perpetuated this uneven playing field are symptomatic of a deeper malaise that afflicts India's shipbuilding industry. Understanding the hindrances that inhibit private shipbuilding, along with the current state of private shipbuilders, is essential to implementing reforms.

State of India's Private Shipyards

A snapshot of India's private shipbuilding sector speaks of the many woes afflicting it. Most shipbuilders are debt-ridden or function at break-even levels with hardly any of them generating profits. The three most recent and prominent casualties have been Western India Shipyard, Bharati Defence and Infrastructure (formerly Bharati Shipyard) and ABG Shipyard, which have either declared bankruptcy or been ordered to liquidate themselves by the National Company Law Tribunal (NCLT).[13] India's biggest dry dock, capable of accommodating an aircraft carrier, was purchased by Reliance Naval and Engineering Limited (RNEL) in 2015. Within five years, the shipyard went bankrupt and is up for sale with a debt of 90 billion rupees.

The only private enterprise in a reasonably healthy state is Larsen and Toubro Shipbuilding, with yards at Hazira and Kattupalli. Awarded a contract to build seven offshore patrol vessels (OPV) for the Indian Coast Guard in 2015, this shipyard reportedly completed the order faster and at a lower cost than a public sector yard, which was also given orders for a similar OPV.

Some of the reasons for this bleak picture in the private sector are listed here.

- Private shipyards lack an even playing field when pitted against public sector yards as governments openly give preference to the latter.
- Public sector shipyards can claim more experience in warship building, which gives them an advantage over private yards that may be more efficient but lack experience/expertise in weapon systems. At the same time, assurance of orders from the navy and coast guard has led to complacency on the part of public sector shipyards and fostered inefficiency as well as time and cost overruns.
- The absence of government initiatives to provide assistance or support in the form of financial tools, subsidies, tax benefits, loans at low-interest rates and capital funds has severely hampered the private shipbuilding industry and made it uncompetitive not only in the international market but also domestically. Shipping companies, therefore, prefer to buy merchant ships from China, Japan or South Korea rather than at home.
- Since the private shipbuilding sector has failed to take off in a meaningful way, no ecosystem of ancillary industries, critical to shipbuilding, has ever taken root. This has imposed a further handicap on private shipyards.

Reforming Shipbuilding in India

Asian nations such as China, South Korea and Japan have demonstrated a great deal of enterprise, initiative and innovation to attain the enviable position as the world's leading shipbuilders. While India can draw many useful lessons from the journey of these countries, it may not be possible, for cultural and political reasons, to emulate them in every way. India must, therefore, draw up its own roadmap of changes and reforms required to pull its shipbuilding industry out of its current state of depression.

A Few Recommendations

- A major policy decision must be taken to nominate shipbuilding as a 'strategic industry'. This is vital for the nation's security as well as industrialisation, skilling of youth and job creation. It deserves to be revived, nurtured and encouraged.
- A strategy and vision for shipbuilding must be created at the national level along with a roadmap and phased implementation plan.
- A level playing field must be created between the private and public sector shipyards. The MoD practice of 'nominating' selected yards must be replaced by open tendering of all defence contracts. Progressive privatisation of some government shipyards must be considered.
- The financial impediments holding back the private shipbuilding industry must be addressed in all seriousness. Given the massive investments required in shipbuilding, private shipyards must have easy access to capital, be provided tax benefits, given subsidies and afforded loans at lower interest rates. FDI must be sought in the industry.
- Consideration needs to be given to setting up a 'shipbuilding fund' for providing shipyards with working capital.

- The government, through policy intervention and fiscal measures, must incentivise the creation of ancillary industries to support shipbuilding in the private and public sectors.
- Access to state-of-the-art shipbuilding technology for shipyards along with the development of institutions are vital; implementing policies that boost research and development in the industry ought to be encouraged.

The Shipping Industry

A Strategic Asset

Our merchant fleet plays an important role in the Indian economy with around 95 per cent of India's trade by volume and 70 per cent in terms of value being transported by sea. With a share of only 1.2 per cent, India ranks No. 17 in world shipping while China, with 10 per cent of world shipping, ranks No. 3. While India's overseas seaborne trade has been growing exponentially over the years, there is a sharp decline in the share of Indian ships in the carriage of the country's overseas trade from about 40 per cent in the late 1980s to 7.9 per cent in 2018–2019.[14]

It is not often realised that a nation's merchant fleet is a strategic asset and vessels like oil tankers, natural gas carriers and roll-on/roll-off (ro-ro) ships could be almost as important as warships in the nation's security matrix. During a war, it will be an adversary's objective to deprive the opponent's industry of vital raw materials and fuel and to starve her civilian population by the imposition of a 'trade blockade' or 'exclusion zone'. Such measure would send marine insurance rates skyrocketing and deter foreign-flagged vessels from approaching blockaded ports. Ideally, therefore, the country should own and control as much of its shipping as possible so that it can ensure the adequate and regular receipt of vital supplies during times of crisis.

In this context, a good example is provided by India's twenty-three oil refineries, which need a daily input of 3.1 million barrels of crude. This demand requires that at least two VLCCs (very large crude carriers) must discharge crude at the Vadinar terminal in Gujarat every single day of the year. Any interruption in shipping traffic will have a negative impact on the refineries and supply chain within days.

Impediments to Growth

India's national merchant fleet has shown feeble growth for some years, and as per the Economic Survey 2018–2019, it has a strength of 1,405 vessels, totalling 19.2 million deadweight tonnes (DWT). This fleet carries less than 10 per cent of India's EXIM trade and around 60 per cent of domestic cargo in FY 2018–2019. It is not only woefully inadequate for India's needs but also lacks container ships as well as product and specialised carriers.

According to a study by an INSA official,[15] at a conservative estimate, India's freight bill is approximately $63 billion, a huge proportion of which goes into foreign coffers because India does not own adequate shipping. This situation can be reversed by simply bringing all these EXIM cargoes onto ships owned by Indian companies. INSA estimates that with an expenditure of just $5.2 billion (or 10 per cent of freight charges being paid to foreign shippers) every year, India can acquire shipping that will add 10 per cent cargo carrying capacity annually.

However, since the Indian government has no policy for the promotion of shipping, we continue to pay and support merchant fleets of other nations to carry our cargo. The question that begs an answer, then, is: why can we not expand our shipping fleet?

The answer seems to lie in the stark fact that it is the government's perverse policies and tax structures that discriminate against India's own shipping and make it cheaper to acquire the services of a foreign shipping company. The higher rates of Indian shipping companies are not due to their higher 'operating costs' (most Indian companies can operate their ships quite efficiently) but because they suffer double jeopardy. They have to pay taxes for services that foreign ships do not and also pay higher costs of capital and debt as compared to foreign competition. This is what makes our shipping non-competitive in the fiercely competitive international freight market.

Universally, consumers are encouraged to purchase and use goods or services that are available locally, and sufficient disincentives, in terms of duties, are imposed on imported goods and services to make them relatively costlier. Curiously, this policy does not seem to apply to shipping, and Indian companies (both public and private) are allowed to employ foreign shipping without paying any tariff. At the same time, import of all inputs by an Indian shipping company, including the ship itself and stores, spares, fuel, etc., as well as services that are needed to provide an Indian flag shipping service are heavily taxed. In terms of output, foreign shipping companies are exempt from tax when carrying goods between two Indian ports.

All these discriminatory policies effectively incentivise the import of shipping services rather than promoting, facilitating and encouraging the use of Indian shipping services. This works to the detriment of India's national interest, diverting cargo away from Indian companies that pay taxes in India, employ only Indian seafarers, train Indian cadets and contribute to the Indian economy.

'A strong and diverse indigenous shipping fleet will not only lead to foreign exchange savings ... but would also reduce excessive dependence on foreign shipping,' said a Press Information Bureau release of 14 July 2021,[16] announcing a subsidy scheme for Indian shipping companies bidding for carriage of government cargo. While the actual benefits of this 16 billion rupees subsidy spread over five years are unclear, it could be a sign that the neglect of this vital component of India's maritime sector is being acknowledged.

Some Remedial Measures

In 2019, almost 90 per cent of EXIM and 40 per cent of coastal trade were carried by foreign ships, who took home the freight fees tax-free. This represents not only a colossal haemorrhaging of national wealth (about $50 billion) but also a strategic vulnerability. Declaration of a 'trade blockade' by an adversary would frighten away foreign flag shipping and bring our economy to its knees in a few days.

In the interests of national security, India must acquire a national fleet large enough to carry at least 50 per cent of its EXIM cargo and energy. In 2020, the average age of the Indian merchant fleet was over 20 years and many ships need replacement. Moreover, we lack many types of specialised vessels for carrying volatile fluid and gaseous products.

The government has made sporadic attempts to encourage the growth of Indian shipping and even offered occasional policy incentives. But these efforts have been rendered infructuous because the basic input cost structure of the shipping industry is not structured to help its growth. The government needs to initiate a focused endeavour with the triple aim of making Indian shipping competitive vis-a-vis domestic road and railway traffic as well as foreign competition in the coastal and EXIM trade. To this end, INSA has recommended some ambitious targets in the next five to ten years:

- Increase in the current 7 per cent share of coastal shipping in the domestic modal mix to 15 per cent by 2025
- Growth of EXIM trade carried by Indian ships from 8 per cent to 16 per cent
- Growth of India's merchant fleet from 1 per cent to 2 per cent of world shipping

In order to attain these targets, there is a need for speedy redressal/change of policies and rules that so obviously discriminate against Indian shipping companies in a broad range of areas ranging from manning norms and cost of fuel to the imposition of GST as well as personal and other taxes. A prime example of this irrational discrimination is a 2018 regulation that permits foreign flag vessels to transport EXIM containers of certain commodities between two or more Indian ports without obtaining a license from the director-general of shipping. This is detrimental to the interests of Indian shipping, with no tangible benefit to the Indian economy.

The government needs to assemble a group of experts to draw up a time-bound plan of 'affirmative action' to provide impetus to the national shipping industry.

Among numerous other steps, the following need early consideration:

- The Indian shipping industry is directly exposed to global competition and it is, therefore, necessary that the costs imposed on this sector match those of international competition. The industry needs long-term funds at competitive rates as are available to global players.
- Currently, there is a great difficulty in obtaining funds from Indian banks. Banks that do participate in the funding of shipping assets provide money at very high costs and shorter periods as compared to sources available to foreign companies.
- The constitution of a 'Maritime Development Fund' to provide funding for India's maritime sector at internationally competitive rates.

As an alternative to the aforementioned, a competitive subvention scheme of interest costs must be considered, which will help the Indian mercantile marine fleet grow by replacing ageing ships with bigger, better and newer hulls in a timely manner.

The Fishing Industry

Soviet Admiral Gorshkov points out in his 1979 book thus:

> The fishing fleet is a constituent part of the civil fleet and an important component of the sea power of the state. The role of this fleet has grown sharply, as a result of the mastery, by mankind, of the World Ocean and ... its most important task consists in ensuring a solution of the acute food problem facing mankind.[17]

He adds, 'In the two world wars, fishing vessels were widely used as part of the navy for auxiliary and combat tasks such as port defence and minesweeping.'

It would seem that China's leadership has taken serious note of Gorshkov's commentary. Over the past two decades, the ocean economy, or 'blue economy', has been assuming growing importance in China's planning. Since the dwindling availability of farmland has forced China to become a net importer of foodgrain, it has mobilised the fishing industry to meet the increasing demands for protein in the Chinese diet.

Consequently, China is today a fishery superpower. It has the largest deep-water fishing (DWF) fleet in the world. In 2016, China captured around 20 per cent of the global total and consumed 38 per cent of total global fish production. A relative latecomer to deep-water fishing, China began overseas fishing in 1985 and now fishes freely in the exclusive economic zones (EEZs) of other countries. China's push to expand its DWF fleet has been supported by tax exemptions and subsidies for ship construction. Fuel subsidies have been a particularly important component of this boom, given the long trips from ports in China to distant fishing waters.

Interestingly, China uses a proportion of its fishing fleet as a 'maritime militia'. Indistinguishable from other boats, and normally engaged in commercial fishing, the militia receive military training and are occasionally called on to assist the PLA Navy or Chinese Coast Guard in their tasks.

In India, too, fisheries are an important source of food, nutrition, employment and foreign exchange earnings. The sector provides livelihood to about fifteen million fishers and fish farmers at the primary level and almost twice the number along the value chain. Fish being an affordable and rich source of animal protein is one of the healthiest options to mitigate hunger and malnutrition in India.

Since Independence, India's marine fishery sector has been dominated by the 'artisanal sector'—poor, small-scale fishers who use non-mechanised craft. Although their livelihood depends exclusively on the sea, the artisanal sector delivers only 2 per cent of the marine fish product while 98 per cent comes from the mechanised and motorised sectors. Commencing as a purely traditional activity, India's fisheries have now transformed into a commercial enterprise. The sector has been showing steady growth and has been one of the major contributors to foreign exchange earnings, with India being one of the leading seafood exporting nations in the world.

However, since India has not invested in a DWF fleet, our trawlers do not venture too far out and most of the fishing is undertaken in coastal waters. A consequent problem in the restricted fishing grounds adjoining Sri Lanka and Pakistan is that of trawlers drifting (inadvertently or deliberately) into foreign waters. This often leads to apprehension by navies/coast guards and prolonged imprisonment of fishers, causing much distress. Moreover, the rich fishery resources in India's EEZs remain underexploited and a lot of catch from our fishing grounds is taken away by trawlers of Southeast Asian nations.

As in other sectors of the maritime domain, India needs to evolve a long-term vision for its fishing industry with a focus on a few main areas:

- Mechanisation and modernisation of fishing vessels by providing communication links and electronic fish-detection devices. Artisanal fishers will need financial assistance for this.

- Developing a deep-water fishing fleet, which will call for bigger trawlers with longer endurance and refrigeration facilities on board. A DWF fleet will have to be built around the 'mother ship' concept, wherein a large vessel would accompany the fleet to provide fuel, medical and processing facilities.
- Development of modern fishing harbours with adequate berthing and post-harvest facilities, including cold storage, preservation and packaging of fish.
- Currently, only 23 per cent of India's fish catch is processed and the rest is marketed fresh. Most of the exports are at a low level of value addition—in frozen and chilled form—without going for higher-order 'ready to eat' or 'ready to cook' fish products.

In September 2020, the Indian government announced the launch of Pradhan Mantri Matsya Sampada Yojana, a flagship scheme for sustainable development of the fishery sector with an estimated investment of 200.5 billion rupees for its implementation during five years as a part of the Atmanirbhar Bharat campaign. Designed to address critical gaps in fish production and productivity, quality, technology and post-harvest infrastructure, it may address some of the existing lacunae if implemented in earnest.

Seabed Exploration

The last issue that needs focus and attention is that of seabed exploration. Based on its substantial investments and extensive exploration work, India, along with France, Japan and the then USSR, was accorded the status of 'pioneer investor' in deep seabed exploration by the UN Convention on the Law of the Sea (UNCLOS) in 1987.

India was allotted an area of 150,000 square kilometres in the Central Indian Ocean Basin by the UN International Seabed Authority (ISA) for exploration and mining. The contract was for fifteen years, but since advanced technologies required for this challenging project were not in sight, India's area was reduced by half and an extension was granted up to 2022. Awaiting discovery and commercial exploitation on the seabed are:

- Polymetallic nodules (PMNs) are found in abundance in the ocean depths. Besides manganese and iron, they contain nickel, copper, cobalt, lead, etc., which are of economic and strategic importance.
- PMNs are also believed to contain rare earth elements (REE) and metals, which are essential for the manufacture of items, such as computer memory, rechargeable batteries, cell phones, catalytic converters and permanent magnets, etc.
- At shallower depths are gas hydrates, a crystalline form of methane and water that exist in seabed sediments of outer continental shelves. They are envisaged as a viable major energy resource for the future.

There are estimated to be 380 million tonnes of PMNs in the retained Indian allotment, but the development of deep subsea technology for mining these resources involves two major challenges. One is the development of a remotely operated vehicle (ROV), which can dive to depths of 6,000 to 10,000 metres and retrieve seabed samples for analysis. Should the exploration render positive results, technological solutions have to be found for extracting the seabed resources in commercial quantities for refining.

The task of developing these technologies has been assigned to the National Institute of Ocean Technology (NIOT)[18] under the Ministry of Earth Sciences (MoES). Earlier, the ministry had initiated the development of a deep-water ROV by NIOT in collaboration with a Russian design bureau. However, it is understood that in 2019 this task was assigned to the space agency ISRO[19] and an ROV design is awaiting validation in Germany. NIOT is also said to be working on a mining concept where a crawler-based mining machine collects, crushes and pumps nodules to a mother ship. Here again, as a measure of self-assessment, it is useful to cast a glance at our neighbour China and note their progress in seabed exploration.

China, as the world's largest manufacturer of electronics, solar panels and wind turbines, has a huge demand for metals essential to these products, such as copper, nickel, manganese and cobalt, as well as for rare earth, which it already produces. But with land reserves of key minerals dwindling, extraction is becoming harder and more expensive. China has, therefore, shown a keen interest in the investigation of seabed resources since the 1980s and has had forty years of reliable funding and outcomes since then due to government support via its 12th and 13th Five Year Plans.[20]

In 2001, the ISA granted exclusive deep seabed exploration rights for PMN in a zone off the northwest Pacific to the China Ocean Mineral Resource Research and Development Association (COMRA), affiliated with the State Oceanic Administration. In 2011, China was also authorised by the ISA to undertake exploration in the southwest Indian Ocean. In 2012, it was reported that COMRA had extracted a 1.2-tonne sample from the seabed of the South Pacific from a depth of 3,000 metres.

As reported by *Global Times*, in July 2020, China's unmanned submersible Haidou-1 created a world record by diving to a depth of 10,907 metres in the Mariana Trench of the Pacific Ocean.

Of the thirty contracts signed by the ISA with nations and corporates, China holds five (the maximum), covering an area of more than 240,000 square kilometres wherein the country has extensive exploration and mining rights. According to the head of ISA,[21] China is likely to become the first country in the world to start mining seabed minerals if the international rules relating to permits and royalty for exploitation are approved next year.

Conclusion and Recommendations

In conclusion, it bears a final reiteration that India's neglect of its maritime domain not only represents an economic missed opportunity but also creates potential security vulnerabilities. The absence of a long-term vision and a coherent policy framework for the maritime domain is attributable to myopia that a five-year election cycle seems to inflict on our political fraternity.

The foregoing text contains repeated references to China for several reasons. First, China offers a close analogue to India since it is a contemporaneous nation state and a fellow Asian 'developing' nation. Second, a visionary outlook, resolute decision-making and tenacious plan implementation, the keys to China's success, offer a worthy example for Indian politicians to study and emulate. Finally, it is now clear that China is determined to be India's rival-cum-adversary in every field from geopolitics and economics to the military and maritime domain. It is, therefore, prudent for India to keep a watchful eye on China's progress in every sphere.

There is a need to remind ourselves that election manifestoes and political promises or slogans are used mostly to leverage votes and therefore cannot be trusted to deliver change. In this specific instance, there is a need for the formulation of an overarching vision document or 'national strategy' that envisages maritime security as the advancement and protection of India's national interests through the active management of risks and opportunities in the maritime domain.

This 'national strategy for maritime security' must place the maritime domain in context and explain the objectives we wish to achieve for each sector, which will allow us to strengthen and extend the nation's prosperity and security. The governance structure, which will enable change and effective implementation of the reform, should include:

- a ministry of maritime affairs with departments for each sector.
- a national oceanic administration with cross-government representation, which will aim to safeguard and promote India's interests and prosperity by mitigating national security threats and exploiting opportunities throughout the maritime domain.

Since the implementation of the national strategy for maritime security will be spread across a period of twenty to twenty-five years, a provision will have to be made that it survives elections and regime changes. It may, therefore, be necessary to have it approved by Parliament as a resolution or bill.

4

Army Capability Development

LIEUTENANT GENERAL D.S. HOODA(RETD)

India's western and northern land frontiers have always presented a significant security challenge but the Indian Army has remained confident about dealing with these borders. It was felt that the threat from Pakistan could be kept under check through limited use of force combined with military coercion. Escalation could be controlled because Pakistan would be hesitant to initiate a major conflict due to the conventional superiority enjoyed by the Indian military.

Along the northern borders, there was an uneasy peace, but also an impression that differences with China could be handled primarily through diplomatic and political steps. The situation was unlikely to escalate to an armed conflict. The standing army remained large mainly due to its involvement in internal security duties and the requirement of manning the vast length of unsettled borders.

With a reducing budget (as a percentage of GDP) and rising numbers due to additional manpower raisings in the last decade, the army's revenue budget has ballooned and its modernisation has suffered. There is a realisation in the army that pay and pensions are making a significant dent in the budget, but efforts to reduce manpower have primarily focused on logistic services. These efforts have yielded only limited results. However, as long as there was no spectre of a major war, it was felt that the army was adequately prepared for border management and localised conflicts.

The recent Chinese assertiveness along the Line of Actual Control (LAC) has been a rude shock. Even if the current crisis is resolved peacefully, deep suspicions will remain. There is a strong likelihood that the LAC will now see the permanent deployment of additional infantry, armour and artillery units backed by logistic elements. This has already started with the operational responsibility of 1 Corps being shifted from the western to the northern border.[1] In addition, a Rashtriya Rifles Force (equivalent to a division) has been inducted into eastern Ladakh[2] and the 14 Infantry Division based in Dehradun is being converted into a mountain division for deployment along the Chinese border in Uttarakhand.[3] The cost of maintaining these additional forces in high-altitude areas will put further strain on the revenue expenditure.

There is almost unanimous agreement that India needs to enhance its military capability. Delivering the second Manohar Parrikar Memorial Lecture in December 2020, Foreign Minister S. Jaishankar said, 'There are the daily security challenges of long borders and large sea spaces. The thinking and planning of a polity that operates in such an uncertain environment naturally should give primacy to hard security.'[4]

The real dilemma facing the army is that the size of the budget imposes limitations on the acquisition of hard power.

Approach to the Chapter

This chapter is focused on how the Indian Army should approach its capability development in light of the reality that the country's financial state will not permit any significant increase in the defence budget in the near future.

I am also starting with the premise that in looking at future capability building, the major challenge to be addressed is the current size of the Indian Army.

There could be an argument that the army's commitments require it to maintain a large force. Some experts have called for increasing the army's strength by completing the raising of the mountain strike corps that was stalled due to lack of funds.[5] However, unless we tackle the extremely high revenue component of the budget, capability development will suffer.

This chapter will assess the current threat perceptions that have shaped the army's force structure. It will explore the viability of a manning model in the army that is based partially on a reservist component. Some other recommendations on integration within the three services, a rethink of operational responsibilities and technology adoption will also be made. The chapter will finally suggest a capability development plan for the Indian Army.

The Land Threat

The Indian Army has significant continental challenges. India has a 4,056 kilometres long-contested border with China that has defied any settlement since independence. A series of border agreements since 1993 kept an uneasy calm between the two armies, but that calm has now been shattered. The Chinese intrusions in May 2020 led to a series of clashes along the LAC and the first deaths of soldiers in military action since 1975.[6] More than two years later, the deadlock at the LAC continues, with no immediate resolution in sight.

The Himalayan watershed that marks most of the length of the India–China border is a formidable defence barrier.

However, impressive infrastructure development by China in Tibet up to the LAC now enables the People's Liberation Army (PLA) to rapidly mobilise and launch forces across the border. On the Indian side, the development of roads has been tardy. Despite the inadequate infrastructure, the need to control the border has necessitated the physical deployment of large forces along the LAC. In the last decade, the army has raised two mountain divisions and a mountain strike corps (partially) to strengthen both the defensive and offensive capabilities along the northern border.[7] This has now been bolstered by the additional deployments mentioned earlier in the chapter.

On the western border, Pakistan remains an intractable foe. The Line of Control (LoC) has been highly active since 2016, and 2020 saw 4,000 ceasefire violations, with increasing use of artillery in the fire exchanges.[8] The continuing infiltration from Pakistan into Jammu and Kashmir has forced the army to adopt a two-tier deployment. The first tier is deployed all along the LoC to ensure that there are no territorial violations while the second tier is in the depth along the border fence for countering any infiltration. Firing has significantly reduced after a ceasefire agreement came into effect in February 2021, but there is no change in the force posture on the LoC.

Pakistan has a well-trained, conflict-experienced and reasonably well-equipped military force. The 550,000-strong army is directed only against one foe—India. To maintain its conventional superiority, the Indian Army had deployed seven defensive corps and three mechanised strike (offensive) corps along the western border.[9] One of these corps (1 Corps) has now been assigned to the northern front.

Apart from preparing for conventional operations, the army's commitments to counter-insurgency in the North East Region (NER) and Jammu and Kashmir require additional forces. To ensure that this commitment does not impact its conventional capability, the army raised the Rashtriya Rifles, specialised counter-insurgency units, in 1990. There are currently five division headquarters and sixty-three battalions of the Rashtriya Rifles, all deployed in Jammu and Kashmir. While this has freed most of the regular army from counter-insurgency, there is an additional burden as the manpower for Rashtriya Rifles units is provided by the army and the funds come out of the defence budget.

The Indian Army is currently 1.2 million strong and takes up 61 per cent of the overall defence budget. Within the army's allocation, 89 per cent of the budget goes towards salaries, pensions and other revenue expenditure, leaving only 11 per cent for modernisation.[10]

Approach to Reform

It is clear that the military cannot expect a significant enhancement in defence budgets in the near future. Since the last few years, the trends have been evident with allocations for the military decreasing as a percentage of the GDP. With the economy having taken a substantial hit due to the Covid-19 pandemic, the money available to the military is unlikely to increase despite the heightened Chinese threat.

In times of stressed budgets, the army has two options. The first is to continue with its manpower-heavy structure and put modernisation on the backburner. Some necessary inductions of new equipment will take place but at a slow pace. This is an incremental approach that causes the least turbulence in the existing system. It is also not an entirely unworkable approach because there is nothing to suggest that the Indian Army is currently failing to perform its role both along the borders and on internal security duties. However, this approach sticks to the comfort of the past and ignores the uncertainties of the future—for instance, how the character of warfare is changing and the need to be prepared for the next conflict.

The second approach is to recognise that deep reform is necessary for the army, and this means trading off size for modernisation. And we need to distinguish between reform and restructuring. All our efforts in the past have been directed at restructuring efforts where the emphasis has been on cutting down logistic units. Despite having stripped logistic units to the bone, there has been little impact on the revenue budget or the availability of funds for modernisation.

To undertake significant reforms, the army will have to look at its basic manning structure, review its operational responsibility, integrate common roles in the three services, undertake a doctrinal study of future warfighting and develop high-end capability. It must also be understood that a reduction in the army's strength does not necessarily equate to a decrease in capability. A leaner, technologically-advanced force supported by a coherent doctrine, high standard of training and good human capital will be more effective.

Rethinking the Army's Manning Structure

The Indian Army is a wholly regular force prepared to undertake conventional operations at a few days' notice. All units are at 100 per cent manning level (less the shortage of officers) and ready for swift mobilisation from peace to war conditions. The questions before us are: Do we need such a large standing army? Or can we organise it into a mix of regular and reserve forces? Let me first outline the proposal, and after that discuss its pros and cons.

It is recommended that those army units that are permanently located in peace stations—for example, logistic units, signals, armoured, mechanised infantry and specialist units of artillery, air defence and engineers—could have a mix of 70 per cent regular and 30 per cent reserve soldiers. Some combat units like the infantry, artillery and engineers that regularly rotate from peace to field every two to three years will necessarily have to be entirely regular.

The reserve force will comprise retired army personnel who would maintain a reserve liability for three years after retirement. They will be geographically assigned to the nearest unit (depending on their arm or service) and report for duty for two months a year during the annual exercises. During this period, they will be paid their full salary. Depending on the number and trade of soldiers retiring each year, it could take up to five years to build up the reserve force to the desirable 30 per cent.

The obvious advantage of this proposal is significant manpower savings without diluting the quality of the human resource. The reservists are soldiers with decades of experience in the army, are well trained and could easily slip into their assigned wartime role with minimal disruption.

One possible drawback with this proposal is that the army's doctrine calls for extremely high levels of readiness with operations planned to be launched across the western border within seventy-two to ninety-six hours.[11] The absence of 30 per cent of a unit's soldiers and the time taken to recall the reservists could delay the mobilisation of units for war. There could indeed be some delay in mobilisation, but two points are worth noting here. The last time the Indian Army was fully mobilised was during Operation Parakram, twenty years ago. It is also unlikely that the political leadership will decide to go to a full-scale war within a few days. The army must make a reasoned assessment on whether it wants to continue with its 100 per cent manning model.

In my view, the benefits of reducing manpower costs and transferring the savings towards modernisation far outweigh the risks in keeping a component of reservists in the army. The army could start with a testbed in some of the units in Punjab or Rajasthan and, if successful, incorporate the reservist model through the force.

The other proposals on restructuring that are currently underway—for example, the shift to independent battle groups—must also continue. Leaner, agile, faster and flexible organisations will achieve better wartime results than large forces that are slow-moving and vulnerable to accurate enemy attacks. Manpower cost savings will enable existing organisations to be equipped with better sensors, precise firepower and greater mobility.

Rethinking Operational Responsibilities

India's existing policies and the responsibilities of the ministries of home and defence have resulted in a lack of synergy in two areas—border management and internal conflicts. This lack of synergy results in the application of forces that are both excessive and wasteful. Let me first take up the issue of border management.

The responsibility of peacetime border management along the India–China border is with the Indo-Tibetan Border Police (ITBP). This may surprise many since it is always the army that is most visible during any standoff with the PLA along the LAC. That is because the army also maintains a heavy presence along the LAC and has a better response capability against PLA transgressions.

Thus, we have two forces under different ministries deployed along the same disputed border. This makes very little strategic sense. The Group of Ministers (GoM) constituted to follow up on the recommendations of the Kargil Review Committee noted:

> At present, there are instances of more than one force working on the same border and questions of conflict in command and control have been raised frequently. Multiplicity of forces on the same border has also led to lack of accountability on the part of the forces. To enforce the accountability, the principle of "one border one force" may be adopted while considering deployment of forces at the border.[12]

More than twenty years after the Kargil conflict, we are continuing with an irrational arrangement on the LAC. Not only does this make a cohesive response to PLA actions difficult but it is also entirely wasteful. The army and the ITBP are independently raising forces without making a joint plan for deployment and warfighting. Recently, the ITBP established two command headquarters, neither of which is co-located with the relevant command headquarters of the army.[13]

The ITBP at the LAC should be placed under the command of the army. A similar arrangement is in place at the LoC in Jammu and Kashmir with the Border Security Force under the army's command. This will improve operational functioning along the LAC and result in significant savings for the government if a unified capability development plan is drawn up jointly for the army and ITBP.

A somewhat incongruous situation also prevails in areas where the army is deployed for counter-insurgency counterterrorism operations. The army and the Central Armed Police Forces (CAPF), such as the Central Reserve Police Force (CRPF), are both operating in Jammu and Kashmir but under different ministries. While there is a lot of talk about synergy, the absence of a unified command leads to independent planning with regard to the requirement of forces for internal security. The army continues to maintain a force level of sixty-three Rashtriya Rifles battalions in Jammu and Kashmir although levels of violence and the number of terrorists have reduced significantly from their peak in the early 2000s.

Taking a combined approach between the ministries of defence and home, it will be possible to carry out a realistic requirement of force levels for internal security in Jammu and Kashmir and the NER. This could reduce the army's commitment, particularly in areas where insurgent activity has reduced significantly.

Integration in the Three Services

There is a lot of focus on achieving integration among the three services. At one level, integration implies a unified command structure, such as a theatre command, with elements of all three services under a single commander. At another, we could consider combining specific capabilities under one service. Let me explain with an example.

The army and the air force operate similar unarmed aerial vehicles (UAVs). In some cases, both services are operating Searcher and Heron UAVs from different bases in close vicinity to each other. There is no formal system for a regular exchange of information gathered from UAV missions. As a result of this, each service independently procures UAVs at great cost and raises separate units with very little integration of capability.

There is a similar situation with air defence, light helicopters, long-range vectors and attack helicopters. It is quite inexplicable why the air force insists on procuring the attack helicopter that is primarily a platform to support a ground manoeuvre. The lack of a combined inter-service approach has led to both the air force and the army separately procuring AH-64 attack helicopters from the US.[14]

The army must also reconsider its decision to induct long-range vectors, such as the BrahMos missile. This is a very effective weapon system but the army does not have the means to acquire targets or carry out battle damage assessment at a distance of 300 kilometres beyond the border. It would be better if the BrahMos is handled by the Strategic Forces Command that has the capability to engage long-range targets.

The integration of the three services should not only be limited to weapon systems but extend to training. All air defence training can be combined at the army's air defence college, and helicopter training should be conducted by the air force for all pilots. A similar model can be adopted in many fields in which the services run their independent training establishments.

Combining capabilities, putting in place inter-service systems that can communicate with each other, sharing information, joint planning and getting rid of service biases could result in significant savings by more efficient resource utilisation.

Technology vs Boots on Ground

There is a constant technology vs boots on the ground debate within the army. It is argued that the enormous challenges posed by the rugged terrain conditions along our borders limit the scope of technology implementation. Ultimately, these borders will have to be physically manned, and therefore there is little scope for reduction in manpower. There is no doubt that the disputed Indian borders will require a minimum force level for manning, but it is also true that technology adoption in the Indian Army has been extremely slow. In 2018, the Vice Chief of the army told the parliamentary panel on defence, 'The state today is 68 per cent of our equipment is in the vintage category, with just about 24 per cent in the current and 8 per cent in the state-of-art category.'[15]

It is not only in equipment but also in niche technologies, such as artificial intelligence (AI), robotics and the cyber sphere, where there has been little progress. Would the adoption of technology help reduce manpower in the army? The answer to this question is yes. Modern equipment is simpler to maintain; more accurate weapon systems enable effective targeting using lesser platforms while AI and robotics can replace certain manual functions. This can undoubtedly lead to reducing manpower without sacrificing efficiency.

One fundamental issue in the army is that the absence of high-end technology has limited our understanding of how future technologies can be incorporated into warfighting strategies and doctrine. Therefore, there is extreme reluctance in cutting down manpower in combat arms and an over-reliance on boots on the ground. This will have to be addressed by creating an organisation within the army that is completely dedicated to future technologies.

A 'Future Technology Directorate' should be raised for the army. This should have a mix of army officers who will bring in user requirements, and scientists, who will provide technical expertise. To ensure that the technologies being considered are aligned with the army's doctrinal thinking, the organisation should be placed under the commander of the Army Training Command. This will get the organisation out of the bureaucratic set-up of the Army Headquarters and enable it to freely interact with the academia and industry to work on disruptive, cutting-edge technologies for adoption in the army.

Capability Development Plan

In times of stressed budgets, each arm or service attempts to push its requirements as a priority. This often results in procuring equipment that is easier to acquire rather than what is essentially required. The budget is spent, but it does not lead to a balanced capability development. In such a situation, the focus is on service-specific platforms, such as guns, tanks, etc., while capabilities that cut across all service domains such as information warfare, cyber technology, command and control, intelligence, etc., are ignored.

Ideally, a capability development plan must be founded on a defence strategy drawn out from the National Security Strategy. Unfortunately, India has been unable to articulate a national security strategy. However, even in the absence of this, the army can undoubtedly carry out a detailed study on future security contingencies, enemy capabilities and force employment options. Based on this study, the army must draw up a five-year capability development plan that strikes a balance between traditional weapon platforms and future warfighting technologies. Areas where the army needs to enhance its capability are:

- The army should look at technology enhancement in networked unmanned systems, robotics, AI, surveillance, and command and control.
- It should carry out greater investment in electronic warfare and cyber technology as these will become increasingly important in future wars.
- India's intelligence shortfalls are well known. There must be a strengthening of both technical and human-intelligence capabilities vis-a-vis PLA activities in Tibet.
- Strategic and tactical airlift capability must further improve. The ability to quickly move troops to threatened sectors could reduce the requirement to deploy ab initio a large number of soldiers on the ground. This could also contribute to an overall reduction of manpower in the Indian Army.
- The Indian Army must improve its battle awareness and lethality.
- The military must find ways to counter China's conventional missile threat. This will require the building of both missile defence and an offensive capability comprising short- and medium-range

ballistic missiles. The Strategic Forces Command needs to be suitably reorganised and tasked for this purpose.

Funding to a Plan

It has often been a military complaint that the government shies away from approving any long-term capability development plan for the three services. This leads to a complete mismatch between the military's annual demand for funds and what is ultimately allotted in the defence budget. According to details provided by the Minister of State for Defence Subhash Bhamre to the Lok Sabha, in the budget of 2108–2019, the armed forces were allocated 76,765 crore rupees less than what had been demanded towards capital procurement.[16]

This massive difference in expectations of the services and the allocation by the government leads to ad hocism in planning. Unspent capital expenditure goes back into the government's coffers, and to avoid surrender of funds, the services could end up buying not the most-needed equipment but that which is readily available. In 2017, the Parliamentary Standing Committee on Defence recommended creating a Non-Lapsable Capital Fund Account for defence modernisation. If created, this could bring some long-term stability to defence purchases.

There is one more concern that is internally debated within the army. There is no surety that if the army cuts down its manpower, the funds saved will be made available to the army for modernisation. There is apprehension that the budget would be reduced and the money accruing out of manpower savings could be diverted for other purposes. This could leave the army with a force that is both too small and insufficiently modernised to carry out its task effectively.

The government needs to step in to allay the apprehensions of the army. As a first step, the Ministry of Defence, with the sanction of the Cabinet Committee on Security, should approve the five-year capability development plan of the army. The budget allocation must be based on this plan and not an ad hoc grant or a fixed percentage of the GDP. This will ensure that the money is being spent on a well-thought-out path. In case any capital expenditure remains unspent, it should be rolled over to the following year.

The government must also commit to plough back into the army budget any savings that accrue due to manpower cuts. This harmonising of the budget, restructuring and capability development will require the government and Parliament to take a deeper interest in military affairs. The Indian Parliament routinely passes the defence budget without any discussion. This has permitted the military to frame its own threats and make demands for force accretions with little intervention from the political leadership except through budget allocations. A better model of civil-military interaction could be considered.

Conclusion

In a 1989 speech at Princeton University, General Colin Powell said, 'All of the sophisticated talks about grand strategy is helpful, but show me your budgets and I will tell you what your strategy is.'[17] The Indian Army must face this reality—unrealistic expectations about financial allocations will only delay reform.

The primary issue to be addressed is whether it is possible to reduce the size of the army while maintaining its combat effectiveness. This will require a review of the army's basic model of keeping all units at 100 per cent manning levels. Synergising border management and internal security with the CAPFs, integrating capabilities across the services and incorporating technology will lead to further reductions in manpower.

Austerity demands that the government and the military work in complete harmony to ensure that we get the biggest bang for the buck. The government must approve all capability development plans and ensure that funds are provided according to these plans.

Frustrations about the defence budget are understandable, but the army must also realise that there is a need to change existing structures and doctrines to be prepared for a future warfighting role.

5

Trajectory of Indian Air Power

AIR VICE MARSHAL MANMOHAN BAHADUR (RETD)

There are various drivers to a nation's power-building campaign; the drive is modulated or gets moderated by numerous factors such as availability of monetary resources, technological expertise, quality of human resources and internal political stability, among others. Rarely, if ever, has public health emerged as an important determinant—in fact, an arbiter—of the trajectory that national power would acquire. India finds itself at such a crossroads, with an external security environment that is far from benign, a challenging internal melange of socio-ideological movements, an economy that has been severely affected by the Covid-19 pandemic and an armed forces' inventory that is in crying need of upgradation and modernisation.

This essay looks at the positioning of Indian air power in the maze that constitutes national security—its role and capabilities that would meet the requirements of the political leadership of the country. For sure, a nation's air power comprises capabilities of both the civil and military (all three services) spheres, but the fact is that the Indian Air Force (IAF) is *the* determinant of the potency of India's air power; hence, the terms air power and IAF will be used interchangeably to mean India's air power.

Is the IAF the prima donna in India's security posture? While this would be analysed through the course of this essay, it would be instructive to see how air power has been viewed in the past as a medium of force application to enforce a nation's political will on another. Writing in the *USI Journal 1912*, Lieutenant L.V.S. Blacker laid out the advantages of investing in aeroplanes:

> It is therefore obvious that a country which means to take war seriously must ensure having more aeroplanes than the enemy, and faster ones. Otherwise, the day after the declaration of war will see the wiping out of the slow aeroplanes and their pilots, and the 'command of the air' for the enemy, carrying with it the most minute knowledge of his opponent's entire dispositions and movements and laying open all important points ... open to damage or destruction from high explosive shells dropped by the enemy.[1]

In the October 1919 issue, Lieutenant H.T. Geary commented on the 'Instructional Methods in a Scout Training Squadron of the Royal Air Force,' pointing to the fact that aviation had, till then, been considered an appendage of the ground forces. However, the fact that an aircraft was still looked on as an adjunct to land forces was very clearly stated by Major H.G. Martin in his essay 'India and the Next War' in the October 1922 issue of the *USI Journal*. Major Martin writes, 'The conclusion is that, while aircraft are invaluable in their legitimate role as adjuncts to our land-forces, they are quite incapable of replacing them.' This was a land-centric view, the army being the older service, in contrast to what an aviator felt. Flight Lieutenant R.L. Stevenson writes on 'The Army

Cooperation Squadron' in the July 1925 issue of the *USI Journal*,[2] and it is interesting to note that while the Royal Air Force (RAF) author describes the various roles that the Army Cooperation Squadron undertook, he ends up with the advice that army and air force officers must visit each other's units to understand their operations.[3] This century-old reference is to what is now the buzzword in war studies—jointness.

Wars in the last century were witness to the fact that air power slowly became the politician's preferred choice of hard and soft power used to impose a nation's will on another. The attributes of reach, speed and mobility, and lately of persistence (permanence of 'stare' through UAVs and satellites) and precision attack, have given air power an aura of being a panacea for all the troubles that an adversary may be causing, and hence the politician's love for it. This, however, is a faulty understanding of what air power can, and/or cannot do; but what is certain is that technology has given air power the capability that was part of fiction just a few decades back. Thus, swarm technology and artificial intelligence–enabled systems will soon lead to non-contact warfare, and manned–unmanned teaming will keep the man behind these destructive machines out of harm's way; the militarisation of space is already a reality, and weaponisation is not far behind. But this technology is niche and expensive—in fact, very expensive. Notwithstanding the costs, an air force that falls behind in ensuring technological asymmetry—or rather technological superiority—vis-a-vis its adversaries, will be greatly handicapped. The US Air Force Chief of Staff General Charles Q. Brown Jr titled his message to airmen on taking over command in August 2020 as 'Accelerate Change or Lose'[4] and dwelt on the need to stay ahead of adversaries despite cost constraints. Though stated vis-a-vis the challenges expected of the US from China and Russia, the deeper message of the statement is true for any fighting force of any country, especially an air force, due to air power's extreme dependency on technology. So, as the third decade of this century gets underway and nations move up the technology curve, especially China (as also Pakistan), this essay will analyse, through four steps, the trajectory Indian air power could take in the Covid-19 impacted milieu.

First, does the present doctrine of the IAF, which is of 2012 vintage, require a revamp to take into account not only the changed security environment but also the reduced financial resources available for defence? Second, where does the present inventory lie in terms of meeting the doctrinal aspirations in the coming two decades or so? Third, since all indicators are that the monies available for capability accretion will fall short of the requirement, how should the IAF adapt to the shortfall in its assets and the associated capability gaps to meet the threat from both its adversaries? And last, since defence planning needs to be looking far into the future, what foundational changes should the IAF be making *now* so that they fructify to meet the challenges of the mid-century, three decades hence, when the national economy will have, hopefully, rebounded?

The character of war keeps changing as Giulio Douhet, the Italian air power strategist, said in 1921: 'Victory smiles upon those who anticipate the change in the character of war, not upon those who wait to adapt themselves after the changes occur.'[5] A doctrinal makeover for the IAF is the need of the hour because from that will flow correct acquisitions and realistic training.

Doctrine of the IAF

In 2012, the IAF published the *Basic Doctrine of the Indian Air Force 2012*, an unclassified version of the foundational underpinning of how it planned to prosecute the tasks given to it.[6] As a text that was to guide IAF operations, the doctrine lays out the roles and missions of the IAF, which were not too different from those of any other modern air force. It was a good beginning to declassify IAF doctrinal thought. The doctrine includes the complete gamut of operations in the conflict spectrum from peace to a no-war-no-peace scenario and from a limited war under the nuclear overhang to a nuclear engagement via the conventional conflict route. It also talks of an expeditionary role in protecting Indian overseas interests.

Doctrine, in simple terms, is 'the best way to do a task'. The task of the IAF should flow from the nation's national security strategy, which has not been issued to date. Hence, its foundation rests on the defence minister's operational instructions given to the service chiefs and is a classified document. Service plans, as they stand, flow from these operational instructions. Over the years, the expanding ambitions of the Indian state have also been visible through the environmental review contained in the Annual Reports of the Ministry of Defence (MoD). The 2002–2003 report defined India's area of strategic interest as 'from the Persian Gulf in the west to the Straits of Malacca in the east and from the Central Asian republics in the north to near the equator in the south'. The 2012–2013 report declared, 'India's size and strategic location ... links its security environment with the extended neighbourhood, particularly with neighbouring countries and the regions of West, Central Asia, South East Asia, East Asia and the

Indian Ocean.' The latest published report (2018–2019) states that India's relations with a host of countries in almost all continents had deepened, with special reference to those in the Indian Ocean and Indo-Pacific region. It identifies Pakistan as a country that would be problematic while China came in for a rosy assessment as 'relations with China moved towards greater stability in the overall context of Closer Development Partnership'.

This assessment of China's intentions was, surely, extremely faulty as the summer of 2020 saw incursions into India's side of the Line of Actual Control (LAC) and associated violent clashes, one of which, at Galwan Valley, resulted in the deaths of twenty Indian soldiers and an unknown number of Chinese personnel.[7]

India, thus, has a live northern frontier with China and a simmering Line of Control (LoC) in Jammu and Kashmir with Pakistan.[8] As it beefs up its defences and prepares for the long haul due to Chinese intransigence in returning to the status quo ante,[9] the IAF is being seen as the X-factor in New Delhi's deterrence posture. While its doctrine talks of full-spectrum operations (nuclear deterrence not included here), it is silent with respect to the impact of the availability of monies on the capability acquisition wish list and hence the capability that can actually accrue. Since the allocation towards capital acquisition has been diminishing by the year, the doctrine needs a relook to factor in the 'best way of doing India's defence' with the availability of finances bringing in a modicum of realism.

According to one study, the fund for capital acquisitions for the three services put together was 27 per cent of the MoD expenditure in 2011–2012 (when the doctrine was written); they have decreased over the years to 19 per cent in the budget estimates of FY 2020–2021.[10] Capability gaps are bound to affect the ability of the services to deter adversaries, a situation that should not be acceptable. Some would say that a doctrine is a theoretical construct and that the effect of finances would be taken into account by the strategy that is devised. While this argument has some merit, can a foundational document be so divorced from reality? The roots of the doctrinal tree assimilate the environment and the experiences of an organisation and its personnel, and the recommended 'best way of doing a thing' gets modulated accordingly.

The availability of resources forms an important part of the 'experiences', and in the case of the IAF, is a critical input since in real life it has had to make do with the sub-par allocation of funds for capability accretion. The idiom 'cut your coat according to your cloth' is apt here, and the doctrine must take this into account for building a realistic road map for the type of posture it can help India build in future against its two adversaries. A careful reading of the doctrine does show that it has exercised some latitude. Theoretically, doctrine drives technological R&D and innovations, but, as Doctrine 2012 puts it, 'In the Indian context, it may not always be possible for doctrine to drive technology due to resource and technological constraints. Instead, doctrine is maybe limited to playing an interactive role with technology.' 'Resource' as an input to doctrine formulation has, thus, not been given its due. This is an omission in the document and, in fact, an admission of the lack of resources having an impact on two important principles of war—concentration of force and economy of effort. Can the principle of concentrating the required mass economically (which is what the two referred principles jointly imply) in the required time and space be circumvented by increased effectiveness through the use of better technology and strategy? That's what the IAF is trying to do with the reduced numbers it has. Its success with this idea will be limited because it has peer, and maybe more resourced, competitors on the other side, and the mass has its own unique quality in ensuring deterrence. This will be covered in detail in the next segment of the analysis, but before that, it is necessary to analyse where the IAF is placed vis-a-vis its two adversaries.

The Basic Doctrine states that the IAF is a strategic force that can create strategic outcomes in an offensive mode; while this was always true against Pakistan, the posture against China has changed over the years from 'holding action' to 'dissuasion', hinting at a change in strategy—from deterrence by denial to one of deterrence by punishment.[11] This was also an acknowledgement of the fact that the Indian nation was facing the reality of a two-front war.

The switch in strategy was visible in the acquisitions by the IAF, with the Su-30MKI becoming the mainstay of taking the battle deep into the enemy heartland; besides the Su-30 and the upgradation projects of the Mirage 2000 and MiG-29, other acquisitions, such as flight refuelling tankers, AWACS, precision munitions and modern, ground-based radars added to this posture. This changeover started at the beginning of this century and was a counter to the fast-paced modernisation of the Chinese military that came about after the 1991 Gulf War, when they realised how far behind the US they were in armament technology. The Chinese modernisation happened in conjunction with a rapid build-up in communication infrastructure in the Tibetan plateau and a network of roads and railway lines coming up in quick time. The momentum in capability accretion of the IAF, however, soon sagged due to a decision-making paralysis that affected the government's acquisition bureaucracy, as witnessed in the delays in moving forward on the MMRCA[12] requirement as also the imperative need of acquiring more combat enablers, such as flight refuelling aircraft (FRA) and AWACS. Publicly available information[13] suggests the IAF planned to acquire a mix of twenty AWACS and AEW&C aircraft by the end of the 14th Five Year Plan (2027); some defence writings suggest that the number is fifteen—thirteen AWACS and two AEW&C built by DRDO.[14] Similarly, six more FRA were to be procured, taking their numbers to twelve. This has not happened to date, with the FRA being shortlisted twice in the past decade after flight trials, only to be shelved due to lack of funds.[15]

With the phasing out of the MiG-21/23 and MiG-27 aircraft, the squadron numbers have depleted to a precarious thirty, as against a minimum requirement of thirty-nine and a half squadrons to meet a two-front contingency[16]; the Jaguars and MiG-29s, too, will get phased out in the next two decades or so. The acquisition of just thirty-six Rafale fighters is grossly inadequate, as is the stopgap proposal of purchasing twenty-one mothballed MiG-29s from Russia.[17] With the production of the indigenous Tejas fighter currently being just about eight aircraft a year, the government dragging its feet on fast-tracking the 114 fighter aircraft project eximport (even the request for proposal has not been sent to vendors, only the request for information has been made)[18] and a severe Covid-19 induced financial crunch looming, the IAF will need to have a relook at what its basic doctrine enjoins it to do since no new doctrine has been issued after the 2012 edition.

Realistic Capability, Circa 2040

This section evaluates where the present inventory lies in terms of meeting the doctrinal aspirations in the coming two decades or so if no revisions take place and the present doctrine holds good. That there needs to be a doctrinal revision is a given and is covered in the last part of this chapter.

The 2012 doctrine states, 'Control of air becomes a prerequisite for the effectiveness of all military activities.'[19] This is true, but a strategic-level doctrine must acknowledge that adversaries are well equipped too. Airspace will be highly contested and planning parameters must help create favourable, situations to ensure mission accomplishment. The doctrine also states that the 'generation and sustenance of favourable symmetry' is one of the principles of war.[20] It is in honouring this principle that the capabilities and capacities of the IAF will get called into question as the following examination shows.

The shortage of fighter aircraft is well known, with the strength down to thirty squadrons:[21]

Su-30MKI – 12 squadrons
Mirage 2000 – 3 squadrons
MiG-29UPG – 3 squadrons
Jaguars – 6 squadrons
MiG-21 Bison – 4 squadrons (to be phased out in the next 5 years)
Tejas Mk1 – 1 squadron with another under raising
Rafale – 1 squadron with another under raising

The numbers would increase if—and it is a big if—HAL augments its Tejas Mk1 and Mk1A manufacturing capability to at least sixteen aircraft per year in quick time.

The director of the Aeronautical Development Agency (ADA), which is developing the Tejas Mk1A, stated in a 30 September 2020 webinar hosted by the New Delhi-based Centre for Air Power Studies that the deliveries of the Mk1A will be completed by 2027–2028; if HAL does not ramp up its production rate, then the complete order of 123 would take the better part of the next decade to complete. The IAF has placed its faith in the Tejas Mk2, with its chief giving a firm undertaking that twelve squadrons of the Mk2 will be acquired;[22] these will be replacements of three Mirage 2000, three MiG-29 and six Jaguar squadrons.[23]

The Tejas Mk2 is a new design with canards and the more powerful American GE-414 engine. It is still on the drawing board, and the prototype, scheduled to fly in 2022, with a service entry in 2025–2026, is nowhere on the scene.[24] This timeline was reiterated by the ADA director at the 30 September conference. Despite the optimistic claims of DRDO that the fifth-generation Advanced Medium Combat Aircraft (AMCA) will fly by 2032,[25] this aircraft will not enter operational service before 2040, as acknowledged by the IAF chief in a 3 August 2020 webinar organised by the leading think tank MP-IDSA.[26] The only answer seems to be 'more imports', a decision that would strike at the very root of the 'buy local' drive of the government.

How the government will work this policy decision in the 114 fighter aircraft contract will be interesting to see; what can be said with surety is that these 114 fighters (roughly five squadrons) are an absolute must if the IAF squadron strength has to go up in the next decade to meet the threats on both the northern and western frontiers.

The IAF, in the 1980s, had a 4:1 ratio in combat aircraft vis-a-vis Pakistan, a CIA 1987 study had concluded.[27] China was still rising in that period and did not pose any threat to India. In fact, it was in those years, and later in 1993, that India–China relations got better after Prime Minister Rajiv Gandhi's 1988 visit to Beijing and the many confidence-building measures adopted in subsequent prime ministerial interactions. As the LAC stayed fairly dormant for the next two decades or so, it was Pakistan that was seen as the adversary to be countered. The IAF squadron strength, meanwhile, started dwindling from a high of thirty-nine and a half squadrons in the early 1990s[28] to thirty squadrons now. It will go up to 'around 37 Squadrons (but be a more capable fleet) only by 2030 or so', as stated by the IAF's deputy chief who looks after acquisitions.[29] It is, however, important to remember that the operational impact of today's thirty squadrons and the thirty-seven squadrons in future will depend on the availability of combat enablers in required numbers and capability.

Combat enablers are an inalienable part of the force mix that will be needed to meet the threat of any war now or in the future. The IAF, however, suffers from an inadequate number of FRA and AWACS. For the FRA, two acquisition tenders to supplement the six IL-78 refuellers have been withdrawn in the past decade due to non-availability of finances even though the Airbus 330 Multi-Role Tanker Transport (MRTT) was shortlisted in both attempts. The third acquisition attempt has started,[30] so it would be at least six to seven years before the first machine arrives. This is if all clearances are given in time and adequate funds are made available on schedule.

For airborne surveillance, there are just three AWACS and two AEW&C indigenous systems on an Embraer platform. This is grossly inadequate considering the volume of air space that has to be scanned and protected.

To make up for the shortfall, the government has decided that indigenous AEW aircraft will be built on six Airbus A-320 airframes being bought from Air India.[31] Given that extensive R&D and flight testing of the basic airframe with the balance-beam radar mount would be necessary to clear it, followed by radar trials, one is looking at the better part of a decade before the first aircraft enters operational service; by this time, some present holdings of frontline fighter aircraft will have started reaching obsolescence.

Many of the legacy aircraft designs (the Su-30MKI, which was inducted two decades back, is entering this classification too!) need an avionics and weapon upgrade to stay relevant. The loss of the MiG-21 in the Balakot strike in Pakistan could have been due to the pilot's radio transmissions being jammed[32] as the IAF does not have an encrypted system. Data linking is still a work in progress. Though the ground segment of the Integrated Air Command and Control System (IACCS) is well established, the airborne element is lagging. Software-defined radios, which are mandatory for secure data linking and voice, have just started arriving.[33] Thus, the ambitious and vitally necessary IACCS is not yet fully in place.

This is the inventory the IAF has to counter the People's Liberation Army Air Force (PLAAF), which has around 600 combat aircraft, including modern fourth and 4.5 generation fighters.[34] Indeed, all these will not be ranged against India as China has to look after its Pacific coastline too, but its fighter aircraft—comprising a mix of J-11 variants, Su-27/30 and J-10B/C—have been stationed in airfields in the Western Theatre Command. Some media reports state that the fifth-generation J-20[35] has also been spotted in a Tibetan airfield as also H-6K bombers.[36] PLAAF's combat enablers are a mix of KJ200

AEW and KJ-500 and KJ-2000 AWACS (only four on an IL-76 airframe, with a total of all types being twenty-nine).[37] China is ramping up production of its airborne sensors by using its indigenous Y-20 transport aircraft as the base aircraft for its AWACS. As this gathers pace, the availability of AWACS will increase rapidly for PLAAF.[38] This will also be the case for FRA, which at present are limited in number with added technical restrictions: the IL-78 can refuel only Russian origin aircraft and H-6K refuellers are compatible only with Chinese-origin designs (this is a big operational handicap).

On the western front, Pakistan has around 500 combat aircraft, all ranged against India.[39] Latest reports indicate that it is acquiring twenty-five J-10C fighters from China to counter India's induction of the Rafale.[40] They are supported by Chinese-origin AWACS ZDK-03 and six Swedish Erieye AEW&C aircraft[41] for its vastly smaller airspace. There are four IL-78 FRA,[42] while ELINT and SIGINT is done through dedicated platforms. In addition, the Pakistani strategy has been based on having a powerful air defence system; it thus has a wide array of land-based radars and SAM systems dovetailed with its airborne elements.

So the current IAF inventory falls short of the ideal requirement of its doctrine: to give air cover to India's ambition of increasing its area of influence in the neighbourhood and beyond. The IAF has the wherewithal for a limited engagement in space and time, but an assured capability status is mandatory for meeting its doctrinal aspirations, irrespective of these two determinants. Even in the case of a two-front war across its land frontiers, the shortage of almost all critical systems, fighters as well as combat enablers, will be felt though the IAF hierarchy is on record to say that a collusive China and Pakistan threat will be addressed appropriately.[43] At the same time, the underlying assessment, in fact, an almost persuasive wish, is that the conflict will be short (but sharp), which may not be the case. This equipment shortfall will affect the deterrence quotient as it (deterrence) is built on two equally vital prongs—capability and resolve. Resolve rings hollow if capability falls short.

The shortfall in capability will be in terms of sustaining the tempo of operations as, besides fighter aircraft, the combat enablers are woefully inadequate. As stated earlier, it's almost a persuasive wish that the future war will be sharp and swift. No one can guarantee that, and India has to be prepared for the long haul too. Indian strike power will degrade due to a reducing inventory as the conflict progresses, and the adversary, knowing our limitations, could stretch the crisis. China's indigenous industry is very strong and will help Pakistan to keep India engaged. The extended activation in eastern Ladakh in 2020, which is continuing in 2022, has been a drain on manpower and equipment. Even though a partial disengagement of forces has taken place, it is inconceivable that India will reduce its manning and readiness status to one that existed before March 2020, when the crisis started; additionally, a similar beefing up of defences in the North East Region has been undertaken to prevent another Ladakh-like crisis. This extensive deployment will continue throughout the year and in subsequent years as well—to avoid any further surprises like what happened post-Kargil—putting further strain on manpower planning and the exchequer. An equally critical eye would have to be maintained on the western borders, lest Pakistan takes some inimical steps in collusion with China, notwithstanding the 'agreement' reached between

New Delhi and Islamabad on 25 February 2021 to dial down tensions on the LoC.[44] In such a security scenario, the wear and tear of equipment—indeed the drain on the life of the flying assets due to increased usage—is an aspect that does not get due weightage in common discourse but makes a significant mark on the budget.

IAF's Budget Challenge: Doing More with Less

As the foreword of this book says, when there is a crunch in war fighting wherewithal, it boils down to which side is smarter—the one that uses assets in an innovative way like the Megarians who used the humble pig to confront the highly-trained Indian battle elephants of the king of Macedonia, or the latter, who lost despite having the elephants. Since all indications are that the monies available for capability accretion will fall well short of the requirement (the defence allocation for FY 2021–2022 is 1.35 trillion rupees vis-a-vis 1.14 trillion in FY 2020–2021),[45] how should the IAF adapt to the shortfall in its assets, and the associated capability gaps, to meet the threat from both its adversaries? The challenge before the IAF is how to do more with less (monies, and hence equipment).

First, a deep and honest view has to be taken on whether India is biting off more than it can chew. The World Bank has predicted that the Indian economy would shrink.[46] In the coming years, a standard growth of capital and revenue budget for planning purposes in the defence sector, as was the practice hitherto, will not be possible.[47] So with the inventory not keeping pace with its ambitions on the geopolitical stage, is it time to restrict the nation's ambitions of achieving regional supremacy to a more credible one that can be serviced by the reduced inventory? Should the focus be on augmenting military tools rather than modifying objectives if the tools are not forthcoming? Or should the tools themselves be modified considering the rapid improvements in, and generation of newer, technology? It must be remembered that the army and navy have a similar problem of obsolescence of equipment and lack of finances to upgrade them or acquire new modern ones. The budget allocation will thus be assiduously wooed by each service for its modernisation and ensuring a minimum inventory is maintained to generate the required mass.

The mass has its relevance, as brought out earlier, and technology will be a key to the vexing question of reducing numbers. The 'mass' available at present has to be conserved till the effects of an augmented financial outlay start taking effect. Even when the economy turns for the better to afford the increase, it will be at least a decade before the accretion of numbers happens and starts getting reflected in the increased availability of assets on the flight lines and in operational squadrons. The required technology has to be garnered by tapping indigenous civilian resources too—both capital and human—in the segments that constitute the IAF's power.

Conserving the IAF's resources for war by using them judiciously in all areas is the key to operating with a restricted budget. Here, simulators could come in handy. While full-motion simulators have been installed for many fleets, they are by no means available for all; this is also valid for support equipment like radars, SAM systems and communication networks, *among others*. Simulators do not come cheap; moreover, money is needed for their maintenance, updating costs and the manpower to run and maintain them. Because fleet and equipment hours have to be conserved immediately, leasing simulators and permitting foreign companies to set up simulator parks, as in the civil aviation sector, should be planned. With AI making giant strides, it should be incorporated for ab initio as well as operational training by partnering with an ally that uses and offers virtual and augmented reality in its training profiles[48]; it would only be right if India's strong AI workforce in the civilian arena is used in this endeavour. Thus, the availability of fighter aircraft airframes and aero-engines, the most critical issue facing the IAF, could be extended by saving substantial hours that are otherwise used in training aircrew—and all this could be done without compromising the quality of training, which would be better (and safer) with augmented reality simulators.

With the Defence Acquisition Procedure 2020 allowing 'leasing' of transport aircraft and helicopters, civilian operators in the defence sector need to be brought in. Many Western nations are already using FRA for their daily operations in benign environments, and with just six FRA in its inventory, the IAF would do well to utilise the leasing option and save flight hours of integral assets for operational tasks only.[49]

With AI, the mode of operations is today undergoing radical change. The advent of UAVs—their transformation from benign tasks, such as photography, battle damage assessment and intelligence, surveillance and reconnaissance (ISR) to an armed role, carrying air-to-ground missiles and now to a proper combat role, has been breathtaking. They are now flying with manned assets under the manned-unmanned teaming concept that will revolutionise air operations. The vulnerability of ground-based assets to coordinated artillery and drone attacks was televised worldwide in the Armenia–Azerbaijan conflict of 2020 and the Russian–Ukraine war of 2022.[50] While lessons are being drawn by the IAF, it is a little worrying to note that its unmanned air assets are woefully inadequate, considering the volume of air and ground space that has to be covered. Loitering munitions, such as the Harpy drone that target electromagnetic emitters, are available in limited numbers,[51] but it is the non-availability of small munition carriers such as the Turkish Bayraktar TB2—which can fly long hours carrying light munitions—that is critical. Some emergency purchases are indeed being made[52] and Project Cheetah to arm the Israeli Herons is underway,[53] but the numbers are just not enough. DRDO's Rustom project is floundering,[54] while Pakistan and China have a flourishing indigenous industry producing armed UAVs, with the latter already in flying prototypes of unmanned combat aerial vehicles (UCAVs).

The limited budget from the IAF will need to be judiciously spent, with R&D for unmanned technology getting the required share of the pie. With India's software skills and entrepreneurial talent, the private sector can produce results in a shorter time frame than the public sector; it needs to bear in mind that many start-ups have already demonstrated swarms of UAVs[55] and all they need is institutional support to show results. In the interim, leasing could be an option, as has been done by the Indian Navy[56] to ensure 24x7 operational coverage in the Indian Ocean Region (IOR) by networking all platforms.

Linking all elements of a war-fighting system requires that they be networked seamlessly. The IAF's Integrated Air Command and Control System (IACCS) is still a work in progress, and when it is ready, it will have a force-multiplier effect in more ways than one. It will, for instance, help to some extent in offsetting the negative impact of falling squadron numbers by sharing data among the networked members; without networking, more aircraft will be necessary to generate the necessary effect and bring the required force to bear in the time frame required. With the acquisition of Software Defined Radios (SDRs), the necessary encryption of voice and data and networking of airborne assets with other elements of the IACCS will happen, a process that augurs well for the IAF's plans to have the necessary kinetic potential with a reduced fighter inventory. The panacea lies in tapping the latent potential of young entrepreneurs in the private sector and merging their output with the huge infrastructure in public sector undertakings that have, unfortunately, been used in a sub-optimal manner in capability development, accretion of assets and overall defence planning. Planning for the future must take into account these and other likely developments so that a new doctrine, as and when crafted, will be a true guide to the optimal use of the nation's air power.

A New Doctrine

Since defence planning requires looking far into the future, what foundational changes should the IAF be making *now* so that it is ready for the challenges of the mid-century when the economy will hopefully rebound? As stated earlier, the IAF's Basic Doctrine 2012 is a dated document and needs a revamp. Here are a few suggestions for a new doctrine.

Doctrines do not change overnight as they are a reflection of past experiences, present reality and future projections. To be effective, it has to be a live document and the IAF needs a new one due to significant new factors. Technology has progressed exponentially, with quantum computing being the next big thing after digital computing. AI and machine learning have come of age and are getting refined even further to come as close as possible to human cognitive abilities and intuition; autonomous machines are straining at the leash, being held back only because mankind is debating the morals and ethics of granting them the power to decide whom to kill. Covid-19 has been a speed breaker that will severely restrict financial support for cutting-edge R&D. With monies likely to remain elusive for another decade or so, manufacturing capacity and capability accretion will take a hit. The challenge will, however, be a test for the IAF's leadership. It will have to factor in the galloping advances in technology that cause early equipment obsolescence. The fact that the numbers of fighter squadrons will remain at around thirty in the coming decade (and only then increase) and the reality of a severe monetary crunch will affect operational capability.

Planning for the mid-century requires a leap of faith in the national work culture and decision-making apparatus to get the planned indigenous equipment on time and in acceptable quality for the IAF to operate effectively. It must be remembered that *doctrine drives technology*—and hence, considering the ongoing advancements and future trajectory of armament technology, the IAF doctrine will have to spell out the following to meet the challenges of the mid-century:

- The role and missions of the IAF will have to be redrafted since space, with its enabling technologies and associated capabilities, will have to be incorporated as a major, if not central, player in the doctrinal thought process.

- The weaponisation of space has to be accepted as a given, and incorporating space weaponry in the doctrine will be a must. There is no point sweeping the issue under the carpet as every major power is already doing it surreptitiously, the Outer Space Treaty notwithstanding.
- Air dominance can be won or lost quickly as seen in the case of the victorious French after the First World War when they neglected air power, and the Israelis in the Yom Kippur war after having come out trumps just six years earlier in the 1967 conflict.[57] With the arrival of the Su-30MKI with the R27 BVR, the IAF had the upper hand in air engagements with Pakistan. However, this was lost by 2008 when PAF received the AIM9-120, effectively nullifying the potency of the Sukhoi as seen during the reprisal by the PAF after the Balakot strike; no less than the IAF chief publicly accepted that the IAF had lost the technological edge.[58] This has been assessed as such too by noted strategic scholar Ashley Tellis.[59] Though tactics can, to a certain extent, overcome such disadvantages, one must remember that the lance lost out to the bow and arrow, which in turn became ineffective when the cannon was invented. So since air superiority is the sought-after state in a kinetic war, retaining the technological edge is a sine qua non for any professional force. The IAF's doctrine must expound on this aspect as an imperative that cannot be brushed aside despite the high financial commitment that air power entails.
- A call must be made on how air power, with its niche strike, ISR and precision-attack capabilities, will be

merged in the drive towards jointness. While the Department of Military Affairs and the institution of the Chief of Defence Staff (CDS) are just a year old, a 'flight plan' for the future needs to be incorporated.

- The first use of aviation in the military was for reconnaissance due to the 'high ground' it occupies. So were the balloons (before they were used to throw down flares), the German fighter Eindecker in 1915, the British Mosquito in the Second World War and the Mach 3 American SR-71 or the Russian MiG-25.[60] The case has been the same with UAVs—initially used solely for reconnaissance, they moved to an offensive role. The Indian experience in recent engagements—the Kargil conflict in 1999 and the flare-up in eastern Ladakh in 2020—revealed that lack of intelligence was the reason why the security establishment was caught on the back foot.[61] While a wholesome intelligence appraisal has many components, including Humint (human intelligence), it is the ISR from air and space that, in most cases, becomes the initial trigger as well as the confirmation of a likely trajectory of events. The new IAF doctrine must re-emphasise this as a starting point in its narrative for capability accretion and force projection—and plan acquisition accordingly. This would involve placing greater emphasis on unmanned platforms, both for ISR and strike as well as space assets, including the capability to have satellites on call. That this will be an inter-ministerial endeavour is indeed true but needs to be stressed at the higher decision-making levels.
- Are we entering an era of coalitions? Would India, given the two-front threat (especially an aggressive China) be forced to tilt towards the US? While this

would be a political call, a nuanced statement could be made in the doctrine about 'joint operations with friendly nations'. Here, the reinvigoration of the Quad—exemplified by the March 2021 meeting of the US president and the prime ministers of Japan, Australia and India—needs to be kept in view. Significantly, the joint statement issued after the meeting[62] listed many areas of cooperation, specifically stating that they will work towards a rules-based order in the Indo-Pacific. Among other assertions, the joint statement stated:

> Together, we commit to promoting a free, open, rules-based order, rooted in international law, to advance security and prosperity and counter threats both in the Indo-Pacific and beyond. We support the rule of law, freedom of navigation and overflight, peaceful resolution of disputes, democratic values, and territorial integrity.

The statement added:

> We will continue to prioritise the role of international law in the maritime domain, particularly as reflected in the United Nations Convention on the Law of the Sea (UNCLOS), and facilitate collaboration, including in maritime security, to meet challenges to the rules-based maritime order in the East and South China Seas.

So the thrust was to address the aggressive moves of China in the Indo-Pacific. Though India is firmly opposed to entering any security alliance, it could be asked for certain commitments in partnerships such as the Quad. This important issue needs to be addressed at the policy level by the government and may form part of the revised doctrine of the IAF.

- It is a fact of history that when a nation's economy improves, a time will come when it will have to move beyond its borders for raw materials to fuel its advancement; this, invariably, will put it in adversarial mode against other powers who are doing the same.[63] This points towards an expeditionary requirement that a nation's armed forces have to fulfil. When this happens in real earnest in India's case, the IAF will be tasked with providing an air umbrella for operations beyond the immediate neighbourhood to protect India's economic and political interests. This will call for a substantial restructuring of the IAF's inventory and training syllabus based on a doctrinal foundation that must be expounded in the new document.
- The world has already graduated to multi-domain operations where cyber, space, electromagnetic spectrum and influence operations, among others, are activated together or in stages to get a whole-of-government approach towards meeting national objectives. India, too, has to have an organisational structure to harness all tools of national power in its endeavour to meet its challenges. The IAF will be just one, though an important, cog in the multi-domain power synchronisation for which doctrinal guidance will be a must. All-domain operations are already underway in many advanced militaries. How will the IAF synergise its thinking, training and operational plans to work with the other domains? As an example, the US is graduating to all-domain operations where air, land, sea, space, cyber and the electromagnetic spectrum operations will be seamlessly fused to, in the words of

vice-chairman of the US Joint Chiefs of Staff General John Hyten, 'compete with a global competitor and at all levels of conflict'.[64] It is, as he puts it,

> A concrete effort to build sensors, communications systems, and data fusion engines designed to make it possible for, say, a submarine, a Marine Corps infantry squad, an F-35, an Apache gunship, a P-8 patrol plane, an orbiting satellite or a Navy ship to feed targeting data to any other weapon to ensure the most efficient and lethal response to a threat.

This is where the world is going.

- Managing its human resource will be a very important task for the IAF. Technology will not relieve people of stress but overload them with info. 'Accelerate change or lose' as a slogan may be okay, but for such acceleration of ideas, people have to feel secure—they have to have the psychological high ground to feel confident about coming out with fresh ideas. Since any war is a team effort, it's the management of the team members that is vital. 'High ground' not only gives a sense of physical security but, equally importantly, affords a sense of psychological well-being due to their presence on high ground—this is psychological high ground. As an article on the website War on the Rocks puts it, 'Leaders need to seize and maintain the psychological high ground to provide their subordinates with an environment in which they feel they can contribute without fear of judgment or *ad hominem* attacks by either their teammates or their leadership.'[65]
- The US had nuclear asymmetry after the Second World War and used it as a deterrent against the USSR

mounting any invasion of Europe. But as the USSR came on par, the nuclear card disappeared and the conventional Soviet threat reappeared. To counter this, the US brought in what is called the second offset—overcoming the threat of numbers with quality. Thus started the 'revolution in military affairs' (RMA) where information, precision and the ability to hit from stand-off distances became key research projects and resulted in all three being demonstrated, to some extent, in Op Eldorado Canyon against Libya and finally in the 1991 Gulf War.[66] This turnaround in precision targeting at the tactical level, but deterrent signalling at the strategic level, was not an overnight phenomenon. It took dedicated research teams under programme leadership that had continuity since 1965 and the political backing under different administrations—from Carter to Reagan to Bush Senior—to achieve fruition.[67] Though there is a political tinge in this argument, the IAF doctrine should, in a diplomatic way, hint at 'defence' being seen as a national endeavour and not filter it through the prism of the dispensation at the helm. This is vital for continuous growth in defence R&D and manufacturing, which should not be held hostage to political changes.

Summation

An air force is not just about fighter aircraft and combat enablers such as FRA and AWACS, and one may justifiably ask about the status of the transport aircraft, helicopters, radar assets and other such components that are vital for the efficient working of the IAF. To clarify, this chapter has been about the combat power of the IAF; however, a crisp statement can be made that, thanks to sound planning by the IAF leadership, the availability status of these assets is satisfactory and, in some sub-fields, good. However, complacency and/or lack of planning to cater for their obsolescence in the coming years will land them in the same state as the fighter inventory now. With India trying to cement its place as a regional power of reckoning, these assets are vital for humanitarian assistance and disaster relief, which are important factors of a nation's engagement with other countries; to put it succinctly, they are vital cogs in military diplomacy, which is such a vital aspect of any nation's foreign policy. Neglecting them will be to India's disadvantage, more so because they are vital too in sustaining combat power availability and its sustenance in national defence. The new IAF doctrine must cater to these aspects to guide policymakers.

Indian air power is at a crossroads. While its transport aircraft and helicopter assets have been in the thick of Covid-19 operations and deployed in the wake of the two cyclones that hit India's coastal areas during the pandemic, the combat element (including transport aircraft, helicopters, radars, etc.) has been on alert on both the frontiers, especially the northern one. Their usage must have been beyond the normal, in many cases, resulting in decreased availability in the future vis-a-vis their operational life cycle. Considering the issues involved and the rigid stands taken by the protagonists, the security environment around the country may not turn benign for many decades. The IAF needs to have a guiding document that helps it navigate the tough times ahead. A new IAF doctrine must be formulated to help it live up to its motto: 'Touch the Sky with Glory.'

6

How Can the Indian Army Address the Resource Modernisation Logjam?

COLONEL VIVEK CHADHA (RETD)

National security has remained a serious challenge through most of India's seventy years of independence. Between conventional wars and internal security threats, national security planners have been perpetually tied down in merely sustaining a territorial status quo.[1]

However, now the enormity of the existing challenges seems to have grown beyond anything experienced in the past. This includes the ambition of creating military capabilities in line with India's expectations of itself as an emerging power as well as expectations of others within the region and beyond. This desire has been constrained by a weakening economy, the adverse impact of Covid-19 and the limited resources available within the defence budget for modernisation.

Let us consider the responsibilities of the defence forces, the desired capabilities and the resources available as three variables that form a triangle defining India's defence dilemma. The recent past clearly indicates that when two of these variables become constant, the third is bound to be affected. In this case, with resources and threats more or less constant, capability building is bound to take a hit, unless, of course, ways and means are found to manage resources and responsibilities in a manner that offsets the constraints or a consensus is built to enhance resources over the short term while a major readjustment of the other variables takes place.

The last few years have seen defence budget allocations just about meeting the basic needs of the armed forces and inflation—this, at a time the threat of an expansionist China has emerged in its most belligerent form. The Middle Kingdom's hurry to challenge the status quo in a bid to emerge as the dominant power in Asia is quite evident. The riposte to this, as it were, has been India's desire to play a growing role in the Indo-Pacific.

The fund crunch and the desire to create the requisite capability have resulted in a conflicted trajectory most evident in the case of the Indian Army, given its large numbers; this, in turn, has implications for its revenue budget. This has placed an ever-increasing strain on the ability of the army to manage human resources, deliver on its responsibilities and continue to build necessary capabilities.

How can defence planners overcome this challenge in realistic terms? This is the key dilemma for policymakers and the senior leadership of the military. And this remains more so for the army, which has the largest manpower footprint among the three services as also the largest revenue component of the defence budget.

In light of this reality, this chapter will explore options to offset the existing threat—the resource logjam that the Indian Army finds itself in—through an analysis of each of the three variables and come up with possible solutions.

Threats and Responsibilities

The last five decades have largely witnessed a consistent combination of threats on the external front with Pakistan's challenge on the western border and China on the northern. The threat from China has remained a reality with a certain degree of stability prevailing, while the situation with Pakistan has been more fluid. Over time, this led to the weight of the military capability remaining focused towards the west. The attempt was to manage the dispute with China even as India dealt with Pakistan through diplomatic and military means. It was, therefore, not surprising for Prime Minister Narendra Modi, speaking at the St Petersburg International Economic Forum in 2017, to say, 'It is true that we have a border dispute with China. But in the last 40 years, not a single bullet has been fired because of it.'[2] This indicated that the differences with China could be managed, as had successfully been done in the past.

For some time, there has been an acceptance of the possibility of a two-front war. This was manifested in the defence minister's operational directive in 2008.[3] The military, and more specifically the Indian Army, had been speaking of this challenge even earlier. However, despite Defence Minister George Fernandes proclaiming China as 'potential threat No. 1' in 1998, little has changed in terms of the capability orientation of the army.[4] The three strike corps created over the decades as the offensive arm of the army were equipped to operate across the plains and deserts of Punjab and Rajasthan. Heavy tanks, towed artillery guns and bridging equipment were procured to take the battle into Pakistan, not China. Ironically, the structure of the strike corps did not change even after the defence minister's 2008 directive. What did change was the decision to raise two divisions to fill gaps in the defensive layout against China in 2009–2010.[5]

Over the years, clashes between patrols and claims and counter-claims were not unknown on the India and China border. However, 2013 brought a degree of open challenge. In April that year, in an attempt at forcing their claim, Chinese troops pitched three or four tents and occupied an Indian-claimed territory in Depsang in northern Ladakh. After a stand-off, the Chinese side withdrew in May 2013.[6]

The fears that had been repeatedly voiced over the years seemed to be gaining credibility. Consequently, the government gave the go-ahead for raising a strike corps against China. While this proposal had been pending, it is likely that the incident at Depsang spurred the decision.[7]

Almost on cue, yet another incident took place at Chumar in September 2014.[8] Unlike Depsang, there was no difference of opinion between the two sides in this area. The incident led to a physical clash and, unfortunately, took place during the official visit of Chinese President Xi Jinping.

Three years later, in 2017, a more serious incident took place at Doklam near the India–Bhutan–China trijunction border. This was sparked by China's attempt to change the status quo and unilaterally build a road into the Bhutanese territory. The stand-off that resulted lasted seventy-three days and was accompanied by a vicious media, legal and psychological campaign by the Chinese to thwart the Indian side, though with little success.[9]

The three incidents were followed up by an attempt by both sides to bridge the divide. Strategic guidance was issued from the highest level after meetings between Prime Minister Narendra Modi and President Xi Jinping. Even as temperatures cooled and relations picked up, the unilateral, aggressive attempts at changing the status quo along the Line of Actual Control (LAC) by China began yet again in May 2020.[10] Only this time, it was backed by a larger force and along a much larger frontage.

This backdrop is important to understand how India's threat spectrum has undergone a major change in a short span of about a decade. In this period, moreover, there has been no reduction in the security concerns vis-a-vis Pakistan. The threat of a two-front military challenge had indeed become a reality.

This reality was accompanied by China's growing footprint, including the regular movement of submarines, in the Indian Ocean Region (IOR).[11] A hallmark of this was the setting up of a Chinese base in Djibouti. China's presence and influence in India's neighbourhood and along strategically important ports also became a factor. Separately, a new challenge emerged in relation to the China–Pakistan Economic Corridor (CPEC) passing through an area illegally occupied by Pakistan. There was alarm, too, at the Chinese presence and influence in Nepal. This was, quite evidently, neither coincidental nor unrelated to how China was building its presence and capability in a bid to limit India's rise and influence in the region.[12]

The emergence of China as an overt and aggressive challenger seemed to validate the assessment made by Fernandes twenty-two years ago. Though, in this period, India, too, has enhanced its military capacity to operate beyond its traditional areas of influence. This was evident in the push for the idea of the Indo-Pacific as an area of influence and growing engagements with countries from the eastern board of Africa to the Pacific Ocean.

Despite this, the quantum jump needed to realistically cater for a two-front threat has fallen far short of expectations. In the previous wars with Pakistan, China was more of a potential, rather than an actual, military player. However, the reality of 2013, 2014 and 2017 suggested a change in Chinese behaviour. This was reinforced and magnified in 2020 with the Galwan clash that saw casualties on both sides.[13] Even though these were not an outcome of an exchange of fire, the oft-repeated contention of 'no casualties due to bullets' has become increasingly tenuous.

The growing concerns over China's decade-long assertiveness on the border led to India attempting to procure light tanks, howitzers, transport aircraft and heavy-lift helicopters and deploying military equipment, such as the existing tanks, apart from strengthening border infrastructure to include roads and advanced landing grounds. After Galwan, emergency powers were granted to the services to undertake procurements.[14]

The Indian military establishment has been struggling with budgets to deal with a threat, such as from Pakistan, while expecting to maintain the status quo with China. But the emergence of Beijing as a serious military player on the LAC now requires a fresh direction in the capability development. The question that arises is: where will India find the resources for this requirement?

Monetary Outlay

The changing Chinese posture has come at a time when there is an increasing pressure on the defence budget outlay. As it is, there has been a virtual cap on the percentage of growth of the defence budget, which, in any case, barely kept pace with the annual inflation rate.[15] From the government's perspective, the need to push infrastructure development, education and health, among its other responsibilities, required a fine balancing act. And this led to a defence outlay that barely, if at all, covered committed liabilities.

The Sixth Pay Commission resulted in an across-the-board spurt in salaries and pensions, including those relating to the defence services. The Seventh Pay Commission and the acceptance of the concept of One Rank One Pension (OROP) pushed this up further.[16] The impact on manpower cost was most pronounced in the army compared to the other two services. As a result, recent statistics suggest that the army spends almost 82 per cent of its budget on revenue expenditure, with a mere 18 per cent available for capital or force modernisation needs. This, quite obviously, is inadequate for an army that is deployed along active borders and has remained involved in countering terrorism as part of Pakistan's proxy war against India.

The answers suggested from an accountant's perspective are not surprising: as the armed forces can't do without modernisation, they must cut their revenue expenditure. And since vehicles will continue to need spares and tanks and aircraft fuel to operate (both components of revenue expenditure), the only option is to tweak the pay, service conditions or pensions of personnel. The second and third elements seem to have become the most obvious options for 'rationalisation' as salaries must also relate to those of other central government services.

There have been suggestions to reduce the term of service in the armed forces, thereby limiting the number of soldiers eligible for pension.[17] The option of bringing the armed forces within the ambit of contributory pension schemes has also come up.[18]

Proponents have related these proposals to the experience of countries in the West, especially the US, the UK, Australia and France,[19] or of the paramilitary and central police organisations within India. Rarely has any effort been made to correlate them to the actual service conditions of military personnel, the country's economic condition and its job market, the comparative demands on the armed forces and the impact on their morale from applying a different yardstick to the armed forces. It has usually been about numbers and numbers alone!

Capability Development

If the threats have grown along with financial constraints, what will be its impact on capability development?

The Indian Air Force has repeatedly highlighted the declining numbers of its squadrons.[20] The Indian Navy has made the case for a third aircraft carrier if India wants to pursue its ambitions and security agenda that has been defined in the Naval strategy document of 2016.[21] The Indian Army remains saddled with equipment that should have long been replaced, and the process for the replacement of yet another lot should have been underway. However, this process remains stuck because of a lack of money.

The progress of these initiatives has been documented extensively in the reports of the Parliamentary Standing Committee on Defence, which, for its part, has repeatedly underlined existing shortfalls and gaps in capabilities.

Former vice chief of army staff, while deposing before the Parliamentary Committee on Defence, said in 2018:

> The Budget of 2018-19 has dashed our hopes and most of what has been achieved has actually received a little set back. To highlight a few cases, the marginal increase in BE (Budget Estimates) barely accounts for the inflation and does not even cater for the taxes. Allocation of Rs. 21,338 Crore [213.38 billion] for modernisation is insufficient even to cater for committed liabilities of Rs 29,033 Crore [290.33 billion] for 125 on-going schemes, emergency procurements.... Committed liabilities of 2017 which will also get passed on to 2018 will further accentuate the situation. Therefore, liquidation of this committed liability will hardly leave any funds for new schemes in 2018-19.... As far as we are concerned, the state today is 68 per cent of our equipment is in the vintage category.[22]

The vice chief added that while 'Make in India' was a great initiative, the army did not have the requisite funds to support it. Similarly, the initiative to undertake strategic partnerships will also get delayed in light of the budgetary stringency.

Capital expenditure has a critical role in building and retaining the capability of the armed forces. However, its proportion to the overall budget has been coming down over the years. Table 6.1 indicates the demand and allocation of the capital budget for the three services.[23]

TABLE 6.1 Projection and Allocation of Capital Expenditure from 2015–2016 to 2020–2021

Year	*Service*	*BE*		*RE*		*Expenditure*
		Projected	*Allotted*	*Projected*	*Allotted*	*(in Crores)*
2015–2016	Army	31,938.67	27,342.42	27,845.33	24,230.47	20,703.70
	Navy	26,268.13	25,003.24	25,152.20	19,740.06	19,874.69
	Air Force	46,191.96	33,686.75	35,780.78	30,442.15	31,198.32
2016–2017	Army#	37,960.18	26,935.81	34,489.90	24,017.86	28,462.11
	Navy	30,223.31	22,000.09	22,530.04	19,596.28	19,996.88
	Air Force	41,266.41	29795.42	36,512.95	28,239.86	30,414.79
2017–2018	Army	42,485.93	25,205.71	40,791.43	25,205.71	27,148.26
	Navy	28,591.56	19,348.16	27,717.41	19,348.16	20,118.58
	Air Force	62,048.85	33,570.17	52,548.50	33,570.17	34,917.60
2018–2019	Army	44,572.63	26,815.71	41,614.41	26,815.71	27,438.66
	Navy	35,695.41	20,848.16	30,735.65	20,890.87	21,509.60
	Air Force	77,694.74	35,770.17	68,579.46	35,770.17	36,451.74
2019–2020	Army	44,660.57	29,511.25	46,032.00	29,666.90	19,817.19
	Navy	37,220.98	23,156.43	40,123.18	26,156.43	23,050.79
	Air Force	74,894.56	39,347.19	81,301.99	44,947.19	37,154.79
2020–2021	Army	50,373.60	32,462.38			
	Navy	45,268.31	26,688.28			
	Air Force	66,207.29	43,281.91			

(# Includes allotments to NCC, military farms, Rashtriya Rifles and ECHS, which were shifted to modified Grant No 20-MoD (Miscellaneous) in FY 2016–2017, for the purpose of comparison with previous as well as future years. Except for military farms and ECHS, other organisations were transferred back to Defence Services Estimates in FY 2017–2018. In FY 2019–2020, military farms and ECHS also reverted to DSE)

A survey of the capital and revenue budget of the three services for the year 2020–2021 provides a perspective of the comparison between the two heads:

TABLE 6.2 Service-wise Projection and Allocation of Revenue and Capital Expenditure[24]

Service	Revenue (Net)		Capital		Total Allocation (Revenue + Capital)
	Projection	Allocation	Projection	Allocation	
Army	165,228.28	145,785.88	50,373.60	32,462.38	178,248.26
Navy	27,905.69	19,495.10	43,707.48	25,666.49	45,161.59
Joint Staff	4,332.27	3,439.65	1,560.83	1,021.79	4,461.44
Air Force	43,904.17	29,962.66	66,207.29	43,281.91	73,244.57

The process of capability development within the three services follows a model wherein, based on the directive issued by the defence minister, a long-term integrated perspective plan (LTIPP) covering a period of fifteen years is prepared. This identifies specific weapons and equipment for procurement, which will help create a certain capability. Each service has its own procurement plan for five years based on this plan. An annual acquisition plan covering a period of two years further contributes to this plan.[25]

And finally, to put this in perspective, the figures for each financial year have been translated to percentages for both capital and revenue expenditure, as shown in Table 6.3:

TABLE 6.3 Percentage of Revenue and Capital Budget from 2014–2015 to 2010–2021[26]

Year	Service	Revenue	Capital
2014–15	Army	84	16
	Navy	38	62
	Air Force	38	62
	Total Outlay	63	37
2015–16	Army	83	17
	Navy	43	57
	Air Force	40	60
	Total Outlay	65	35
2016–17	Army	80	20
	Navy	46	54
	Air Force	43	57
	Total Outlay	66	34
2017–18	Army	82	18
	Navy	48	52
	Air Force	44	56
	Total Outlay	68	32
2018–19	Army	83	17
	Navy	49	51
	Air Force	44	56
	Total Outlay	68	32
2019–20 (RE)	Army	83	17
	Navy	49	51
	Air Force	43	57
	Total Outlay	66	34
2020–21 (BE)	Army	82	18
	Navy	46	54
	Air Force	41	59
	Total Outlay	65	35

It is quite evident from the table that the primary challenge in terms of the correlation between revenue and capital expenditure is being faced by the army. The vice chief of army staff confirmed in his oral evidence to the parliamentary committee that the ideal ratio between revenue and capital expenditure should be 60:40. He ascribed the skewed ratio, which had been prevailing for a few years, to the challenge of unresolved borders and the internal security environment. There can be little doubt that, given the percentage of allocation to the defence budget, the revenue budget of the army is unlikely to see a major change. And if this situation prevails, capacity building is bound to be affected.

We have seen that there have been some emergency procurements to offset the immediate challenge of every major national security crisis we have faced. However, it is also clear that this cannot provide a lasting solution to the almost-intractable problems of military modernisation.

Way Forward

It may be appropriate here to discuss the changing character of war before we discuss the options available to bring the three ends of the triangle into a seamless connect.[27] This will dictate how armed forces will fight in the future and, logically, should also dictate today's priorities, structures and procurement patterns.

The easiest mandate given to the armed forces, more often than not by their own senior leadership, is to prepare for a 'full spectrum' capability. This will, of course, be eminently feasible if the armed forces also had a full spectrum budget. Therefore, it is for the military commanders to clearly lay down their priorities. And for that, there is a need for a professional assessment of the future battlefield. Given India's budgetary reality, no army can prepare simultaneously for a major conventional war on multiple fronts, terrorism in multiple regions, defensive and offensive cyber operations, a nuclear war, aid to civil authorities and simultaneously transform into an AI-driven, network-centric force, even while functioning as a net security provider in the neighbouring region and beyond. The results are bound to remain sub-optimal.

The Indian Army needs to reorient its conventional force structure, which reflects the reality of the industrial age. The doctrines and tactical manoeuvres—both in conventional and sub-conventional operations—have not kept pace with the benefits that technology provides. And this is not merely aimed at reducing numbers; the attempt must also be to enhance the combat efficiency of fighting units.

The context of the existing realities with Pakistan and China indicates the importance of maintaining deterrence against any conventional threat. For this, does the army need three strike corps arrayed against Pakistan despite having concluded that Pakistan has since long undertaken a strategic shift to employ hybrid warfare—a mix of terrorism, information campaigns, cyberwarfare and subversion—against India?[28] As the Kargil action of 1999 indicated, this does not suggest that conventional wars are a thing of the past. However, it does suggest that it represented the lower end of the military spectrum that may have since transformed into the higher end of the same spectrum in the present (and future) scenarios. If that indeed is the case, has the capability development initiative been readjusted to this reality? Does India still need a standing army of the size that we have? Can there be a different way to approach the challenges being faced from Pakistan and China?

The strategy adopted in the 1980s aimed at striking deep inside Pakistan, and force structures and equipment profiles were created for this objective. Surely, then, with changes in the objective, should not the structures and profile change? Similarly, if the logistical model in place in the past was created to support deep thrusts inside enemy territory, does it need to remain the same when that is no longer feasible? A similar assessment can also be made for other affiliated actions and organisations in support of the larger objective.

Despite the manpower-intensive nature of the army's responsibilities, there is little escaping the fact that cuts are necessary. The army has two choices to make in the face of its budgetary imbalance. Either it accepts a change in its service conditions—in terms of pay, perks and pensions—or costs will have to be controlled by reducing numbers. From the accountant's point of view, it is always easier to rejig service conditions. When they are argued for by military professionals, numbers are difficult to counter by accountants. Changing service conditions for the worse will have an impact on morale, motivation and the quality of people being recruited and is, in a sense, an intangible that can be glossed over. But the detrimental effect of such moves is obvious. For far too long, the army has chosen the maximalist approach of continuing with the status quo even as it demanded modernisation. The reality of the present times suggests that this will no longer remain a viable alternative.

A number of options have been suggested by the committee of experts headed by Lieutenant General D.B.

Shekatkar (Retd).[29] Some of these are being implemented and will see a reduction in numbers by around 50,000–100,000.[30] It may also be the time to consider some other major options.

The first is handing over counterterrorism duties fully to the Central Reserve Police Force (CRPF) and terminating the useful experiment of the Rashtriya Rifles, which has over 70,000 personnel, including headquarters and officers.

The army alone is not meant to fight threats, such as terrorism. In the past decade and more, there has been a significant increase in the numbers of the Central Armed Police Forces who can take up the burden. The CRPF's sanctioned strength in 2019 was 324,810, the Border Security Force (BSF) 263,905, the Central Industrial Security Force (CISF) 156,013, the Sashashtra Seema Bal (SSB) 99,221, the Indo-Tibetan Border Police (ITBP) 89,438 and, finally, the Assam Rifles 66,408.[31]

The total strength is just short of a million. This increase is related to their taking over enhanced counterterrorism responsibilities. There cannot be a simultaneous increase in two organisations, with responsibilities that overlap to an extent that goes beyond the logic of redundancy and contingency.

Second, serious thought will also have to be given to the need for three strike corps to handle the threat from Pakistan. A reduction of one strike corps can further lead to a cut of over 60,000 personnel. These are just two examples that can lead to a 10 per cent reduction in the size of the army.

There has been a long debate about the lateral induction of soldiers into central police organisations. While the mechanics and details of the proposal can be evaluated, there is little doubt that such an induction will go a long way in reducing the Indian Army's pension burden. It is perhaps time for such options to be seriously considered again.

A number of options have been discussed in the past to reduce personnel and costs. However, these suggestions must be viewed from the right perspective. One of the more common suggestions recommends the use of technology to reduce the manpower-intensive responsibilities of the army. The use of robotics and AI have opened up options that have created a dramatic impact on organisational efficiencies. Three examples immediately come to mind. While some are already making an impact, others have shown remarkable potential.

A recent incident saw the assassination of an Iranian scientist. Tehran contended that a weapon mounted on a vehicle, controlled remotely, was used to carry out the killing.[32] The incident opens up the option of controlling weapons at sensitive locations without the employment of manpower. This, along with the possibility of improving optical, thermal and radar-based systems, can offset the heavy requirement of manpower along sensitive parts of the disputed borders.

Another element is the use of remotely controlled and piloted air and undersea vehicles that can partly provide an alternative to manned platforms.[33] Similarly, self-driven vehicles are being experimented with in a major way by a number of manufacturers.[34] Can a future army have its vehicles driven in this manner? This will substantially reduce the employment of drivers and pilots in certain specific scenarios.

The possibilities are endless, though some of them are years away in terms of their acceptance and induction, especially in the relatively more unpredictable and harsher operational situations required by military services.

This is especially in the case of the army, which finds most of its manpower-intensive needs coming from the disputed borders it guards. It is not easy to do away with the physical presence of forces given the special circumstances we have seen on the Line of Control with Pakistan and the LAC with China. Therefore, for now, while technology will undoubtedly enhance force capability and efficiency, it is unlikely to make an immediate difference in reducing numbers. This has been seen with the introduction of computers, networks and GPS-based navigation systems in the past. Technology must cross a tipping point for it to create a paradigm shift to function effectively. This tipping point in manpower-intensive responsibilities, however welcome, is unlikely to emerge in the next decade and perhaps beyond.

This raises the important question of the cost of technology. Experience has shown that given its research and development costs, new technology will initially require increased investments. It is only in the long run that overall costs can be reduced. Economies of scale and returns on investment are a must for long-term reduction in costs. In the meanwhile, budgets may have to be expanded to improve capability and invest in the future. India's experience suggests that both an increase in size and enhancement in quality led to a budget increase. While the former took place after the 1962 Sino-Indian war. The latter happened after the victory of 1971 over Pakistan.[35]

Defence budgets saw a substantial increase after the 1962 war when it was realised that capability development was a critical national security requirement. Similarly, after the 1971 war, when the recommendations of the experts' committee headed by Krishna Rao for modernising the army were taken up (as were similar options for the other two services), budgetary allocations were increased substantially to meet the requirement for weapon and platform procurement through the 1980s.

Therefore, the induction of new technology or platform for any major transformative shift must go beyond the existing capital allocations. An actual increase in outlay is the only route open for this. However, beyond that, on a more routine basis, it would be useful to analyse options that can be applied on a more regular basis to ensure greater efficiencies.

The final aspect relates to organisational issues. There is no magic wand that can bring in efficiencies. It comes from rethinking structures, systems and procedures. There is little denying that the army continues with practices that are a legacy of British India. Ironically, even as the British Army has reformed itself and brought in a degree of simplicity and prudence, the same has not been witnessed in adequate measure in the Indian Army. It is time to ask a simple question: how does an existing system enhance operational or functional efficiency? And if it does not, is it perhaps not time to discard it? And if it is felt that such a process is not feasible in-house, is it time for an international professional consultant to provide the recommendations that the army itself may be hesitant in outlining?

The reality of the situation is staring the Indian Army in the face. It is time for a self-generated systemic change or to be pushed to change. The latter might bring with it unintended consequences that could adversely affect operational efficiency. For change to be truly holistic and long-lasting, it must come from within. It is for the Indian Army to create congruity between reality and change. And this can only happen by balancing the triangle of threats, capabilities and resources.

7

Vectored Thrust: The Future of Indian Air Power

GROUP CAPTAIN KISHORE KUMAR KHERA (RETD)

The development of kinetic capability is an intricate process in which finite financial resources need to be channelised to achieve strategic objectives. The process is most complex in a technologically intensive domain, such as aerospace, where all the components have the multirole capability and high-sustenance costs. The complexity only increases if strategic goals are ill-defined. At this juncture, with aggressive neighbours, enhanced hybridisation of conflict,[1] the increasing role of technology, a waning combat aircraft fleet and an acute economic crunch as a result of Covid-19, the capability-building plan for Indian aerospace power needs a de novo assessment.

Wars in the next decade will be won or lost in the information domain, and the entity that knows more will invariably dominate/devastate the opposing force even without a matching military capability. With finite resources, there is bound to be a battle within a force over allocation for systems to enhance information and systems capable of packing a punch. The debate around butter versus guns now has a clearly articulated subset within 'guns', which is information versus strike. Both information and strike capabilities are important and are, indeed, useless without adequate support from each other.

A balance is necessary for optimisation, but often 'strike' has a predominant role. It is time to relook at this.

A time frame of ten years is appropriate to chart out a course of action. It should take into account assessments of the geostrategic landscape, the foreseeable technological road map, resource availability and the time required for the fructification of various aspects of capability development from acquisition to operationalisation. How should Indian aerospace power traverse the next decade, ensuring the protection of national interests while remaining within the available means?

The first part of my argument covers qualitative and quantitative assessments of the current aerospace power of China and Pakistan and compares them with Indian capability. The second brings out key attributes of conflict of the coming decade. Finally, I examine the aerospace capability that India needs to have by 2030 to remain relevant. I also discuss various methods that India can employ to reach the desired capability goals.

The Current Aerospace Equation

Security-wise, India faces two challenges: China and Pakistan. A comparative analysis of TEAM (thoughts, equipment, application philosophy and management)[2]—including inventory and capability of combat aircraft, weapons, systems, airlift, force multipliers, space-based assets, infrastructure, helicopters, unmanned systems, training and experience, logistical support, the indigenous aerospace industry—of all three players throws up an interesting matrix. For military hardware, infrastructure and personnel strength, China holds a 3:1 advantage over

India[3] but the Chinese advantage in military industry, technology, organisational power and economic resources is far greater. Where India has an advantage over China, specifically for aerospace power, includes geography and exposure to best practices of major air powers of the world. But are these enough to handle China? Probably not.

As regards Pakistan, in terms of hardware and numerical strength, India has an edge.[4] However, over the last two decades, Pakistan has been successful in neutralising this advantage by making conventional power irrelevant with its low-intensity conflict strategy and nuclear threat.[5] A new normal in the India–Pakistan military equation was initiated by the Indian surgical strike in 2016 and the Balakot strike in 2019. The qualitative and quantitative edge of Indian aerospace power over its counterpart in Pakistan has been gradually diminishing, and events of February 2019 support this assertion.

So, now to the critical question. What should India's relative aerospace power equation be with respect to China and Pakistan? To reach a realistic assessment, a look at conflict dynamics in the next decade is a prerequisite.

Conflict Dynamics in 2030

The character of conflict is under transformation. On the one hand, several non-kinetic aspects have dominated the change, and on the other, kinetic power projection and enforcement have undergone a metamorphosis. The last decade hardly saw any force-on-force, large-scale encounters, although peaceful coexistence was elusive. The role of controlling and manipulating media, including social media, has been an easy and cost-effective strategy implemented by states and non-state actors and by states through non-state actors. The results have been phenomenal. Add to this the ease with which events in cyberspace can be orchestrated, the defensive mechanisms of almost all states and organisations continuously remain under stress. But the game in kinetic power too has evolved with technological advances in sensors, communication, processing power and artificial intelligence. An attack on a well-defended oil refinery deep inside a large and powerful state[6] and the assassination of two powerful and crucial Iranian military officers,[7] one during his visit to Iraq and the other within Iran, are indicative of an ability to hit targets precisely, anywhere in the world. The implications of such events are far-reaching and, in many cases, more than a conventional war. So targeting has evolved and the focus has shifted from armed forces and military hardware to the identification of key capabilities and enablers and eliminating them. Even in a conventional clash between Azerbaijan and Armenia in 2020, the outcome was governed by technological superiority and precision targeting.[8] So how will a conflict look like a decade from now?

To look at a future conflict scenario objectively, it is important to assess four defining parameters of any conflict: battlespace, timeline, targeting and outcome. The infusion of long-range kinetic weapons and platforms has allowed battlespace expansion. Unlike in the last century, key enablers can be hit anywhere in the world. The risk for the attacker is further minimised by the use of unmanned systems[9] and collateral damage is also minimised by the use of smart sensors enabled by artificial intelligence. Consequently, looking across the border, though important, has lost its salience. Now, security involves a 360-degree view and protection of key enablers, mostly individuals, but could be systems and subsystems too. The attack could emanate from any dimension: land, sea, air, space or cyberspace.

The second aspect is about timelines. The declaration of war is passe. The intents are unambiguous but seldom supported by a formal declaration. The ongoing 'no war, no peace' situation is likely to continue. Under these circumstances, the window of opportunity to unhinge an adversary will be very small. As an event that necessitates a reaction unfolds, a quick decision and fast kinetic force application will be necessary. In case an opportunity is missed, there is likely to be a very long wait for the next chance.

Two terrorist attacks, one in Uri in 2016 and the second in Pulwama in 2019, were responded to after eleven days with a surgical strike on terrorist launch pads and an attack on the Balakot terrorist training camp. Should another terrorist attack take place, India will have to respond faster to hit the terrorists before they disperse and diminish the impact of a strike. Taking into account the likely Indian response, terrorist organisations in Pakistan may disperse as soon as they plot an attack in India. Therefore, the reaction time available for an effective response will be minimal and much smaller than the almost two weeks taken by India in 2016 and 2019. Kinetic tools, consequently, need to be ready to hit back within hours—always and every time.

This aspect is valid not only for countering terrorist attacks but also for military targets. This facet, along with an expansion of battlespace, puts the focus on intelligence operations, with the need for 24x7 reconnaissance, surveillance and intelligence operations. Only with effective surveillance can an attack be prevented and, if required, a punitive strike carried out. The surveillance system will need inputs from all possible sensors—based on land, sea, air or space—and cover the entire electromagnetic spectrum to pick up communications, electro-optical and infrared signatures. The lack of the requisite surveillance capability was the prime failure that led to the Kargil war in 1999. And nothing seems to have changed. If Chinese motives were assessed correctly based on their force concentration, and Indian troops moved accordingly, the ongoing stand-off in Ladakh would have followed a different contour.[10]

The next aspect is about targeting. As the battlespace expands and timelines compress, power will be centred on certain decision-making individuals, and the entire decision-to-execution cycle will depend on fast communication networks. This means that the best way to neutralise a system will be to target key decision-makers and/or communication and decision-assisting networks. Recent assassinations of key Iranians and attacks on government networks across the world support this hypothesis. The significance of networks will further grow as artificial intelligence gathers momentum. Even in the pure kinetic domain, attacks on a few key assets can have a devastating impact, as was witnessed in Nagorno-Karabakh where Azerbaijan successfully targeted air defence systems and rendered the entire Armenian force vulnerable to aerial attacks.[11] More than the loss in the physical domain, the psychological impact of such precision strikes proved decisive in that short war.

The last defining parameter of conflict is the outcome. Killing an individual or subverting a network for a few hours—or at best, a few days—may not have a major impact on a state or a well-oiled organisation. However, the impact of such events will go beyond physical aspects and have a telling impact on the morale of the state/organisation. That will be significant and help achieve the desired goals in the strategic, economic, diplomatic or physical domain. The objectives of future conflict are likely to be power—or perception of power—rather than the accrual of physical holdings. Therefore, psychological aspects will dominate. Azerbaijan's release of videos of attacks on Armenian forces and no trace of any tell-tale signs in the assassination of Iranian Brigadier Mohsen Fakhrizadeh in November 2020 had a devastating impact on Armenia and Iran, respectively.

Overall, the conflict in the coming decade will be defined by the ability to stay ahead in the information battle and have the kinetic capability to hit desired targets with speed and precision. As the battlespace expands, it will be impractical to have forces deployed everywhere. For the physical domain on land, as often the victory is still measured on foot, where the keys to success will be mobility and logistics. The ability to quickly move forces where required and then sustain them with a robust and efficient logistical chain will define the outcome of the conflict. The ongoing stand-off in Ladakh substantiates the necessity for quick mobilisation and a robust sustenance chain.[12]

The most significant change that the coming decade will witness is an unprecedented advantage for the first mover. The battle between offence and defence has always been a balanced one. The attacker needs more resources and power to breach the defensive set-up or dug-in troops. Conventionally, a 3:1 superiority is required in the plains and 9:1 in mountainous terrain for a successful attack. But the attacker overcomes a part of this limitation by choosing the time and place of attack and thereby surprising the defender. With a great deal of technology infusion in kinetic tools, the offence–defence balance is today tilted decisively in favour of the attacker. In other words, the first-mover advantage is incredible.

Apart from choosing the time and place of attack, technology now gives the attacker multiple execution options. The extended ranges of weapons, precision-targeting minimising collateral and unmanned systems minimising risks, favour the attacker; the defender is practically left defenceless as it is impossible to protect every part of the system. The defensive systems against aerial attacks are expensive and often limited in numbers, thus they have limited coverage. Even if the intended target is well covered by a potent air defence system like the S-400, the chances of completely neutralising a well-planned attacking force are low. Moreover, with the use of low-cost unmanned systems and precision smart munitions, the sheer economic cost of firing expensive surface-to-air missiles or air-to-air missiles makes it a lose-lose transaction for the defender.

Aerospace Power Focus Areas

So what should be the capability goals of an aerospace power with two hostile, nuclear-armed neighbours? Indian airpower needs to reinvent itself to face the challenges in the coming decade for two reasons. First, the threat of a two-front war has already come into play. Both China and Pakistan need to be handled—and simultaneously so. Second, the resources available for capability development are shrinking in real terms and will contract further because of the economic crisis triggered by Covid-19. Setting goals to achieve the requisite capability within limited resources will be a challenge. It will thus be prudent to focus on certain subdomains that will give the requisite capabilities for the challenges ahead instead of developing all domains and aspects. Although not an ideal situation for military power, the time has come to switch India's goal from becoming a 'powerful military' to being a 'smart military'.

The most visible and potent aerial platforms are combat aircraft (commonly known as fighter aircraft). The Indian Air Force (IAF) and the Indian Navy are together authorised to have nearly 1,000 combat aircraft,[13] but the number currently stands at less than 700—and receding further. By the end of the current decade, the number is expected to be in the region of 550.[14] No matter what India does, IAF is likely to have no more than twenty-four to twenty-six combat aircraft squadrons by 2030. The force level will be lower in case the productivity at Hindustan Aeronautics Limited remains low. Quantitatively and qualitatively, the die is already cast for the combat aircraft fleet. Everything else, as a part of kinetic capability, in general, and aerospace power, in particular, will have to deal with this reality.

While it is important to have platforms to deliver weapons, these are best utilised in conjunction with battlespace transparency tools. As explained in the previous section, battlespace transparency, or the lack thereof, will govern the outcome. Current resources, equipment and capability fall well short of the required level and, in certain aspects, are even behind Pakistan. There is a clear need to equip the force with battlespace transparency tools. AWACS, AEW&C, reconnaissance and surveillance systems based in space, air or surface ought to be priorities. Unless the position of hostile elements—on the ground, in the air or maritime domain—is known and tracked, it is impossible to neutralise them. Therefore, rather than focus on increasing the inventory of combat aircraft, often exorbitantly priced, better combat potential can be generated by a combination of battlespace transparency tools and combat platforms. Not for nothing are such battlespace transparency tools called force multipliers. The Defence Acquisition Council has set the ball rolling by seeking six additional AWACS.[15] Can the Defence Research and Development Organisation (DRDO) deliver? Looking at the record, the probability of this project getting completed on time is low. There is a need to assign the project 'key mission' status and provide it with capable personnel and priority funding.

The second focus area needs to be a sensor–weapon combination. The induction of the Rafale fighters in the IAF in 2020 was claimed as a 'game changer'.[16] A 4.5 generation fighter, it is the best India has as of now, but the tag of it being a 'game changer' is overhyped as it does not bring any new capability to the force. A range of sensors and weapons on board does give this aircraft its potency and this ought to be the focus area. Re-equipping other combat aircraft with more sensitive and durable sensors, along with long-range weapons, will be a true game changer. The slow pace of upgradation of the SU-30MKI is a case in point.[17] Rather than increasing the number of platforms, the focus needs to be on enhancing potency per platform. That is a cost-effective option. A BrahMos-equipped Su-30MKI[18] and Astra-armed light combat aircraft (LCA)[19] are significant steps in this direction. But more needs to be done. Energising the development of longer range and more precise versions of the BrahMos and Astra is the key at this juncture, and the entire establishment should focus on these two aspects. Once these schemes come to fruition, they will be 'game changers'. Although both BrahMos[20] and Astra currently depend on imported components,[21] their indigenisation will allow further development in this field and help enhance their potency. In line with these projects, more indigenous precise weapons need development and integration with various platforms, including building on the success of initial projects like the Hypersonic Technology Demonstration Vehicle (HSTDV).[22]

The third focus area needs to be effective resource utilisation of aerial assets. A seamless data link that will allow the entire combat force in an area to act as a single, powerful entity. Without a secure data link between various platforms, communication is restricted and utilisation and effectiveness suboptimal.[23] The process of development of an airborne data link is moving at a snail's pace. In an era of network-centric warfare, this is sacrilege. Unless this gross error is rectified, the dwindling number of combat aircraft will be even more ineffective. This approach needs a change. For starters, the initial, limited success in quantum communication[24] needs to progress at the speed of light and evolve to include quantum computing and quantum radars. This research effort needs impetus like no other and can help offset dwindling combat power. Practical advances made in this field will transform the force application, probably leaving the much-touted stealth features of today redundant and taking electronic warfare to another level.[25]

The fourth aspect concerns the development and integration of unmanned aerial systems in the operational matrices. These systems are already playing a significant role in military aviation and kinetic power projection. With low risk and relatively low cost, an unmanned system, equipped with precision-guided weapons, can have a significant impact on the outcome of conflicts. With DRDO unable to meet this requirement for decades, imports[26] have been the preferred option and, of late, some systems are on lease[27] for surveillance purposes. This is an area where the private sector can be incentivised; although baby steps were taken with the Baba Mehar Singh open competition, which indeed was too little.[28]

The last aspect concerns organisational issues. Shrinking resources are a fait accompli and certain organisational changes are required to offset the pinch. First, focus on core competencies. The IAF needs to shed non-core segments: surface-to-surface missiles and the Garud force, to begin with, as both these capabilities already exist with the sister services. Similar duplication within the IAF needs a relook: its Training Command and Directorate of Training, Maintenance Command and Maintenance Branch at the Indian Air Force Headquarters, et al. The reduction in duplication will result in efficient processes and resource conservation. An expansion of the Defence Communication Network[29] to subsume individual networks of all three services will not only reduce communication bottlenecks and inter-operability issues but also lead to resource conservation. Hopefully, integration efforts initiated with the appointment of a Chief of Defence Staff will help cut organisational flab.[30]

The Gestalt Approach

Indian aerospace power needs to reorientate in the coming decade to remain relevant. More importantly, policymakers need to understand that the reduction in resource allocation will leave the Indian armed forces, in general, and Indian aerospace power, in particular, with limited kinetic capability. Therefore, there is a need to keep the geostrategic environment under constant watch and change basic defence policy from reactive to proactive. For far too long, India had been tolerating the aggressiveness of its neighbours, with 'India does not react' becoming the norm. This changed to 'India reacts' after the 2016 and 2019 strikes in Pakistan. This needs to further change to 'India acts' to offset the diminishing military capability. This will align with changing character of war, with the offence–defence balance tilted towards offence. Similarly, changes in military operational philosophy and equipping have often been reactive. This, combined with a labyrinthine acquisition process and non-functional indigenous defence industry, has ensured that India is always ready for a war of yesteryears. Thought processes need a radical change for our forces to be ready for the wars of the future.

In the coming decades, it would be impractical for India to attempt to outmatch or outgun China in terms of equipment and resources. Therefore, a major focus of the Indian establishment ought to be on investing in capabilities that will give the country some viable military options. Rather than an all-domain parity with China, Indian aerospace power would do well to focus on specific areas and generate capability dominance or parity in specific subdomains. The current state of the Indian military is an outcome of the country's failure in the past to invest in its future. Today, India needs to invest in capabilities that will define future battlespace. Focus and resource allocation for R&D in certain key capabilities is the only practical option and needs implementation even at the cost of deferring military hardware imports for sustaining current capability levels. Overall, at this juncture, with very limited resources, only a vectored thrust can prevent Indian aerospace power from stalling.

8

Beyond Equal Opportunities: Women in the Armed Forces

NISHTHA GAUTAM

Widows of military personnel doing smart drills at passing out parades of the Officers Training Academy make for compelling headlines. In the past few years, India has seen many women who lost their husbands in action join the military, ostensibly as a tribute to their departed spouses. The act not only attempts to bring emotional closure—with the advent of a new life—to the newly commissioned woman officer, but it also showcases the Indian armed forces as a caring, embracing 'family'.

However, women's participation in the forces ought to avoid precisely these tropes and cliches of sentimentality when it comes to the discourse on modernisation. Nor should policy decisions be informed by self-perpetuating myths about the suitability of women soldiers in a tradition-driven military.

The argument for a more gender-balanced military should also not be approached merely through the prism of equal opportunity—though equality remains the centrepiece of our national aspirations—but by taking a hard look at the urgent need to build more efficient, economically smarter and sustainable forces.

India needs a dramatically overhauled security structure in terms of both acquisition and organisation of resources. In this schema of India's long-awaited military modernisation, the importance of women's increased participation cannot be stressed enough.

Making the Army Smarter

India's armed forces have been tackling, since Independence, significant and continual challenges of internal security, apart from two hostile armies at the borders. With assimilation being the stated political policy with respect to internal security threats from insurgencies—there's no indication of any policy change in future either—the Indian military ought to see itself in a peacekeeping role even without wearing the blue helmets.

Ashley Tellis[1] notes that handing over the counter-insurgency role entirely to the paramilitary forces is not going to happen anytime soon, and even if there is a drastic change in the allocation of these responsibilities, Indian armed forces will likely stay engaged for training purposes. He also observes that at present, almost 60 per cent of the defence budget is 'eaten up by pay and pensions, a testament to the steady increase in size of India's personnel under arms over the last three decades—during which the 10 biggest defence spenders have done exactly the opposite'.

Despite its mammoth size, the Indian military is spread out thin owing to the twin challenges of guarding its borders and dealing with internal security. This is why the chorus for a military that looks and acts smarter is growing in India. Can women's increased participation achieve it? Perhaps yes, but even raising such a question can put one at loggerheads with scholars, such as Sylvia Chant and Caroline Sweetman,[2] whose idea of 'smart economics', which 'rationalises "investing" in women and girls for more effective development outcomes', can be comfortably extended to the military modernisation discourse. They propose that instead of being the goals per se, women's empowerment and gender equality become tools to make better economic sense. For a country that is staring at growing security challenges along its borders while the economy struggles, thanks to flaws in policymaking and the stress of the Covid-19 pandemic, choosing economics over sociology looks like a wise thing to do.

Let us try and argue for greater participation of women in the Indian armed forces from a purely utilitarian standpoint: increased participation of women is about an improvement in security outcomes. The next few thousand words seek to explain why and how.

New Personnel Paradigms

In their iconoclastic research on the Israeli military's mixed-gender training bases, Orna Sasson-Levy and Sarit Amram-Katz demonstrated that there is rarely any difference in operational suitability of men and women in the time of hi-tech warfare.[3]

On the whole, though, the quantitative data from the studied training courses indicate that the functioning of men and women was relatively similar and, more important, that differences within each gender group were greater than differences between genders. Age differences, prior military experience and education seemed to be more indicative than gender in their chances of graduating with high grades.

The authors, however, state,

> The military schema, in contrast, positions the masculine body of the warrior as a universal military ideal. This is an androcentric rule demanding that all soldiers, men and women alike, shape their bodies and behaviour in accordance with the warrior model, and the closer one gets to the core of the military, the more crucial is his or her resemblance to the combat soldier.[4]

India's military also seems to be stuck in worshipping the masculine body as the gold standard for soldiering, ignoring all other aspects of warfare. At a time when all the three arms, especially the Air Force, are seeking to build intelligence, surveillance and reconnaissance (ISR) capabilities, this insistence on superhero-like physical ability to preclude women from combat formations is counterproductive.

At this point, let's look at what scholar Chris Dougherty recommended to Indian strategists and force planners in light of emerging threats from China.[5] To buttress my argument, these recommendations are worth quoting in toto.

- Offensive cyberattacks to disrupt networks and exfiltrate information;
- Information operations to confuse Chinese ISR and feed bad data into Chinese targeting processes;
- Camouflage, concealment and deception;
- Constant movement of forces to interfere with Chinese operational planning;
- Jamming/dazzling of overhead sensors;
- Exercising emissions control to negate China's electronic intelligence capabilities.

India should, therefore, attempt to avoid dependence on defensive systems in these areas and instead seek to use offensive weapons to negate Chinese systems. A simple example makes this point clearly. China depends on space systems for command, control, communications, computers, intelligence, surveillance and reconnaissance (C4ISR) and position, navigation and timing (PNT) in the Indian Ocean, but it also possesses a robust suite of counter-space weapons.

The above list, read in light of the fact that the Indian armed forces are aiming to modernise in keeping with the demands of changing scenarios of warfare, precludes any extraordinary physical burden on soldiers. Why, then, is it still an anathema to think of a bigger operational role for women? According to data shared by the Ministry of Electronics and Information Technology for FY 2017–2018, more than a third of the IT and ITES sector in India (34 per cent) is made up of women. The ministry also officially shares that about 40 per cent of all students enrolled for a bachelor's degree in computer science are women. Can the military afford to ignore this potential and prioritise customary masculinity over efficiency? Fishing only in a restricted pool of resources will rarely get you a good catch.

It has been a long-standing myth, even in more gender-balanced militaries, that mixed-gender units are less efficient due to limited 'male bonding'. This was dismantled by a 1995 study conducted by the U.S. Army Research Institute for the Behavioral and Social Sciences.[6] The study concludes that 'the relation between cohesiveness and performance is due primarily to the commitment to the task' component of cohesiveness and not the '"interpersonal attraction" or "group pride" components of cohesiveness'. Taking the argument further, scholars Robert MacCoun, Elizabeth Kier and Aaron Belkin demonstrate in a 2006 study that 'all of the evidence indicates that military performance depends on whether service members are committed to the same professional goals, not on whether they like one another'.[7]

Another senior analyst researching the US armed forces Leora N. Rosen concludes that acceptance (institutional and personal) of women had a positive impact on a unit's effectiveness.[8]

A study conducted by the Norwegian Defence Security Department—one of the only two countries to have undertaken such a research project—established that one of the three reasons why women soldiers left the military was their perception and experience of the military as a male-dominated and exclusionary culture.[9]

No organisation with high-attrition rates can boast of efficiency.

Sasson-Levy and Amram-Katz note about the degendering process of the Israeli armed forces: 'Some military resources—such as high-level training, military knowledge and skills, training commands, and especially officer's rank and its accompanying prestige—are no longer allocated strictly along gendered lines.' These are, in Sewell's[10] terms, mostly human resources but their outcome is actual and material: they become 'observable characteristics of real people … and it is their actualisation in people's minds and bodies that make them resources'.

Since the Indian military does not have any comparable studies to refer to, we'll have to be content with transposing these findings with suitable caveats to our context. What is clear, however, is that preparing a leaner, more lethal force is a matter of making smart recruitment choices in line with the changing nature of the job.

Navigating Conflict

Data from Kashmir show that the periods of relative calm are achieved not by successful counter-insurgency operations but by reducing local recruitment into jihadi outfits through peace-building measures complemented by reliable intelligence gathering. Should the Indian military take itself seriously as a peacekeeping force in the region, it can draw lessons from the UN's stated goal of getting more women into the fold for improving operational effectiveness. India, one must remember, is a member nation that sends a significant number of police and military personnel to UN peacekeeping missions.

Talking of UN peacekeeping operations, Sandra Whitworth[11] states, 'The introduction of peacekeeping forces has actually served to increase some local people's insecurity rather than alleviate it.' This seems to hold true for the relationship that insurgency-ridden regions have with the Indian armed forces deployed there.

In its landmark resolution UNSCR 1325, the Security Council recognises how women are disproportionately affected by armed conflict. The resolution also focuses on how women might have a unique way of minimising conflict and initiating peace-building processes, and appeals for increased participation of women at all levels of peacekeeping. Essentially relying on gender stereotypes, the resolution paves the way for a more gender-balanced UN peacekeeping force with a trickle-down effect on national militaries. Canada and Ireland, for example, drew their National Action Plans to attract more women to join the military in different roles soon after. India missed that bus, but it is never too late to get on board, especially when it makes better sense in terms of economics and efficiency.

If a higher number of women soldiers in conflict-ridden regions can ensure a better intelligence network due to increased access—Lieutenant General Kirsten Lund famously said that women soldiers have access to 100 per cent of population—and reduce the 'gender problem' in highly militarised areas, the consequent security outcomes are sure to display an upward tick.

Another positive fallout of the increased number of women in conflict-ridden regions could be turning the women population there into important stakeholders in the peace process. Not so far in the past, the commander of the Srinagar-based Chinar Corps of the Indian Army Lieutenant General K.J.S. Dhillon made a famous appeal to the 'mothers' in the region to cooperate in curbing fresh recruitments to jihadi outfits and helping in the surrender of armed militants.[12]

Women and Conflict Zones

Sasson-Levy and Amram-Katz state that despite the degendering efforts of the Israeli military, denying women certain responsibilities posits them as unequal or lesser soldiers against their male counterparts, thus limiting their participation in decision-making. The absence of women at the high table is even more noticeable in India.

When it comes to policies relating to the welfare of military personnel, an ad hoc arrangement in the form of the Army Wives Welfare Association—and its counterparts in the air force and the navy—has been put in place to address immediate and everyday concerns. It is beyond the purview of this essay to comment on the efficiency and desirability of such organisations that function parallelly and claim precious resources. Since military families are seen as an integral part of India's security structure and wives of military officers are considered capable of addressing their issues because of their access to women, why can we not bring about a structural alteration where women soldiers have a bigger say in welfare matters instead of an NGO pulling extra-official strings? The efficiency of any operational unit depends as much on training or intelligence as on the well-being of the soldiers and, by extension, their families. A happy soldier who is secure in his/her welfare is the basic unit of an efficient formation, and no strategic goals are achieved with a discontented force that puts an additional burden on already stretched resources.

However, in a set-up where women officers are treated as unequal soldiers, 'welfare' responsibilities shouldered by them can be easily seen as 'soft' duties. This can be addressed by according the same weightage to welfare deployments and not treating them as punishment or soft posts. A lack of combat experience (because women in the Indian military do not lead a battalion in a conflict situation) has restricted their ascent to leadership positions and that creates a dual problem of hierarchy. There is an immediate need to decouple strategic and operational thinking; this will help men, too.

Criticism aside, military wives have been picking the slack where institutions failed. It is high time that institutions pulled up their socks and stopped relying on their unpaid labour while also 'unofficially' supporting the parallel structure with manpower and resources. The military must take ownership and deploy women soldiers in welfare roles and stop funding semi-institutional, ad hoc measures.

Marriage, Money and the Military

The rules in India stipulate that if both spouses are employed by the government and posted in the same station, certain allowances, for instance, house rent allowance or HRA, are payable to only one of them.

Military perquisites going to a family where both spouses are in the services—instead of two male officers with separate families—could thus cut that expenditure by almost half. Since Indian armed forces rarely commission research into personnel's attitudes, there are no data to back this, but—anecdotally speaking—there is an upward trend of uniformed women officers/personnel marrying their colleagues.

Researching American marriages—Philadelphia, to be specific—more than a hundred years ago, D.M. Marvin suggests that men and women engaged in the same professional field intermarried in numbers beyond 'chance expectation'. This held true for almost every occupation.[13]

Data crunching of the 2015 US census also brought to light similar trends. Dan Kopf at Priceonomics looked at forty million couples and deduced that people who work in an industry dominated by the opposite sex are very likely to marry within their own industry.[14] Coming to India, data garnered from the Indian Human Development Survey (IHDS-II) conducted in 2016 suggest that 'married couples, wherein both the partners are working, often tend to be engaged in similar occupations'.

Although the military is going to remain a male-dominated profession for a long time despite all the arguments made in this chapter, or several such others, women soldiers will likely continue to find spouses in colleagues. And since these studies and surveys have indicated that military propinquity is likely to be a significant factor in marriage selection, a policy discussion on the same is certainly warranted.

Rebecca A. Adelman observes, 'Both the military and the family operate as "greedy" institutions, placing copious and often non-negotiable demands on their members and potentially absorbing all available resources of time and energy. Inevitably, this leads to conflict between them.'[15] It is worth considering whether a two-personnel military family, which mostly stays stationed together, could be one of the ways to minimise conflicts that burden the military's financial and logistical resources.

Talking of utilisation of resources and the role gender plays in this aspect, a study of the US military by Eileen Patten and Kim Parker for Pew Research Centre in 2011[16] throws up some interesting data points that may inform this debate, even if tangentially. The study found that, as opposed to their male counterparts, women veterans were more critical of the wars in Iraq and Afghanistan, despite being proud of their service. Sixty-three per cent of women veterans shared the sentiment that the Iraq war was not worth fighting and the figure for the Afghanistan war stood at 54 per cent. Male veterans' figures for the same stood at 47 per cent (Iraq) and 39 per cent (Afghanistan).

Is it possible to extrapolate, then, from the study and similar others, to propose that women soldiers tend to assess operations, big and small, less chauvinistically and can, thus, ensure better utilisation and deployment of resources?

It has been established through studies of Western democracies that higher representation of women in the legislature has a direct impact on defence spending.[17] Is this also to be seen as a way to rationalise resources to make vital decisions while leaving 'signalling' behind? Do women military leaders make better use of allotted resources? As women gain greater access to policymaking, the need for female chief executives to prove themselves or overcome stereotypes may diminish. They make decisions that are not to impress with their 'man-like abilities' but to maximise gains.

Defence scholars may want to take this up as a challenge and circulate a questionnaire within the forces to survey how women officers in leadership roles in the military impact conflict behaviour and spending.

Gender and Global Reach

India has gradually moved from the policy of non-alignment to a position of multi-alignment as is evident from its often-tricky navigation of relations with countries with disparate interests and ideologies. As veteran diplomat Kanwal Sibal notes, the military has played a significant role in bolstering India's foreign relations.[18] From training their officers in Indian academies to setting up their own military training institutions, India has helped many nations, including Bhutan in the immediate neighbourhood and several countries in Africa. In Africa alone, Sibal observes, India has military-to-military relations with eighteen countries.

It is also to be noted that as part of UN peacekeeping initiatives, many African countries already have Indian boots on the ground.

With China's intrepid wooing of the African economies, India needs to up its game in this region. Can India's foreign policy be aided by a gender-balanced military? Certainly.

With the increased participation of women in the armed forces, India will be able to offer crucial support to not only the training of women in the militaries of countries such as Angola, Ethiopia, Ghana, Kenya, Lesotho, Mozambique, Nigeria and South Africa but also establish goodwill in parts of some of these countries that still need humanitarian engagement. The presence of more women in Indian military training teams can establish progressive attitudes in local populations and consolidate India's diplomatic ties with these countries. There is a reason why Scandinavia is seen as synonymous with progress and goodwill. There is no reason why India cannot attempt to be a driver of social change in lesser developed countries in Africa.

A consolidation of bilateral relations thus will help India at a time when Chinese economic and military presence is growing in the region. Since India already has a big troop presence in the Democratic Republic of Congo, Eritrea, Ethiopia and Southern Sudan, this is a low-hanging fruit with significant gains on offer. India's women workforce in the IT sector can become its military's powerful asset in many African countries. Africa, as a whole, is looking at an IT revolution, and China has already made inroads in the sector. India can still catch up by combining its goodwill and existing collaborations with a modern outlook, showcased by its women soldiers.

With its commitment to gender equality, and having women in the armed forces as equal soldiers to show for it, India can further its military partnerships with Western countries that already have taken several strides towards creating gender-balanced militaries. Ideological convergence in this regard with countries, such as France, Canada, Norway, the US, Ireland and Germany, among others, can lead to stronger ties that could benefit India in the areas of commercial satellites, space-based systems for maritime domain awareness, cyberwarfare, electronic warfare and information operations.

Looking at the immediate neighbourhood, it is only going to benefit India to have security and intelligence networks that see women as active participants rather than ad hoc and dispensable passive recipients of 'orders'. Multiple studies have found that women can learn and use languages more effectively than men. It has also been suggested that the female brain is more suited for language learning from birth.[19] India's military can capitalise on this gender 'bias' in cognitive learning by employing more women for intelligence and reconnaissance operations. Recruiting women from the border areas will also help the Indian military in its tactical and strategic goals.

Conclusion

The argument for a more gender-balanced military is not approached through the prism of equal opportunity—though the principle remains germane to this chapter—but by taking a hard look at the urgency to build a more efficient and sustainable force. Interventions in the space of gender balance—such as the new policy to grant permanent commissions to women officers—are economically beneficial for the military in both the short and long terms.

In the end, policymakers need to evolve a custom-fit approach for the Indian armed forces.

There are multiple models available to improvise upon, though ultimately, it can be one of two approaches: One, should the military, collectively, think like a man and expect women to reach at-par physical standards and facilitate that through by all means? Norway's all-women Jegertroppen (Hunter Troop) elite commando training is a good case study. Since 2014, Norway trains its commando elites in sex-segregated groups. Women have to achieve the same physical standards as men but are more successful at doing so when they train separately from them. Two, should the military think like a woman and get men to think beyond brawn? The Canadian Armed Forces have challenged the existing physical standards. Unlike the Norwegians, who helped women train to male standards, the Canadians have redefined optimal and more holistic fitness regimes for both men and women. Can it result in maintaining a healthier force that eases the burden on healthcare for military personnel while also addressing the issue of redundancies and attrition?

9

Reforming Indian Intelligence

ANON

In the Mahabharata, counselling Yudhishthira from his *vaan-sayya* (bed of arrows), Bhishma emphasises that the king, among his other duties,

> must have spies who warn him of everything that goes on in his enemies' kingdoms ... [and] ... his spies must be the cleverest of his agents. They must seem like fools before whom an enemy will speak freely, without fear; ... men that are deaf and blind. In fact, they must be wise men, sharp and loyal, a king's eyes and ears, in his streets and in distant parts ... [They must] be the hardiest, most incorruptible men, strong and able to bear privations: exile, cold, heat violence and hunger.[1]

Alas, India's spies may have seemed like fools, and they have not always proved prescient!

In Kautilyan statecraft, too, intelligence was deemed 'indispensable in a conflicted and anarchical world (*matsya-nyaya*)'. Political life—intra- and inter-state—had to be seen in a realist perspective to 'serve offensive and defensive postures'. Kautilya detailed how to recruit and run agents and what cover to use. The Kautilyan secret service played a critically important role not only by acting as an 'early warning system' with respect to economic, social or political aberrations but also to alert or even induce the state to facilitate necessary corrections of its policies. The chancellor (*mantri*) and the secret agents (*sattrin*) operated under the king both in foreign countries and in protecting domestic security. They recruited local informants to nip treasonous conspiracies in the bud, applying the four *upayas—saam*, *daam*, *bheda* and *dand* (conciliation, compensation, division and force)—through the intelligence service.[2] These stratagems seem to have been accepted with great alacrity by our political masters, only to achieve short-term gains.

The main intelligence organisations considered in this analysis are the Intelligence Bureau (IB) and the Research and Analysis Wing (RAW). The National Technical Research Organisation (NTRO) and the Defence Intelligence Agency (DIA) were set up after the recommendations of the Kargil Review Committee, headed by K. Subrahmanyam, and the G.C. Saxena Task Force on Intelligence Apparatus set up by the Group of Ministers on National Security in April 2000.[3] The NTRO was to be dedicated to the collection of technical, communications and cyber intelligence, whereas the DIA would act as a nodal body to process all military-related intelligence.[4]

The National Investigation Agency (NIA) was set up by an act of parliament in 2008. Having concurrent jurisdiction to probe terror attacks in any part of the country, it also performs important intelligence gathering, collation and pre-emptive operational function in fostering national security, as may have been spectacularly emphasised in the arrests in Ernakulam, Kerala, and Murshidabad, West Bengal, allegedly busting a major Al-Qaeda-linked terrorism module.[5]

Other central police organisations such as the Border Security Force (BSF), Central Reserve Police Force

(CRPF), Indo-Tibetan Border Police (ITBP) and Sashashtra Seema Bal (SSB) also act in collaborative, trans-border intelligence roles, as also organisations such as the Narcotics Control Bureau (NCB), Directorate of Revenue Intelligence (DRI) and Enforcement Directorate (ED), the latter two in enquiries pertaining especially to hawala transactions abetting trans-border terrorism.

Except in the context of coordination of all sources of information collection pertaining to national security, these organisations have not been studied sufficiently. Also excluded from the detailed study are the military intelligence agencies: the Military Intelligence Directorate, Naval Intelligence, Air Intelligence and the DIA.

Intelligence Bureau

The IB is India's oldest intelligence agency, evolving from British colonial times. In 1885, General Charles McGregor, Quartermaster General of the British Army, was tasked with watching developments in India. The anti-thuggee operations of Colonel William Henry Sleeman saw the effective implementation of a criminal-police system of intelligence gathering against a focused threat. Later, the IB's role under the Indian Political Intelligence Office (IPIO), from 1909 to 1921, homed in more on reporting about the nationalist movement.[6]

Today, the IB is a very big organisation. The exact details of its staffing are not in the public domain. As an organisation, it permeates into practically all aspects of political, social and economic activities in the country. It covers political movements, student and labour union activities and threats to very important persons (VIPs) from terrorists. It also monitors relations between the Union and federating states. A criticism voiced in this regard by a well-regarded former spymaster suggests that it probably has too much on its plate: 'No wonder, structurally IB has remained overwhelmingly weighted in favour of a collection of political intelligence that has a bearing on the stability of the government. Political snooping units operate at every nook and corner of the country.'[7]

IB is also mandated to watch what foreign intelligence organisations are doing inside India. This important counter-intelligence function has been badly neglected in recent times due mainly to staff shortages and a shift of personnel to more urgent counterterrorism duties. The bulk of its intelligence collection work is carried out through central intelligence officers directly recruited at different levels. Others recruited at a lower level can ascend to the joint director level if efficiency records are obtained. Senior officers are inducted through deputation from the Indian Police Service (IPS). Earlier, they were brought in from the states under the 'earmarking scheme', in which the best from the merit lists were inducted. Now, deputations are carried out more randomly. The IB enjoys a homogeneity or cadre esprit de corps because almost all senior officers belong to the IPS.

Research and Analysis Wing

RAW came into existence in September 1968, divesting the collection of external intelligence from the IB. After the Chinese debacle of 1962, it was decided to set up an Aviation Research Centre (ARC) in 1964 for focused aerial surveillance, monitoring mainly the China border, analysing imagery and signals intelligence. This was placed under B.N. Mullik after his retirement as director of the IB. He was made Director General of Security (DGS). ARC was later brought under the purview of RAW. The director, ARC, is a special secretary-rank officer who enjoys considerable autonomy in the day-to-day functioning of his organisation.

Over the years, RAW has grown in size to cover intelligence collection, operations and analyses of events, political and other developments, in neighbouring countries as well as in other major powers abroad where India's security interests are involved. Telecommunication and electronic intelligence capabilities were added. It has also developed a limited capacity to collect economic and scientific intelligence.

Initially, RAW began its operations by drawing officers from the IPS already serving with the IB. Later, a smattering of other generalists was brought in on deputation from All India Services, such as customs, income tax, forest and even the Indian Administrative Service (IAS) at middle or junior levels, but the IPS has continued to dominate the top leadership positions. Direct induction was tried in two phases but with limited success.[8]

A small contingent of serving or retired defence service personnel are also regularly inducted for the collection and analyses of geostrategic and tactical military intelligence.

Intelligence Lapses and Calls for Reform

Good intelligence has often made the difference between victory and defeat in wars or between life and death while foiling terrorist attacks. Regrettably, India has never been hot on accountability for national security lapses. The politics of intelligence reform in India has moved in fits and starts, with piecemeal restructuring[9] or ad hoc, mostly crisis-driven, tinkering every time a major or minor security lapse occurred. There does not seem to have been any broad-based exercise to reform the country's intelligence apparatus that could address basic and structural flaws in a need-based manner.

After the May 2020 'transgression' of the Line of Actual Control (LAC) by Chinese troops in several sub-sectors of eastern Ladakh, a prominent defence analyst claimed in a damning indictment: 'Insider reports again suggested that intelligence gathering, especially of satellite intelligence, left much to be desired, with planners having to fall back on commercial satellite imagery. Within the DIA, functioning directly under the CDS, there was no cross-verification of satellite imagery obtained from various sources and of signal intercepts.' Moreover, 'there were equal failures in intelligence analysis in the National Security Council Secretariat (NSCS), which functions under the NSA'; there was 'little coordination obtained between military technical intelligence and the four civilian agencies—the NTRO, the IB, RAW and the Ministry of Home Affairs (MHA) through the ITBP'.[10] Other foreign analysts queried, 'Why was India's security establishment seemingly blindsided by China?' despite 'local officials in Ladakh sounding the alarm about Chinese forays into Indian territory for years', pointing 'to a complete breakdown in New Delhi's intelligence gathering and risk assessment'.[11]

B. Raman was perhaps one of few Indian officials who understood the intelligence culture in the country and the need for reform. In his post-retirement avatar, he consistently argued that, despite having many brilliant intelligence officers, 'police or Special Branch culture still largely governed the thinking and functioning of our intelligence agencies'. He stressed that 'a real secret agent is a risk-taker, who foregoes diplomatic and other protections and penetrates the sanctum sanctorum of the adversary—whether it be another State or a terrorist organisation—clandestinely and successfully carrying out' assigned tasks. He felt it was high time Indian intelligence developed 'inner core capability' to take out anti-Indian elements, such as Dawood Ibrahim, in hostile foreign lands a la Operation Neptune Spear of the US Special Forces that eliminated Osama bin Laden in his Abbottabad lair in May 2011.[12]

The reform of existing intelligence agencies has to be predicated on three or four main pillars.[13]

Legal Status

First, all major intelligence agencies should be founded on a legal basis. Though emerging initially from clandestine origins, this has been the pattern of evolution of all modern intelligence organisations. The CIA in the US was provided with a legal status by the National Security Act, 1947; the Russian FIS by the Law on Foreign Intelligence Organs, 1996; the MI-5 in the UK by the Security Services Act, 1989; and the MI-6 by the Intelligence Services Act, 1994.[14] The famous Harman and Hewitt versus UK case in the European Court of Human Rights in 1992 deemed 'lack of a statutory basis fatal to claims' of an intelligence agency (MI-5) to justify that its actions (surveillance) 'were in accordance with the law'.[15] This was clearly emphasised during a conference on the future challenges to India's intelligence organised by the Observer Research Foundation (ORF) in February 2015: there should be a law or separate laws to specify the existence and jurisdiction of all such outfits, both for reasons of accountability and defining the specificity of functions.[16]

In August 2011, Manish Tewari, a Congress member of parliament, tabled a private member's bill—The Intelligence Services (Powers and Regulation) Bill, 2011—seeking legal status and parliamentary supervision for three major intelligence agencies: RAW, IB and NTRO. Among other features, the draft bill proposed a national intelligence tribunal for the investigation of complaints against these agencies, a parliamentary committee for effective accountability and an intelligence ombudsman for efficient grievance redressal from within. Former home secretary G.K. Pillai disclosed in a seminar in July 2011 that this proposal was being looked into by a committee of secretaries.[17] However, the idea seems to have languished thereafter. The bill itself lapsed in October 2012.

Accountability

Second, and most importantly, such legislation must provide different tiers of oversight and accountability of intelligence agencies—executive, financial and legislative.

Addressing the fourth R.N. Kao Memorial Lecture at RAW in January 2010, the then vice president, M. Hamid Ansari, questioned 'why a democratic system like ours should not have' some form of parliamentary accountability?[18] Dwelling at length on the possibility and scope of misuse of intelligence agencies and the widespread perception in the media about instances of intelligence lapses being brushed under the carpet, he said it was essential for India to adopt accountability practices prevailing in democracies worldwide. Ansari identified three models of intelligence oversight:

- Comprehensive: to include both policy and operations, as in the US and Germany
- Limited: to matters of policy and finance, as in the UK
- Focused: on human rights and rule of law, as in Norway

Ansari favoured an oversight body that has some access to operational details to ensure effective supervision and improve the efficiency of intelligence agencies.

If accountability were to come in, it will have to be woven into the aforementioned legislation. Following the British model, a limited beginning could be made to set up a small, say, seven-member committee of the seniormost politicians from across the political spectrum, with four MPs from the Lok Sabha and three from the Rajya Sabha, including leaders of the opposition or their nominees. They would meet in-camera and may not be required to make full disclosures in their reports tabled in Parliament.

Recruitment and Training

Third, recruitment to intelligence organisations, especially for RAW and NTRO, must be made open to induct the best available talent and also to cater to varied needs and different streams. This could be done through the Union Public Service Commission (UPSC) and a separate examination, prescribing specific requirements, including age limits (18–22 years), to 'catch them young'. For the NTRO, minimum technical qualifications could be specified for the entry-level. The quality of intake will then drastically change, even disregarding the bureaucratic structure and limits of career progression, which have, unfortunately, bound agencies down to routine intake of personnel on deputation from different all-India services. An option of 'running a three-year "graduation" course at a residential intelligence academy, run on patterns of a military training establishment'—'a kind of spymasters university'—has also been suggested.[19] This rigorous training will cover investigative skills and language specialisation. A minimum physical toughening-up course of three to four months will be mandatory.

Intelligence collection and operations are highly specialised functions, only some of which can be imparted through systematic professional training. In-depth knowledge of strategic issues, cultural mores of target countries, computer know-how and other technological skills like cryptography may all be needed at different stages of assessing any intelligence input. These capabilities cannot be developed overnight by everybody or by personnel joining an intelligence agency as a temporary haven. It has to be a lifetime profession, where skills are progressively honed 'on the job'.

Addressing a round-table conference on national security at the Indian Council of World Affairs (ICWA) in December 2014, N.N. Vohra, the former governor of Jammu and Kashmir and former principal secretary to the prime minister, recommended[20] the setting up of a National Security Administrative Service, which would be a cadre of dedicated and well-trained officers from all services who have spent a long time in ministries dealing with security issues. A task force headed by him had reportedly given a similar recommendation to a group of ministers (GoM), in 2000, which was apparently accepted 'in principle' but 'was being examined further' for implementation.

Coordination of Intelligence

The fourth important aspect is intelligence coordination. Apex-level political decisions on security issues are taken by the Cabinet Committee on Security (CCS), which is assisted by a core group of bureaucrats, including heads of intelligence agencies. Discussions in the CCS and the core group tend to remain restricted to immediate or emergent security problems. There is seldom the inclination to devote time to debate, analyse and develop long-term policy options, strategies or consequences. Though there is the National Security Council and an advisory board of experts to cater to some of these issues, structural channels to utilise their inputs through pinpointed action agendas have not been fructified.[21]

The organogram below shows the flow chart for coordinated dissemination of intelligence as it exists in India (Figure 9.1):

FIGURE 9.1 A Flow Chart of Intelligence Dissemination Protocol

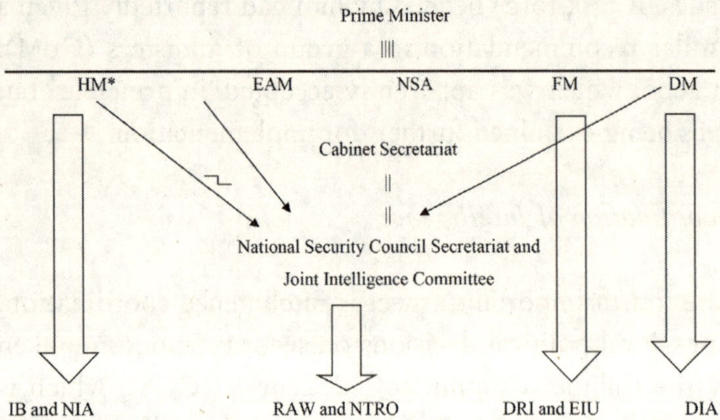

*Abbreviations:
DIA: Defence Intelligence Agency
DRI: Directorate of Revenue Intelligence
EIU: Economic Intelligence Unit
IB: Intelligence Bureau
NIA: National Investigation Agency
NTRO: National Technical Research Organisation
RAW: Research and Analysis Wing
HM: Home Minister
EAM: External Affairs Minister
NSA: National Security Adviser
FM: Finance Minister
DM: Defence Minister

National Security Advisor

The National Security Adviser (NSA) emerged as the nodal authority for the coordination of intelligence. He is assisted by the National Security Council Secretariat (NSCS) set up in 1999. The first National Security Adviser, Brajesh Misra, was appointed in November 1998. He functioned in a dual role—alongside NSA, he was also principal secretary to the prime minister till May 2004. Later NSAs—J.N. Dixit from May 2004 till January 2005, M.K. Narayanan from January 2005 till January 2010 and Shivshankar Menon from January 2010 till May 2014—took on the intelligence and security coordination role exclusively, which extends inevitably to foreign policy formulation. Ajit Doval has been NSA since May 2014.

National Security Council Secretariat

The NSCS was mandated by a 1999 Cabinet Secretariat resolution to 'prepare or cause to be prepared papers for consideration' of the higher policymaking leadership. It was headed by a deputy NSA, who has usually been either a senior, serving or retired officer of the Indian Foreign Service or an intelligence official with a police background. Currently, it operates in four dedicated silos with two deputy NSAs, a chairman, a Joint Intelligence Committee (currently vacant) and a retired general, at the helm of each vertical. Details of their work distribution are not in the public domain.

In addition to the CCS and NSCS, the Multi-Agency Centre (MAC) and Joint Task Force on Intelligence (JTFI) attached to the IB have also come up to effectively coordinate inputs related to terrorism from different field agencies on a day-to-day basis. Though functioning from 2002, the role of MAC and JTFI was formalised through a home ministry regulation issued in December 2008. Subsidiary MACs (S-MACs) were also established at the state level, giving S-MAC responsibilities to different lead agencies for different borders, such as the BSF, CRPF, ITBP and SSB. The S-MACs are also required to create synergy between state police and central intelligence agencies.

Post 26/11 Reforms

In the backdrop of the 2008 Mumbai attacks, the Indian government formed two more intelligence entities—National Intelligence Grid (NATGRID) and National Investigation Agency (NIA).

NATGRID collects data from twenty-one sources and shares it with eleven central intelligence agencies, including RAW, IB and CBI as well as tax, customs and revenue intelligence authorities. Once operational, NATGRID also connects the state and central agencies working on law enforcement and intelligence. Though initially a retired military officer was appointed its chief executive, NATGRID was later placed under the IB. Question marks remain, though, on connecting such a grid to state agencies and police forces.

In 2007, an intelligence task force within the NSC furnished a set of recommendations to revamp the intelligence set-up, suggesting 15 per cent staff accretions in IB and the creation of new centres to tone up counter-intelligence, analysis and to update databases. It also proposed setting up a new maritime intelligence and security centre and a nuclear and missile intelligence centre under the aegis of the NSCS.[22] It is not known if these proposals were implemented.

National Counterterrorism Centre

Addressing the annual conference of director generals of police at the IB headquarters in December 2011, Home Minister P. Chidambaram mooted the concept of a National Counterterrorism Centre (NCTC) to serve as an apex body for effective control of all counterterrorism measures.[23] The NCTC was to derive its powers from the Unlawful Activities Prevention Act, 1967. It was proposed to be part of the IB. It would execute counter-terror operations and collect, collate and disseminate data on terrorism, besides maintaining a database on terrorists and their associates, including their families. It would have powers to conduct searches and arrests in any part of India and respond to terror threats.

As policing and law and order fall under the state list of the seventh schedule of the Indian Constitution, the NCTC proposal faced much criticism from chief ministers of various states, including, notably, from Gujarat's then chief minister, Narendra Modi. They saw this step as a means to weaken India's federalism. In particular, there were apprehensions about its unilateral powers to conduct operations, especially to search and arrest people without keeping state governments in the loop. It was argued, with some justification, that such sweeping powers vested in a central agency would violate the autonomy of state governments. It was also argued that the establishment of the NCTC will only add to the bureaucratic tangle in intelligence sharing and counterterrorism actions.

Later, efforts were made to build political consensus gradually so that this resistance is overcome and the NCTC could start functioning, albeit with fewer teeth initially. The Union home ministry has since suggested that director generals of police and chiefs of anti-terror squads of all states be made members of the standing council of the NCTC. These senior police officers will then have to be informed before the NCTC conducted any operation in their state. These proposals were sent to the CCS, including one to make it a separate organisation outside the IB. A modified draft of the NCTC proposed that it will no longer come under the IB and states will be taken into confidence before the central government carried out any operation in their territories. One idea suggested for consideration was for all states to have an empowered cell or branch, to coordinate and cooperate in the operation of the NCTC, keeping a balance between secrecy and a state's legal prerogatives. Another suggestion was made by N.N. Vohra to set up Joint Terrorism Task Forces (JTTF) with states.[24]

Police Reforms

Improvement in coordination and dissemination of intelligence necessarily involves giving some impetus to police reforms. Compared to central intelligence, major gaps or shortfalls in capabilities and culture of intelligence work and policing were known to exist at the state level. For a police officer at the Union government level, a stint in a central intelligence organisation is highly desirable. Quite in contrast, in the states, the Special Branch, CID or intelligence agencies have been traditionally regarded as backwater dump yards, giving officers much lesser access to the perks of power.

Confronted by the increasing challenge of terrorism, this has slowly begun to change. Many states have taken ameliorative steps to start anti-terror cells or specialised counter-terror branches in their police organisations, where crack teams of able officers are posted and given state-of-the-art equipment on priority. More remains to be done in this regard.

Improvising Analysis and Prescience

Traditionally, most modern intelligence agencies in the world have organised their functioning into two broad areas: analysis and operations. The latter involves collecting intelligence and the former assessing it and adding value before sending inputs to consumers. While the human component and quality of intelligence personnel remain vital, coping with the open-source intelligence (OSINT) revolution may have changed the very nature and approach to intelligence gathering, analysis and operations.

All secret intelligence collection, whether it is based on HUMINT or TECHINT, results from penetrating the adversary—a neighbouring state or an amorphous non-state actor system. This is usually done by a variety of means—either through physical presence or, if that is not possible, through trans-border or third-country efforts. Today, there is also a flood of inputs from OSINT. A good analyst can only perform his function effectively if he can weld together inputs from HUMINT and TECHINT with OSINT without being dishonest to any particular aspect, thus achieving a balance nearest to the truth. This task is easier said than done and requires back-breaking hours of sustained diligence, building up one's background on the subject, searching for grain in the chaff and making mistakes while learning on the job. Experience, area specialisation and the ability to read between the lines count for a great deal in this type of work.

Using modern tools of analysis for sifting intelligence inputs becomes very important. The analyst should be aware of the pros and cons of any intelligence hypothesis. He must try to identify the major causal factors of an event, sort out chronologies or timelines and see the 'decision tree' of that event. He should assign weightage to likely scenarios and undertake a 'sanity check' of the hypothesis. This involves asking searching questions: who is the source? What is his access (from whom is he claiming to get inputs)? How reliable have his inputs been in the past (did they prove correct)? There are several proven methods of hypothesis testing. These include creating a probability tree, comparing the utility of end results, ranking options as well as devil's advocacy or reverse analysis and perceiving a development or outcome not from one's own perspective but from that of the adversary.

This analysis and assessment must be undertaken in an independent and unbiased manner without being affected by the baggage of pre-conceived ideas, conventional wisdom or political compulsions of the political leadership.

For these reasons, many modern intelligence agencies have completely set apart the analysis function to specialists in a separate body attached to a coordinating set-up that is sometimes labelled as a joint analysis centre, especially adopted in the UK for terrorism analysis (JTAC). The Security Intelligence Service (SIS, previously MI-6) in the UK and the CIA in the US have increasingly shifted towards this model, where the focus of the intelligence agency is increasing operations, collecting intelligence and influencing events in target areas/countries. These analysts do not interchange their roles with operators in the field.

A case could, therefore, be made in any agenda of reform to separate the analysis function and assign it to a specialist centre, such as the National Security Council Secretariat (NSCS). In fact, both NSCS and the Ministry of External Affairs have already started appointing interns for area studies and analyses.

Intelligence operations can be broadly divided into three categories:

- Classical intelligence collection: This involves locating and then subverting well-placed HUMINT in sensitive areas of the target subject/country; this is also increasingly being done using TECHINT, but the value of a well-placed HUMINT asset remains irreplaceable.
- Influence operations: These involve the cultivation of prominent policy formulators in the target country to influence, change or continue policies that benefit the home country's larger national security interests.
- Liaison operations: These involve working with intelligence agencies of different countries to share intelligence on issues such as terrorism and pursue common security objectives.

In field operations, an operative has to possess in-depth background knowledge of the target area. They should know the language, local customs and social mores, and also have an understanding of the psychology of the people.

Operational work often tends to get caught up in a 'drift' in most intelligence agencies. Operators try to retain HUMINT assets that may have had access at one time but since have lost utility. They do not often have the honesty to make swift course corrections by quickly discarding them. Abuse of operational practices often tends to be glossed over. One is to artfully cloak open-source inputs (OSINT) from international publications or local media as source reports based on non-existent HUMINT assets and claim expenses for the same.

Another avoidable trend, which has been witnessed especially in the IB of late, has been to divert more or 'better' men to 'high-profile' operational tasks to the detriment of the hardcore, basic and unglamorous field intelligence or counter-intelligence (CI) work. CI branches get denuded and the quality of CI work suffers.[25] Classic CI work involves great patience and diligence. Luck can often transform small snippets into breakthroughs of significance even if detected by low-level functionaries.[26]

Limits of Cooperation

India was invited to join the Fourteen Eyes intelligence collaboration network between the UK, US, Canada, Australia and New Zealand (FVEY), in addition to Denmark, Netherlands, France, Norway, Germany, Belgium, Spain, Sweden and Italy, after the Mumbai terrorist attack in 2008 as the US 'felt strongly' that India's participation in multilateral intelligence sharing will help Indian signals intelligence (SIGINT) agencies.

In June 2010, there was an unprecedented one-time act of cooperation extended to India by American agencies. A team from India's newly formed National Investigation Agency (NIA) was allowed to interrogate David Coleman Headley a.k.a. Daood Gilani, a Pakistani-American serving a jail sentence in the US, who was involved in planning the Mumbai attacks. However, though the attackers' targets were shared, the basis of inputs—from a HUMINT asset who had repeatedly visited both India and Pakistan and interacted with, even penetrated, non-state groups there—was not disclosed.

Though some countries have advanced technical and SIGINT access to activities of militants operating across borders from inside one country, they often share these inputs half-heartedly or partially for fear of compromising their assets. This prevents appropriate analysis and effective remedial security measures. What is needed here is an honest disclosure of access, whether TECHINT or HUMINT, as also a system to assess the reliability of inputs being shared. These glitches need to be sorted out in good liaison relationships. Often these depend on close personal rapport at the leadership level, which requires time, suave sangfroid and mental alacrity at both ends for the chemistry to light up.[27]

'Inner Core' Operational Capabilities

Today, most intelligence agencies worth their salt recognise the need to build capacities to neutralise or eliminate hostile elements enjoying 'safe havens' in adversary neighbouring countries. The manner in which this objective is pursued varies depending on the prevalent political culture of the host nation. More often than not, such requirements may be outsourced to disgruntled enemy nation immigrants in third countries for monetary motivations. Employing professional mercenary outfits could be another option.

In India, if the adequate political will exists, intelligence organisations may develop small, professionally-trained cells within for carrying out specialised commando actions. Training and simulation exercises will be crucial for such an endeavour. A start may have been made in this direction but spelling out details may not be prudent.

Cyber-terror and Information Warfare

Post-mortems of the Mumbai terror attacks and subsequent busting of several Al-Qaeda/Islamic State-linked terror modules by agencies such as NIA demonstrate emphatically the importance of coping with cyberwarfare.[28] Already, our intelligence agencies have had to devote separate sections dealing with psy-war and psy-operations. This will be an abiding task for intelligence agencies to hone and upgrade their capabilities constantly in the future.

Outsourcing of Tasks

World over, intelligence collection, analysis and operations are now being augmented by tasking private industrial and technology organisations, such as IBM, SAIC and Boeing. In the US, information data stored in social networks and automated monetary transactions can all be utilised in intelligence work.[29]

In 1998–1999, Dr Ruth David, a former CIA deputy director for science and technology, and her deputy, Joanne Isham, proposed handing over some aspects of the agency's work to someone in the private sector. Norman Augustine, a former CEO of Lockheed Martin and four-time recipient of the Department of Defense's highest civilian award, the Distinguished Service Medal, was brought in to start In-Q-Tel. By February 1999, the corporation was established as a legal entity, and in March, it received its first contract from the CIA.[30] Set up as an independent, not-for-profit corporation, it pursued research and development (R&D) to produce solutions to some of the most difficult IT problems facing the CIA.

In-Q-Tel began first with unclassified work, combining gradually with commercial potential to focus on a set of strategic problem areas for the corporation:

- Information security: intrusion detection, monitoring and profiling of information use and misuse, and network and data protection
- Use of the internet: secure receipt of information, non-observable surfing, authentication, content verification and hacker resistance
- Distributed architectures: methods to interface with custom or legacy systems, mechanisms to allow dissimilar applications to interact, automatic handling of archived data and connectivity across a wide range of environments
- Knowledge generation: geospatial and multimedia data fusion or integration and computer forensics

Technological Upgrades

With the advent of the World Wide Web, the commercial market started setting the pace in IT innovation. Intelligence agencies cannot compete for IT innovation and talent with the same speed and agility as those in the commercial marketplace can, whose businesses are driven by 'internet time' and profit. Many of the underlying technologies that are driving the information revolution are now directly applicable to the intelligence business. Examples of commercial applications that support intelligence functions are:

- data warehousing and mining
- knowledge management
- profiling search agents

- geographic information systems
- imagery analysis and pattern recognition
- statistical data analysis tools
- language translation
- targeted information systems
- mobile computing
- secure computing

Similarly, information security (INFOSEC), a critical enabling technology for all intelligence information systems, is now a mainstream area of research and innovation in the commercial world, due in no small part to the exponential growth in internet e-commerce. There are a number of commercially available security technologies providing:

- strong encryption
- authentication and access control
- auditing and reporting
- data integrity
- digital signatures
- centralised security administration
- remote or travelling users

Indian agencies should already be taking a leaf out of the CIA's book and developing their capacities for better intelligence collection and analysis. If corporate social responsibility (CSR) tax-deductible investments are permitted, many Indian private sector companies like TCS, Mahindra, Wipro or even other, newer, low-profile companies will be willing to undertake such start-ups having defence/security/surveillance-related applications, which could be utilised to enhance the capabilities of intelligence agencies.

Another interesting innovation worthy of emulation is in the realm of financing. British authorities set up the National Security Strategic Investment Fund (NSSIF)[31] as a venture capital fund after their 2017 budget with an initial outlay of £85 million. It has recently made a series of investments in British start-ups, including in OneWeb, a struggling satellite business. These start-up companies benefit from direct communication with the government, and their technology is assessed by the National Security Interface Centre (NSIC), a highly specialist agency that reviews private sector technology and gives it a stamp of approval for use by the intelligence services. CIA's In-Q-Tel also started a venture capital fund that has backed companies, including Palantir and Keyhole, the mapping service now known as Google Earth. Israel's national intelligence agency, Mossad, also has its own investment fund, Libertad.

Just as technology advances enhance intelligence capacity, some aspects of intelligence work may become more difficult. Operating with multiple identities or cover stories may not be possible with facial recognition software or biometric identity cards being used to check travel. In counterterrorism work too, technology upgrades are needed but could have a double-edged effect. Our NATGRID facility is yet to acquire sufficient prowess to aid intelligence agencies in using facial recognition techniques to prevent operations of terror networks having foreign linkages.

A question arises: could we take assistance from advanced country agencies to enhance our own capacities under liaison arrangements? Earlier spymasters always favoured caution, indeed self-restraint, over such cooperation; but lately, under possible political pressure to deliver instant results and undue media exposure, caution has sometimes been thrown to the winds with possible negative effects. This should be a sobering thought.

Modern data analysis entails numerous risks in terms of data abuse. The growing volumes of data used in the intelligence sector sometimes overwhelm de facto guarantees of legal safeguards, excessive surveillance, encroachment of individual privacy rights and effective oversight. Intelligence agencies in Western countries have already started facing problems in this regard.[32]

The Way Forward

An overhaul of the 'Intelligence Leviathan' was never going to be easy, as another doyen of India's intelligence community B.B. Nandy tellingly brought out,[33] detailing why successive administrations never made a sustained effort toward comprehensive reform. New agencies were created after every fresh crisis without properly sorting out turf wars, perpetuating 'a tradition of bungling'. He also listed several grave lapses of senior officers in RAW, including in the defection episode of Rabinder Singh, which were either brushed under the carpet or not taken to their logical denouement. This would not have happened if parliamentary oversight existed. But, as Nandy lamented, 'Who will bell the cat?'[34]

Appropriate national consensus and sufficient political will need to be built to urgently take up an action agenda for intelligence reform, which must start with legislation, separately for each agency, if need be, providing for common grievance redressal mechanisms like a tribunal and an ombudsman. The police leadership's reluctance to reform must be overcome and better, open systems of recruitment should be experimented with sooner than later. There is also a need for effective parliamentary oversight as a means of democratic control of intelligence.

10

India's Counter-insurgency Crisis

PRAVEEN SWAMI

Soldiers arrived one morning at Darzo, a tiny village deep in the Mizo hills some 200 kilometres south of Aizawl, in the summer of 1967. 'My orders,' the bureaucrat Vijendra Jafa recorded the commander as saying, 'were to get the villagers to collect whatever moveable property they could, and to set their own village to fire.... I also had orders to burn all the paddy and other grain that could not be carried away by the villagers.' The villagers, the officer went on, refused to comply with this order, forcing him to begin setting light to their huts himself. 'My soldiers also started torching other buildings, and the whole place was soon ablaze.'

Pigs were running about, mithuns were bellowing, dogs were barking and fowls setting up a racket with their fluttering and crackling. One little girl ran into her burning house and soon darted out holding a kitten in her hands.[1]

Late that night, after their relocation to the government-designated protected and progressive village of Hnathial was completed, the village elders of Darzo were lined up at gunpoint to obtain an alibi 'that they had burnt down their own village, and that no force or coercion was used by the Security Forces'. Since 1966, ethnic-nationalist insurgents in Mizoram had been seeking independence; the ruins of

Darzo were part of the debris left behind by the Indian state's efforts to stamp it out.

In the decades since the events at Darzo, India's counter-insurgency thinking has cast Mizoram as a template for the successful resolution of conflicts.[2] In most accounts of the Mizoram story, the use of large-scale violence against civilians—the bombing of Aizawl by combat jets in 1966 or the mass relocation of the civilian population of which Darzo was part—has been gently elided.[3] The more optimistic historians of counter-insurgency in Mizoram hold that the use of violence paved the way for political negotiations and lasting peace. In Jafa's somewhat less roseate telling of events, peace was simply purchased by 'getting some of the important dissidents amongst the insurgents into the Congress (I) fold and pouring in enormous quantities of money for the enrichment of this class along with the bureaucracy and the new breed of local contractors'.

Either way, the idea that the use of large-scale military force is essential to the creation of the necessary preconditions for peace has become deeply embedded in Indian thinking on counter-insurgency. The idea is remarkable for its tenacity, all the more so because even a cursory glimpse of the course of Indian insurgencies makes it clear that the experience is an outlier. In Punjab, the application of force proved effective although that did not lead to political negotiations.[4] Through the North East Region (NER), the application of military force has reduced levels of violence but left in its wake violent and criminalised polities, which the police officer E.N. Rammohan memorably described as 'degenerated insurgencies'.[5] Experiments of various kinds have yielded nothing resembling peace in either Kashmir or the Maoist heartlands.

For students of counter-insurgency in India, the lesson ought to be obvious: India's policymakers have been seduced by force, imagining that the use of military means is an almost magical device that can defeat the complex social fractures and processes that drive violent ideological conflict. In this chapter, I shall argue that India might be better off using a policing-led model that involves less force, effectively coupling lower numbers with better intelligence and training, freeing troops and resources in the process, for more compelling strategic purposes.

There is no memorial in Darzo to the events of 1967. A bungalow for tourists who might pass by has, however, been thoughtfully erected, which is perhaps a good place to visit for students of counter-insurgency seeking to rethink India's strangely medieval means as well as the ends it seeks to secure through them.

The Limits of Coercion

In 1951, as summer rose over Kashmir, a great hammering and sawing began across the Valley: a socialist utopia was being constructed. Perhaps some thought it odd that the National Conference ended up winning all 75 seats, of which 73 of them uncontested—45 out of 49 candidates of the Hindu-nationalist Praja Parishad were barred from contesting in the elections on dubious grounds but they chose to be silent. Land reform and mass education were introduced; for the construction of a utopia, newspaper censorship was a small price. Each cluster of villages got a radio set, opening the Valley to the world, but each set was 'tuned to Radio Kashmir, fixed and sealed'.[6]

The case of Kashmir, where the crisis has confronted the Indian state since the moment of its birth in 1947, is a useful starting point to consider the limitations of India's coercion-based counter-insurgency paradigm, which focused on the use of coercion rather than seeking an end to the crisis.

At first glance, the idea that India has failed in Kashmir might appear absurd. In 2020, Jammu and Kashmir recorded 320 fatalities in terrorism-related violence, including those of combatants.[7] The toll of 2.5 victims per 100,000 population compares favourably with intentional homicide rates both in countries marred by large-scale organised violence, such as Afghanistan and Mexico, as well as the US and India as a whole (Figure 10.1).

The data suggest, of course, that there is room for reflection—exactly what levels of violence constitute a threat to the state systems?—but also demonstrates how successful India has been in significantly reducing violence from its peak in the 1990s.

FIGURE 10.1 Intentional Homicides (Per 100,000 People)[8]

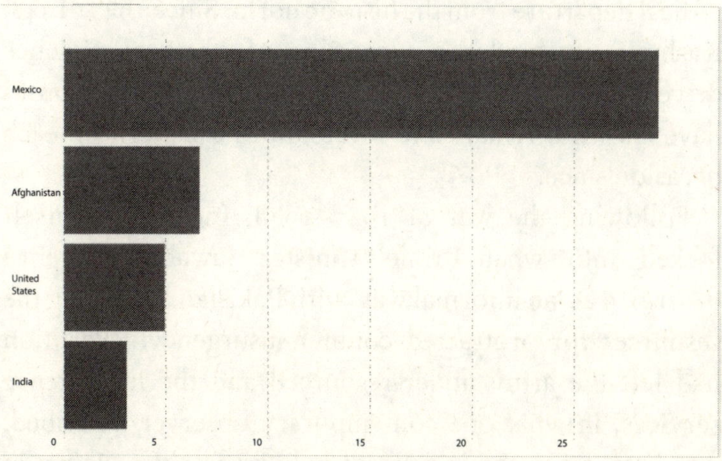

Yet, it is far from clear that the reduction of violence has yielded the necessary strategic *end* of a counter-insurgency, that is, the creation of a political system and, more fundamentally, a polity that is successfully enmeshed in the wider state system. In 2016, years of declining violence notwithstanding, an Islamist-led popular uprising effectively evicted the Indian State from southern Kashmir. In 2008 and 2010, similar uprisings crippled Jammu and Kashmir for months on end. India's decision to end Kashmir's special constitution status in 2019, driven in no small part by these crises, could only be imposed on a foundation of large-scale curfews and arrests.

Efforts to rebuild the political system since 2019 have had, at best, limited success, with voter turnout in south and north Kashmir's secessionist heartlands approximating their historic lows.[9] In addition, traditional fractures of ethnic and religious identity have remained in place; recruitment into jihadist groups is reported to be at levels higher than in 2018.[10]

This ought not, of course, surprise us. The jihad that arose in 1988 was not, contrary to popular imagination, a radical departure from the historic norm. Since 1947/1948, Kashmir has battled a succession of crises of violence driven by ethnic-religious identity; New Delhi's responses have shown a remarkable reversion to a pattern on each occasion since.

Following the war of 1947–1948, India found itself locked into what Prime Minister Jawaharlal Nehru described as 'an informal war' with Pakistan.[11] Lacking the resources for protracted counter-insurgency—Partition had left the army under-resourced and the intelligence services, in what one contemporary observer described, was in a 'tragi-comic state of helplessness'[12]—Nehru in effect allowed Kashmir's pre-eminent political leader Sheikh Muhammad Abdullah to create an authoritarian, one-party state. From 1952, however, beset by pressures from the Hindu nationalist opposition and the growing economic resentment, Abdullah began considering independence. He was incarcerated and his one-time lieutenant Ghulam Muhammad Bakshi installed in his stead.

The imposition of state power, however, proved short-lived. In 1963, a religion-fuelled uprising led to the rise of 'an unauthorised parallel administration, controlling traffic, commerce and prices', which compelled New Delhi to evict Bakshi.[13] In a letter to Nehru, the politician G.M. Sadiq noted an underlying malaise that guided New Delhi's policymaking: 'a primordial fear of the people'.

> Based on this fear, policies have developed and influenced every sphere of our lives. The rule of law was thrown overboard and all executive agencies, as well as the judiciary, were bent to the service of a clique in the National Conference. Corruption in all branches of administration and political life was considered to be something inevitable.[14]

The pattern, however, continued. The 1975 agreement between Prime Minister Indira Gandhi and Abdullah significantly subordinated Kashmir's autonomy in the Indian Union, which ended up empowering the Jama'at-e-Islami in Kashmir and stoking Hindu nationalism in Jammu. The concord between Prime Minister Rajiv Gandhi and Chief Minister Farooq Abdullah, followed by the rigging of the 1988 elections, is widely acknowledged to have had a direct role in precipitating the subsequent Islamist insurgency.

New Delhi's political management strategies since the 1990s have not been a roseate outcome either. The effort by the intelligence services to co-opt and corrupt significant sections of the secessionist leadership, as has been candidly documented by A.S. Dulat, led to the degradation of the political ecosystem, allowing it to be swept aside by the uprisings of 2008 onwards.[15] Similarly, New Delhi's efforts to engineer the rise of political opposition to the National Conference in the late 1990s had the proximate consequence of pushing that party to instrumentalise ethnic and religious divisions to buttress its legitimacy.

In each of the many crises that have punctuated India's tortured relationship with Kashmir—and the wars of 1947–1948, 1965, 1971 and 1999—coercive instruments of state have succeeded in ensuring that violence did not escalate to a point where secession became a real possibility.

The stark fact is, however, that they have also failed to bring about anything that can be said to meaningfully constitute a resolution of the conflict. This is a learning that nation states across the world, confronted with similar situations, have been compelled to absorb.

Perpetuating Conflict

In 1961, the controversial French special forces officer Roger Trinquier authored his findings on why military-led counter-insurgencies were fated to fail. The French military in Algeria and Indochina, he noted, persisted 'in studying a type of warfare that no longer exists and that we shall never fight again'. 'The result of this shortcoming', he went on, 'is that the army is not prepared to confront an adversary employing arms and methods the army itself ignores. It has, therefore, no chance of winning.' He concluded memorably: 'Our military machine reminds one of a pile-driver attempting to crush a fly, indefatigably persisting in repeating its efforts.'[16]

Trinquier's solutions—among them, the use of torture and irregular forces—have since been emulated in counter-insurgencies across the world, from Central America to Iraq and Afghanistan. The strategic outcomes of these conflicts, though, have been less than impressive. In Algeria, where Trinquier's methods were widely applied, France was able to impose tactical defeat on its National Liberation Front adversaries, but only at ultimately unjustifiable economic costs and grave peril to its own polity.[17]

Elsewhere in the world, military after military has had much the same learning. The magisterial work of Caroline Elkins has shown colonial Britain interned a significant proportion of the population in Kenya and institutionalised industrial-scale torture and rape.[18]

'Things got a little out of hand,' a former Kenya Regiment officer reminisced of the time he brought a Mau Mau insurgent into the interrogation centre at Embakasi near Nairobi. 'By the time I cut his balls off, he had no ears, and his eyeball, the right one, I think, was hanging out of its socket. Too bad, he died before we got much out of him.' The judge at a 1953 torture trial wrote up the moral consensus in colonial Kenya thus: 'It is easy to work oneself up into a state of pious horror over these offences, but they must be considered against their background. All the accused were engaged in seeking out inhuman monsters and savages.'

Yet, we know that the savagery did little other than delay the British Empire's inevitable retreat from Africa. Paul Dixon's work on the legendary Gerald Templar—the author of the 'hearts and minds' doctrine that has become counter-insurgency orthodoxy in military academies across that world—establishes that the reality of the British war in Malaya was at some distance from the myth.[19] Large-scale torture and extrajudicial killings were the norms. Again, however, the use of force failed to succeed in its strategic objective of keeping Malaya within the empire.

The perverse consequences of the application of force, similarly, have haunted India's counter-insurgency landscape. For all its counter-insurgency gains, the Indian State was, for all practical purposes, evicted from large swathes of southern Kashmir by an Islamist-led jacquerie in 2016, leading to an implosion of the political system from which the structures of the state are yet to fully recover.

Like in the wars in Afghanistan and Iraq, Indian governments have repeatedly discovered that even overwhelming force cannot achieve their end: a polity that does not engender and perpetuate violence against the state or itself.

Flailing Fight

In November 2009, when Home Minister P. Chidambaram launched what the media called Operation Green Hunt, the task seemed simple. India's national security was persuaded, drawing on the then-fashionable clear-hold-and-build counter-insurgency doctrine, that pumping huge forces into under-policed Bastar will sever links between the Maoists and Adivasis, degrading the insurgency. It was a classic medieval response: move in a few risalas to stamp out the bandits and fly the imperial flag. Thus, Union Home Secretary G.K. Pillai announced: 'Within 30 days of security forces moving in and dominating the area, we should be able to restore civil administration there.'[20] Early the next year, Pillai announced that the troubled district of Gadchiroli would be Maoist-free within a year.[21]

Events, however, proved resistant to the bureaucratic script. Fatalities in 2009 stood at 359, more than in 2008, which had seen 169, and fell only marginally in 2010 to 322. Fatalities of security forces more than doubled, from 67 in 2008 to 150 in 2010; this included a sharp rise from 214 to 312 and civilians from 220 to 391.[22] 'Green Hunt' had the proximate consequence of making the region less secure not more. In the years since, levels of violence have ebbed and flowed, true to the historical pattern, without any evident correlation with force levels.

This should not surprise us. Indian counter-insurgencies have often flailed in the face of their own unanticipated consequences. In spite of its own self-image as relatively benign, Indian counter-insurgency tactics in Kashmir through the early 1990s centred around the less-than-surgical application of force. Torture, extrajudicial executions and, on occasion, the destruction of entire quarters of cities marked the course of the fighting. 'India', the scholar Manoj Joshi has noted in his rich account of the jihad in Jammu and Kashmir, 'has often been compared to an elephant. The lumbering vegetarian pachyderm is not a natural predator, yet, in fear or anger, it can and does kill, often with the greatest brutality.'[23]

India's counter-terror was not, as I have argued, far from the historical global norm; indeed, large-scale human rights abuses continue to mark counter-insurgency operations across the world—witness the obscenities of Abu Ghraib or atrocities involving Australian special forces in Afghanistan.

Yet, these practices were also profoundly counter-productive. Perhaps most important, those practices entrenched anti-India hostility among two successive generations of young Kashmiris, perpetuating the conflict. Even though Pakistan had sought to build armed resistance to Indian rule through several earlier decades, those efforts found little mass resonance until the deinstitutionalisation of democracy in the 1980s.[24] In those cases, political accommodation and adroit policing proved effective in stalling—if not fully addressing—the threat of terrorism.

Though India has indeed succeeded in maintaining order in Kashmir, it has been able to do so through saturating the state with forces, which in turn impedes the emergence of a functional polity. Though reliable figures are hard to come by, the Indian Army's then-northern command chief, Lieutenant General H.S. Panag, revealed in 2007 that some 337,000 troops were committed to Kashmir.[25] In my estimation, some sixty-two Rashtriya Rifles battalions and five reserve brigades—some 80,000 troops or 50,000-60,000, excluding personnel on leave—are committed to counter-insurgency duties, the rest guarding the Line of Control or serving in logistical roles. In addition, some 83,000-plus Jammu and Kashmir Police and up to 60,000 Central Reserve Police Force personnel remain committed to the state.

Even though these numbers might have brought about a stalemate, they clearly have been unable to constitute a solution to the problem to which they were committed. There is also a glaring asymmetry between the problem and the resources committed to it. The bulk of terrorists operating in 2020 possessed no weaponry more substantial than a pistol.[26] Few had received any form of military training; jihadist groups suffered from chronic shortages of weapons and ammunition.[27]

The time has perhaps come for New Delhi to acknowledge the limitations of what force can achieve, acknowledging that massive force commitment and the militarisation of institutions and the polity that it entails are part of the problem. Rule of law-led policing can provide an alternative, but substantial issues lie in the way.

Anaemic Armies

Little insight is needed to see that the capacities of Indian police forces need thoroughgoing reform. In November 2008, the world watched as Lashkar-e-Taiba's assault teams savagely exposed India's doddering police system. The killers faced Mumbai police personnel armed with nothing but lathis, lacking even the rudiments of counter-terrorism training. The State's anti-terrorism unit hadn't fired a practice round in over a year because of shortages of ammunition. The police's command and control system collapsed amidst the chaos, leaving personnel to battle and die. Even the elite National Security Guards botched the siege of the Taj Mahal Palace hotel, infamously setting alight rooms in a bid to flush out terrorists, asphyxiating hostages in the process.

Though very significant investments have since been made, the results have not been unvaryingly heartening. The tactical limitations of police forces involved in counter-insurgency operations continue to be exposed with depressing regularity.[28] In 2016, compelling evidence emerged that the NSG had spent days battling a non-existent terrorist following an attack on the Pathankot Air Force Station.[29]

From data published by the Bureau of Police Research and Development, it is clear that training is one core issue. In 2016–2017, only five states—Delhi, Rajasthan, Maharashtra, Madhya Pradesh and Uttar Pradesh—saw fit to spend more than 5 per cent of their budget on training personnel.[30] In spite of its significant insurgency problem, Chhattisgarh spent just 3.05 per cent of its budget; Andhra Pradesh only 3.18 per cent and Odisha 3.54 per cent. Large numbers of states at risk spent next to nothing on training despite the obvious need for specialist counter-terrorism skills, Jammu and Kashmir spent only 0.02 per cent of its budget on training; Manipur, hit not only by terrorist violence but zones of near-anarchy, spent not one single rupee. In 2016, just 44,083 police personnel across the country—a dismal 0.03 per cent of the national police force—received any form of in-service training, let alone tactical training.

In addition, funding for policing remains anaemic at best. Put together, India's states and union territories spent 906.62 billion rupees on policing in 2016–2017. That might sound impressive till one considers that 900 billion rupees are not a lot over twice the budget for New York alone, a city with a population of 8.5 million, which is less than that of Delhi. The UK, for its part, was scheduled to spend £12.3 billion in 2016–2017, which for a country of 65 million is stupendous against India's 1.35 billion people. These are indeed rich countries, but it's just not possible to get First-World policing on Fourth-World cash.

Police spending in India, moreover, is overwhelmingly swallowed by salaries. In 2016–2017, just 15.46 billion rupees of police budgets were spent on modernisation, marginally up from 13.30 billion rupees in 2015–2016, largely drawn from central grants. That is just 1 per cent of the overall spending—a pathetically small amount to invest in upgrading police capacities. The New York police, by contrast, has a separate capital commitment of $2 billion for 2017–2021, equivalent to about ₹150 billion.

Then, police personnel remain grossly underpaid and overworked, a formula guaranteed to deliver inefficiency and corruption. Even though there is no provision for overtime and a typical working day runs to over sixteen hours, a constable in most states starts on a basic salary of 5,200 to 25,000 rupees take-home. In cities, there's also a chronic shortage of police housing.

Finally, investments in policing have emphasised growth in numbers over adequate training and capacity building. In 2006, India's population stood at 1,123,993,000 and was to be served by 1,632,651 civil and armed police personnel. That meant 145.25 police personnel to serve every 100,000 population. This was well below the United Nations recommended norm of 250 per 100,000. Ten years after the 26/11 Mumbai terror attacks, things are somewhat better. India's projected population, based on the 2001 census, reached 1,277,770,000 in 2016, a growth of 13.68 per cent. There are now 2,464,484 police officers, a dramatic growth of over 50 per cent.[31] Thus, India now has a police-population ratio of 192.87 per 100,000 citizens, slowly inching towards the desired level.

However, there are enormous regional variations, with states hard-hit by insurgency still showing anaemic police numbers, especially when one looks at the actual numbers of police personnel they have hired rather than their theoretically sanctioned strength, the numbers the state government has committed to hire and pay for.

Though Jammu and Kashmir has a relatively robust 626.98 police personnel per 100,000 population, insurgency-torn Chhattisgarh has 228.60, well below its sanctioned number of 269.86. Jharkhand has a pathetic 174.81, well below its sanctioned strength of 251.41.

From the numbers, it is also clear some states have hired police personnel in gross disproportion to their apparent need. Arunachal Pradesh, whose only insurgency problem is the spillover of small numbers of Naga insurgents, has 878.37 police personnel per 100,000 population. Mizoram has 702.15. Perhaps worse, State Armed Police Forces—the corpus from which specialist counterterrorism and counter-insurgency units are drawn—have grown by only 12.69 per cent, slower than population growth. This means that, while there are plenty of personnel in uniform, there isn't enough nationwide investment in elite units.

The shortages in the police are part of a system-wide malaise. The National Investigation Agency has, by my estimation, a staff strength of 800, only 600 of whom are executive personnel. The Federal Bureau of Investigation has 34,019 staff, of whom 12,979 are agents or trained investigators. Even the Intelligence Bureau, the heart of India's counterterrorism apparatus, is a third short of its authorised strength of 32,000, with the agency's training facility barely able to cover attrition from retiring staff. The Research and Analysis Wing suffers, too, from a lack of language and area specialists as well as technical experts.

Conclusions

'I wished to have depopulated the country of Roh', wrote Emperor Sher Shah Suri, as he contemplated the Mughal offensive that would end in the destruction of his empire in 1555, 'and to have transferred its inhabitants to the tract between the Nilab and Lahore, that they might have been constantly on the alert for the arrival of the Mughals, and not allow anyone to pass from Kabul to Hind.'[32] He went on to add: 'Another is to have entirely destroyed Lahore, that so large a city might not exist on the very road of an invader, where immediately after capturing it on his arrival, he could collect his supplies.'

The ideas driving the emperor's thinking would not be unfamiliar to rulers through history as they confronted restive populations and external threats. India's policies in Mizoram were, after all, derivative of those used by the French in Indochina and Algeria and the UK in Malaya and Kenya. Indeed, the idea of large-scale demographic engineering as a conflict-resolution tool can be traced back to the Roman legions.

History, though, has demonstrated that counter-insurgency-by-force more often than not fails. In the absence of appropriate political instruments and the reconstruction of civic institutions, which can ensure rule of law, it can, at best, bring about a stalemate. India's own insurgencies, particularly those of Kashmir and the Maoist heartlands, demonstrate that these stalemates can be fragile, erupting into conflagrations that sap resources and energy away from more important strategic objectives.

The beginning of reform has to be the acknowledgement of a problem and an open-minded willingness to discuss alternatives. The financial and strategic crisis that the pandemic of 2020–2021 has brought on the Indian State ought to be the impetus for such a conversation.

Afterword

MANOJ JOSHI

The trigger for this book was the developments of 2020: the great Covid-19 pandemic that accelerated some global geopolitical trends and decelerated others and the crisis in eastern Ladakh that focused Indian minds on its security predicament. But we are conscious that a book of this kind can, at best, deal with just a thin slice of the reality we confront in our lives and time. So what we have to offer through this book is not some total approach but one that deals with the here and now and wherever we think that the chapters in this volume will provide a sum that is greater than its parts.

As it is, the book was written before another major geopolitical event—the February 2022 Russian invasion of Ukraine—occurred. But it happened after most of the chapters of this book had been written. In any case, this is an ongoing development which will upend an already roiled global system in ways that are not easy to forecast.

The thing to remember is that our geography may be fixed but geopolitics is an ever-changing affair. Along with it are alignments of nations, which can change 180 degrees as has been the case in the previous century, say, with Russia, Germany, the US, China and Japan. The rise of nations has, for example, in the case of China, been a visible affair, but their decline can often be slow and imperceptible. The past and present of a nation most certainly provide us with a glimpse of its possible future, but neither the life of a nation nor that of an individual is foreordained.

Today, our ever-increasing obsession with data allows us to track everything—GDP growth, demographic shifts, political preferences, resource flows—in considerable detail and enables us to cast trajectories into the future. But there are events like wars, financial crises and pandemics that cannot be predicted, nor can the proclivities of human beings. The role of the big man in history has been debated a lot. A Xi Jinping or a Vladimir Putin, or, for that matter, a Narendra Modi or a Donald Trump, can and does disrupt historical pathways. But large groups of small people can also do the same by their behaviour and preferences—and make history.

What we have offered in this book is an examination of the issue of national security in the narrow frame of our time. It is often common to speak of living in an era of change. But the reality of change is that it happens all the time. Time and tide, as is famously said, wait for none. For the past two decades, writers and analysts have followed the rise of China and India, the shift of power eastwards and also its diffusion in all directions brought on by technology. But no one would have been prepared for the Covid-19 pandemic, whose imprint on the geopolitical developments of our time has yet to fully reveal itself. Sure, it has accelerated the trend towards reshoring and near-shoring of supply chains, something that began as a result of the development of additive manufacturing. But in all likelihood, we will only understand what Covid-19 has wreaked in the fullness of time.

But the pandemic was only the last layer that settled on the existing security template of the country, which, as the chapters in this book revealed, is rusting in several parts and is in urgent need of reform and refurbishment, whether in internal or external security. There are some issues, say, for instance, with regards to China and Kashmir, where there is a distinct regression, but there are others that are missed opportunities. There are also prospects that the powers that be seem oblivious to.

The authors of the chapters have examined various facets, sifted through the data carefully, offered critiques, but more importantly, come up with practical suggestions that could help in not only stemming losses but turning things around. But whether there is an inclination to accept their advice or, for that matter, any advice, is something that is not easy to determine because it involves the complex intersection of the country's politics, governance system and priorities, which need not necessarily be the ones we have urged.

What the data does tell us is that slogans, whether it is atmanirbharta (self-reliance) or 'Make in India', cannot substitute for systematic planning and effort. Neither can nations easily defy their geography and prevailing geo-economic and geopolitical realities.

As a country that possesses nuclear weapons and a large military and paramilitary force, India does not face an existential threat from abroad. In the larger perspective, a border skirmish with China or jihadi terror from Pakistan is a pinprick. But there is a significant danger from within.

When we look at the India of today, we see a vast and varied land with many religions and cultures. But we also see a country where religion-related social hostilities are *very high*, according to a Pew research survey.[1] In a country destined to have 1.3 billion Hindus by 2050 and be home to the largest Muslim population in the world at 311 million, this is not good news.[2]

Another trajectory that has been witnessed is that of a slowing, rather than growing, economy.[3] This has implications for both economic development and military modernisation. There is very little, as one of our chapters suggests, that can be done in the next decade to change things here. The danger of the demographic dividend of today transforming into a nightmare of tomorrow is very real.

Contributors to this book have not hesitated to call a spade a spade. But neither have they thrown in the towel in despair. What they have sought is to craft solutions that require purposefulness and teamwork and, in certain cases, get the nation to bite the bullet. At the end of the day, nations, like tailors, must cut the coat according to the cloth. Here, for India, retrenchment is not necessarily a bad word if it seeks to address the excesses of the past. And who can deny that India has not only had aspirations of being a 'major power' or 'great nation', if you will, but often played out that role in regions and areas in a manner that did not quite make any difference.

At this crossroads of our history, the need of the hour is a 'whole-of-the-nation' approach to problems. This may be a good time to take a lesson from Deng Xiaoping's famous 24-character strategy. True, it will not be possible for an open society like India to hide its capacities, but certainly, there are other lessons to be taken, such as the importance of inculcating harmony and calm in our domestic polity, working on key issues, keeping our heads down globally and putting our economy on a fast but sustainable growth trajectory. And last, India must retain a sense of humility and modesty in the face of the challenges we confront.

Postscript: As we have noted, the book had been largely completed before the Russian invasion of Ukraine. This has had the effect of not only upending global geopolitics but also led to revised thinking on several military issues.

On the one hand, it has solidified the China–Russia quasi alliance, on the other, it has helped re-energise the Western alliance. It has also persuaded the two proto–great powers, Japan and Germany, to sharply increase their defence spending, a development that has portents for the future.

The war in Ukraine, and an earlier conflict between Azerbaijan and Armenia, has a bearing on a range of issues discussed by various authors in the book—the character of war, the nature and use of air power, the role of air defence, precision targeting by missiles and artillery, robotics, drones and so on. There are many lessons already evident in the conduct of the war so far—the resilience of logistics, the quality of military commanders, the consequences of poor political leadership, etc. But the bottom-line lesson, Lawrence Freedman recently suggested, was to be wary of the tendency to overestimate what the 'raw force of arms' can achieve and 'the familiar but catastrophic mistake of underestimating the enemy'—in short, understanding the limits to military power.

And, even as we were in the last leg of the preparation for the publication of this book, the Government of India announced the Agnipath Scheme, which will have a transformational impact on the manning of the Indian military. Most of our writers have focused on the issue of manpower reform in the military, but none of them came close to suggesting something as drastic as the Agnipath, which could see the Indian military's profile change from a 100 per cent professional force to one that will consist of 25 per cent professionals and 75 per cent volunteers who will serve for just four years.

The government has sold the scheme as a means of making the military profile younger, but it is really born out of the unsustainability of the military's fiscal situation described so graphically in this book. With the recent Supreme Court judgement that will see OROP revised every five years, the budgetary situation could actually get worse.

The military implications of the scheme in its current iteration are quite serious, especially in relation to the quality of the manpower that the military would need to field in the coming years. The Agnipath savings will only start coming in after a decade and a half, so they cannot meet the military's short-term needs. Whether they will be a longer-term panacea, only time will tell.

NOTES

INTRODUCTION

1 Polyaenus, *Strategems in War*, eds and trans. Peter Krentz and Everett L. Wheeler (Chicago: Ares, 1994), 33.

2 For example, see Sanjaya Baru, *India and the World: Essays on Geoeconomics and Foreign Policy* (New Delhi: Academic Foundation, 2016).

3 Lawrence Freedman, *Strategy: A History* (Oxford University Press, 2016), 18.

4 Gomez, Eric, Christopher Preble, Lauren Sander, and Brandon Valeriano, 'Building a Modern Military: The Force Meets Geopolitical Realities,' Cato Institute Washington, D.C., 26 May 2020.

5 Ashley Tellis, 'Troubles Aplenty: Foreign Policy Challenges for the Next Indian Government,' Carnegie Endowment for International Peace, 20 May 2019, https://carnegieendowment.org/2019/05/20/troubles-aplenty-foreign-policy-challenges-for-next-indian-government-pub-79161

CHAPTER 1 INDIA'S WORLD

1 See, for example, Stephen P. Cohen, *India: Emerging Power* (Washington DC: Brookings Institution Press, 2001); Teresita C. Schaffer and Howard B. Schaffer, *India at the Global High Table: The Quest for Regional Primacy and Strategic Autonomy* (Washington DC: Brookings Institution Press, 2016); Naunihal Singh, *India: A Rising Power* (New Delhi: Authors Press, 2013); Rajesh Basrur and Kate Sullivan de Estrada, *Rising India: Status and Power* (London: Routledge, 2017); Shyam Saran, 'Premature Power,' *Business Standard*, 21 January 2013, https://www.business-standard.com/article/opinion/shyam-saran-premature-power-110031700019_1.html; T.V. Paul (ed.), *Accommodating Rising Powers: Past, Present and Future* (Cambridge: Cambridge University Press, 2016).

2 Ministry of External Affairs, Government of India, Media Center, 'EAM's remarks at Asian Leadership Conference 2020,' 11 November 2020, https://www.mea.gov.in/Speeches-Statements.htm?dtl/33187/EAMs+remarks+at+Asian+Leadership+Conference+2020

3 Samuel Huntington, 'The Lonely Superpower,' *Foreign Affairs*, March/April 1999, https://www.foreignaffairs.com/articles/united-states/1999-03-01/lonely-superpower

4 Ministry of External Affairs, Government of India, Media Center, 'IISS Fullerton Lecture by S. Jaishankar, Foreign Secretary in Singapore, 20 July 2015,' https://mea.gov.in/Speeches-Statements.htm?dtl/25493/IISS_Fullerton_Lecture_by_Foreign_Secretary_in_Singapore

5 Angus Maddison, *The World History, Vols 1 & 2* (OECD, Paris: Academic Foundation, 2007).

6 Henry Kissinger, *Diplomacy* (New York: Simon & Schuster, 1994), 23.

7 Condoleezza Rice, 'Campaign 2000: Promoting the National Interest,' *Foreign Affairs*, Jan–Feb 2000.

8 Sanjaya Baru, *Strategic Consequences of India's Economic Performance* (New Delhi: Academic Foundation, 2006), 29–56.

9 Baru, *Strategic Consequences*, 14.

10 Baru, *Strategic Consequences*, 43.

11 Sanjaya Baru, 'Conceptualising Economic Security,' in Baru, *Strategic Consequences*, 75–86. Also, Kaushik Basu et al., 'The Evolving Dynamics of Global Economic Power in the Post-Crisis World: Revelations from a New Index of Government Economic Power,' 2011, http://kaushikbasu.org/Index%20of%20Government%20Economic%20Power.pdf

12 Arvind Subramanian and Shoumitro Chatterjee, 'India's Inward (Re)Turn,' *Indian Express*, 14 October 2020, https://indianexpress.com/article/opinion/columns/india-trade-economy-coronavirus-impact-covid-6723899/

13 https://av.sc.com/corp-en/content/docs/Standard-Chartered-Opportunity-2030.pdf

14 See for a discussion of state capacity and national power, Sanjaya Baru, 'Defining National Power and Capability,' *ISPP Policy Review* (February 2020), https://policyreview.in/on-national-power-and-capability-by-sanjaya-baru/

15 Arvind Subramanian and Shoumitro Chatterjee, 'India's Inward Re(turn): Is it Warranted? Will it Work?' *Ashoka Centre for Economic Policy* (16 October 2020), http://dx.doi.org/10.2139/ssrn.3713253

16 Omkar Goswami, 'Prepare for Stress and Pain,' in Sanjaya Baru, *Beyond Covid's Shadow: Mapping India's Economic Resurgence* (New Delhi: Rupa Publications, 2020). Also, Sanjaya Baru, 'The Political Economy of Uncertainty,' in Baru, *Beyond Covid's Shadow*.

17 Gulzar Natarajan, 'Indian Economy Update: Covid Recovery,' *Outlook*, 27 November 2020, http://gulzar05.blogspot.com/2020/11/indian-economy-update-covid-recovery.html

18 Shankar Acharya, 'A Subsidy-Tariff-Permit Raj,' *Business Standard*, 26 November 2020, https://www.business-standard.com/article/opinion/a-subsidy-tariff-permit-raj-120112600047_1.html

19 Robert Ward, 'RCEP Trade Deal: A Geopolitical Win for China,' International Institute of Strategic Studies, 25 November 2020, https://www.iiss.org/blogs/analysis/2020/11/rcep-trade-deal?

20 Shyam Saran, 'Leaving RCEP Was a Short-Sighted Decision,' *The Hindu*, 17 November 2020, https://www.thehindu.com/news/national/leaving-rcep-was-a-short-sighted-decision-says-former-foreign-secretary-shyam-saran/article33118832.ece

21 Zorawar Daulet Singh, 'India's Rising Power: Myth or Reality?' *World Affairs: The Journal of International Issues* 11, no. 4 (Winter, 2007): 70–81.

22 Lowy Institute Asia Power Index 2020, https://power.lowyinstitute.org/

23 Media Center, Ministry of External Affairs, 'EAM's Remarks at Asian Leadership Conference 2020,' 11 November 2020, https://mea.gov.in/Speeches-Statements.htm?dtl/33187

24 Richard Bush, 'The United States and China: A G-2 in the Making,' Brookings, 11 October 2011, https://www.brookings.edu/articles/the-united-states-and-china-a-g-2-in-the-making/

25 On Europe's search for strategic autonomy, see: Ronja Kempin and Barbara Kunz, *France, Germany and the Quest for European*

Strategic Autonomy, SWP-IFRI Note 141, December 2017, https://www.ifri.org/sites/default/files/atoms/files/ndc_141_kempin_kunz_france_germany_european_strategic_autonomy_dec_2017.pdf

26 Huntington, 'Lonely Superpower.'

27 Huntington, 'Lonely Superpower.'

28 S. Jaishankar, 'Indian Foreign Policy: Preparing for a Different Era,' Address to Centre for Strategic and International Studies, Washington D.C., 1 October 2019, https://www.csis.org/analysis/indian-foreign-policy-preparing-different-era

CHAPTER 2 NEITHER GUNS NOR BUTTER: THE INCONVENIENT TRUTH OF INDIA'S DEFENCE FINANCING

1 Krishna Kant, 'India's 10-Year Growth One of the Biggest Laggards in Asia, EM Peers,' *Business Standard*, 1 December 2020, https://www.business-standard.com/article/economy-policy/india-s-10-year-growth-one-of-the-biggest-laggards-in-asia-em-peers-120113001325_1.html

2 For definitional clarity, this chapter classifies all expenditure incurred by the Ministry of Defence (MoD) as defence expenditure. This spending includes expenditure on defence pensions and MoD (civil) in addition to the revenue and capital expenditures on the three armed forces.

3 PRS Legislative Research, 'Demand for Grants 2020–21 Analysis: Defence,' prsindia.org, https://prsindia.org/parliamenttrack/budgets/demand-grants-2020-21-analysis-defence

4 For perspective, the two other major components of the Union government expenditure are interest payments on previous loans (3.05 per cent of GDP) and subsidies for petroleum, fertilizer and food (1.1 per cent of GDP).

5 Nominal growth rates do not account for inflation.

6 PRS Demand for Grants 2021–2022. The 2019–2020 figures are from the 5th Report of the Standing Committee on Defence (2019–2020), 12.

7 Non-defence functions include desirable expenditure on developmental responsibilities and undesirable expenditure on various implicit and explicit subsidies and bailouts.

8 Standing Committee on Defence, 28th Report: General Defence Budget, Border Roads Organisation, Indian Coast Guard, Military Engineer Services, Canteen Stores Department, Directorate General Defence Estates, Defence Public Sector Undertakings, Welfare of Ex-Servicemen, Defence Pensions, Ex-Servicemen Contributory Health Scheme, Lok Sabha, 7 March 2017, http://164.100.47.193/lsscommittee/Defence/16_Defence_28.docx

Further, the spending on defence pensions, which has grown the fastest amongst all other components, is imagined to be in addition to this 3 per cent GDP benchmark.

9 Standing Committee on Defence, 37th Report: Action Taken by the Government on the Observations/Recommendations Contained in the 28th Report (16th Lok Sabha) on General Defence Budget, Border Roads Organisation, Indian Coast Guard, Military Engineer Services, Canteen Stores. Department, Directorate General Defence Estates, Defence Public Sector Undertakings, Welfare of Ex-Servicemen, Defence Pensions, Ex-Servicemen Contributory Health Scheme, Lok Sabha, 12 March 2018, http://164.100.47.193/lsscommittee/Defence/16_Defence_37.pdf

10 Chart recreated based on data compiled from Union Budgets (relevant years). Classification as per PRS Legislative Research's Demand for Grants Analysis for successive years: Salaries are for the three services and include salaries for civilians, auxiliary forces, Rashtriya Rifles, Jammu and Kashmir Light Infantry and Indian Coast Guard. Pensions and capital outlay are of the three services. Pensions include rewards. Capital outlay includes capital expenses on border roads and the coast guard. Stores includes ammunition, repairs, refits and spares. Others include administration expenses, expense on research and development and housing.

11 Vinay Kaushal, 'Should the Legacy of Capital Budget Revenue Procedure (CBRP) Be Perpetuated in Draft DPP 2020?' MP-IDSA Issue Brief, 10 April 2020, https://idsa.in/issuebrief/capital-budget-revenue-procedure-vinayk-100420

12 Laxman Kumar Behera and Madhulika Baniwal, 'Bang for Buck: India's Defence Expenditure in Wider Perspective,' MP-IDSA,

10 July 2020, https://idsa.in/specialfeature/india-defence-expenditure-laxman-madhulika-100720

13 Laxman Kumar Behera, Vinay Kaushal, and Amit Cowshish, 'Defence Pension: A Comparative Study of India, US and UK,' MP-IDSA Policy Brief, 23 April 2020, https://idsa.in/policybrief/defence-pension-india-us-uk-230420#footnote3_ecyycu2

14 Amit Cowshish and Rahul Bedi, 'Anomalies Ail Defence Pension System,' *The Tribune*, 3 December 2020, https://www.tribuneindia.com/news/comment/anomalies-ail-defence-pension-system-179122

15 Growth rate is calculated using the budgetary allocations for 2015–2016 and 2019–2020 (Revised).

16 Press Release, 'Five Years of Historic Decision to Implement OROP; Over Rs. 42740 Crore Disbursed to 20,60,220 Defence Forces Pensioners/Family Pensioners,' Press Information Bureau, Government of India, https://pib.gov.in/PressReleaseIframePage.aspx?PRID=1670633

17 Abraham Thomas, '"Courts Can't Examine One Rank One Pension Changes": Centre to SC', *The Hindustan Times*, 3 October 2020, https://www.hindustantimes.com/india-news/courts-can-t-examine-one-rank-one-pension-changes-centre-to-sc/story-QXoLs5zfIZqHxHXLgZGoGM.html

18 Behera and Baniwal, 'Bang for Buck.'

19 Payments for defence platforms are spread over multiple years. The funds allocated under the capital section of the budget are first set aside to meet these projected committed liabilities. The remaining allocation is distributed to meet the projected requirement for other items (MoD statement to the Standing Committee on Defence, 17th Lok Sabha, Report 3).

20 Standing Committee on Defence, 3rd Report (17th Lok Sabha) on Capital Outlay on Defence Services, Procurement Policy, Defence Planning and Married Accommodation Project, Lok Sabha, 9 December 2019, http://164.100.47.193/lsscommittee/Defence/17_Defence_3.pdf

21 The 'no Covid-19 counterfactual' is created by extrapolating the World Bank *Global Economic Prospects* January 2020 forecast to 2021. This pathway assumes 5.8% real GDP growth in FY 2020–2021 and a steady 6.1% real GDP growth for the next nine years.

The 'quick rebound' pathway is based on extrapolating the World Bank *Global Economic Prospects* June 2021 forecast. This pathway assumes a 7.3% contraction in FY 2020–2021 followed by return to growth rates of 8.5% in FY 2021–2022, 7.5% in FY 2022–2023 and 6.5% in FY 2023–2024. For the sake of this exercise, I have assumed a steady growth rate of 6% for the next eight years. World Bank Outlook link: https://openknowledge.worldbank.org/bitstream/handle/10986/34517/9781464816406.pdf?sequence=7&isAllowed=y

The 'long march' pathway is the pessimistically optimistic economic pathway that assumes +3% growth for ten years starting FY 2021–2022.

World Bank. *Global Economic Prospects* (Washington, D.C.: World Bank, 2021), doi:10.1596/978-1-4648-1665-9. License: Creative Commons Attribution CC BY 3.0 IGO.

22 The nominal compound annual rates are obtained by estimating the rise in these components between FY 2011–2012 and FY 2020–2021 and assuming that the same trend continues. So Stores grows at 4.8 per cent, Others at 8.9 per cent, Salaries at 9.4 per cent. For pension, the nominal compound annual rate assumed is 15 per cent, same as the rate the period after OROP came into effect.

23 Pranay Kotasthane and Lt Gen. Prakash Menon, 'Not Fair to Cut Defence Pay, Pensions and Inject Funds in Airlines, Banks,' The Print, 13 November 2020, https://theprint.in/opinion/not-fair-to-cut-defence-pay-pensions-and-inject-funds-in-airlines-banks/542965/

24 Sudipto Mundle and Satadru Sikdar, Subsidies, Merit Goods and the Fiscal Space for Reviving Growth: An Aspect of Public Expenditure in India, NIPFP Working Paper 282, 8 November 2019, https://www.nipfp.org.in/media/medialibrary/2019/11/WP_282_2019.pdf

25 Nitin Pai, 'Free up the Army's Land,' *Business Standard*, 10 May 2015, https://www.business-standard.com/article/opinion/nitin-pai-free-up-the-army-s-land-115051000748_1.html

26 This idea was first proposed by Lt Gen. Prakash Menon in Prakash Menon and Pranay Kotasthane, 'Covid-19 Warrants Long Overdue Doctrinal Shifts in Military Planning,' *Indian*

Public Policy Review 1, no. 1 (2020), https://www.ippr.in/index.php/ippr/article/view/7

27 Menon and Kotasthane, 'COVID-19 Warrants Long Overdue Doctrinal Shifts.'

CHAPTER 3 INDIA'S NEGLECTED MARITIME DOMAIN: A MISSED OPPORTUNITY

1 The author wishes to acknowledge the invaluable assistance provided by Suchet Vir Singh while researching for this chapter.

2 Bhartiya Janta Party, BJP Election Manifesto (New Delhi: BJP, 2014), 38.

3 *The Economic Times*, 'INSA Urges Government to Formulate Shipping Development Policy.' *The Economic Times*, 27 June 2019, https://economictimes.indiatimes.com/industry/transportation/shipping-/-transport/insa-urge-govt-to-formulate-shipping-development-policy/articleshow/69976634.cms?from=mdr

4 Captain A.T. Mahan, *The Influence of Sea Power Upon History 1660–1783* (Boston: Little Brown & Co., 1905).

5 Admiral Sergei Gorshkov, *The Sea Power of the State* (Florida: Pergamon, 1979), 1–17.

6 Military and Security Developments Involving the Peoples Republic of China 2020, US Department of Defence's Annual Report to Congress, July 2020.

7 Michael A. McDevitt, *China as a Twenty-First Century Naval Power* (Annapolis: Naval Institute Press, 2020).

8 Ministry of Shipping, Government of India, Maritime Agenda 2010–2020 (New Delhi: Ministry of Shipping, 2011), 441.

9 Ministry of Shipping, Government of India, Sagarmala–Vision, https://www.sagarmala.gov.in/about-sagarmala/vision

10 *Business Today*, 'Sagarmala Project Created Nearly 10,000 Jobs in Last 3 Years, Says Minister,' *Business Today*, 15 July 2019, https://www.businesstoday.in/sectors/jobs/sagarmala-project-created-nearly-10000-jobs-in-last-3-years-says-minister/story/364571.html

11 P. Parekh and G. Saini, 'Why India Needs to Finance Its Maritime Sector to Emerge as a World Leader,' DailyO, 5 June 2020, https://www.dailyo.in/business/indian-maritime-sector-financing-shipping-world-economy-shipbuilding-overseas-trade/story/1/33048.html

12 Ministry of Shipping, Government of India, Annual Report 2018–2019, http://shipmin.gov.in/sites/default/files/1405631573Anuleng.pdf

13 P. Manoj, 'NCLT Orders Liquidation of Bharati Defence,' *The Hindu Business Line*, 16 January 2019, https://www.thehindubusinessline.com/companies/nclt-orders-liquidation-of-bharati-defence/article26000863.ece

14 Ministry of Shipping, Government of India, Annual Report 2019–2020, para 5.6, https://shipmin.gov.in/sites/default/files/Shipping%20Annual%20Report%20English_compressed.pdf

15 Rupali Ghanekar, 'Towards a Larger Indian Shipping Industry,' Observer Research Foundation, 24 March 2020, https://www.orfonline.org/expert-speak/towards-a-larger-indian-shipping-industry-63662/

16 Press Information Bureau, Government of India, Press Release, 14 July 2021, https://pib.gov.in/PressReleasePage.aspx?PRID=1735373

17 Admiral Sergei Gorshkov, *The Sea Power of the State* (Florida: Pergamon, 1979), 42.

18 National Institute of Ocean Technology, Ministry of Earth Sciences, Government of India, https://www.niot.res.in/niot1/dst_intro.php

19 Prabhjot Gill, 'ISRO Plans to Dive 6,000 Meters Deep into the Sea by 2022,' *Business Insider*, 4 November 2019, https://www.businessinsider.in/science/space/news/isro-plans-deep-sea-exploration-with-manned-submersible-by-2022/articleshow/71887408.cms

20 China Dialogue Ocean, 'China Dives into Deep-Sea Mining,' Maritime Executive, 29 March 2019, https://www.maritime-executive.com/editorials/china-dives-into-deep-sea-mining

21 Reuters, 'China Leads the Race to Exploit Deep Sea Minerals: U.N. Body,' Reuters, 23 October 2019, https://www.reuters.com/article/us-mining-deepsea-idUSKBN1X213T

CHAPTER 4 ARMY CAPABILITY DEVELOPMENT

1 Amrita Nayak Dutta, 'Army Plans to Keep 2 Strike Corps for Mountains Facing China amid Ladakh Crisis,' The Print, 6 January 2021, https://theprint.in/defence/army-plans-

to-deploy-2-strike-corps-in-mountains-facing-china-amid-ladakh-crisis/579924/

2 Nitin A. Gokhale, 'Eastern Ladakh: Chinese Formations Undertaking Rotation,' Bharat Shakti, 24 April 2021, https://bharatshakti.in/eastern-ladakh-chinese-formations-undertaking-rotation/

3 Nitin A. Gokhale, 'India to Allocate Three More Divisions to China Border,' Bharat Shakti, 15 January 2021, https://bharatshakti.in/india-to-allocate-three-more-divisions-to-china-border/

4 Express News Service, 'India's Global Rise Will Invite Attempts to Limit It: S. Jaishankar,' *The Indian Express*, 13 December 2020, https://indianexpress.com/article/india/indias-rise-will-evoke-its-own-reactions-and-responses-s-jaishankar-7103459/

5 Vinod Bhatia and Anil Ahuja, 'Revisiting Mountain Corps to Deter China,' *The Tribune*, 18 June 2020, https://www.tribuneindia.com/news/comment/revisiting-mountain-corps-to-deter-china-100707

6 Srijan Shukla, '1975 Arunachal Ambush—the Last Time Indian Soldiers Died in Clash with China at LAC,' The Print, 16 June 2020, https://theprint.in/india/1975-arunachal-ambush-the-last-time-indian-soldiers-died-in-clash-with-china-at-lac/442674/

7 Subir Bhaumik, 'More Troops on Sino-India Border,' BBC News, 23 November 2010, https://www.bbc.com/news/world-south-asia-11818840

8 Kalyan Das, 'Pak Using Heavier Artillery for LoC Violations: Army Vice Chief,' *The Hindustan Times*, 13 December 2020, https://www.hindustantimes.com/dehradun/pak-using-heavier-artillery-for-loc-violations-army-vice-chief/story-2aY1eSb1c27EnbV7REFISP.html

9 Walter C. Ladwig III, 'A Cold Start for Hot Wars? The Indian Army's New Limited War Doctrine,' *Quarterly Journal: International Security* 32, no. 3 (Winter 2007/08): 158–190, https://www.belfercenter.org/publication/cold-start-hot-wars-indian-armys-new-limited-war-doctrine

10 PRS Legislative Research, 'Demand for Grants 2021–22 Analysis: Defence,' prsindia.org, https://prsindia.org/

budgets/parliament/demand-for-grants-2021-22-analysis-defence

11 Ladwig, 'A Cold Start for Hot Wars?'

12 Group of Ministers, 'Reforming the National Security System: Recommendations' (New Delhi: Government of India, 2001), https://www.vifindia.org/sites/default/files/GoM%20Report%20on%20National%20Security.pdf

13 Vijay Mohan, 'Amid Stand-off with China, ITBP Rushes to Raise New Command at Chandigarh,' *The Tribune*, 4 June 2020, https://www.tribuneindia.com/news/chandigarh/amidst-stand-off-with-china-itbp-rushes-to-raise-new-command-at-chandigarh-94399

14 Snehesh Alex Philip, 'Army and IAF Fought over Apache Choppers, Costing Us Rs 2,500 Crore More: Blame Their Silos,' The Print, 28 February 2020, https://theprint.in/opinion/brahmastra/army-and-iaf-fought-over-apache-choppers-costing-us-rs-2500-crore-more-blame-their-silos/372553/

15 Press Trust of India, '68 Percent of Equipment Is Vintage: Army to Parliamentary Panel,' The Quint, 14 March 2018, https://www.thequint.com/news/india/indian-army-insufficient-fund-allocation-in-defence-budget

16 Press Trust of India, 'Indian Army: India's Armed Forces Got Rs 1.21 Lakh Crore Less than What They Demanded in Budget,' *The Economic Times*, 21 March 2018, https://economictimes.indiatimes.com/news/defence/indias-armed-forces-got-rs-1-21-lakh-crore-less-than-what-they-demanded-in-budget/articleshow/63400023.cms?from=mdr

17 Joseph Da Silva, Hugh Liebert, and Isaiah Wilson III, *American Grand Strategy and the Future of U.S. Landpower* (San Diego: Didactic Press, 2015).

CHAPTER 5 TRAJECTORY OF INDIAN AIR POWER

1 Lt L.V.S. Blacker, 'Aviation,' *USI Journal* XLI, no. 188 (July 1912), https://usiofindia.org/wp-content/uploads/2019/02/Part1.pdf). The *USI Journal* maintains in its library a pdf version of this article and all the articles referred in this chapter.

2 Flt Lt R.L. Stevenson, 'The Army Cooperation Squadron,' *USI Journal* LV, no. 240 (July 1925), https://usiofindia.org/wp-content/uploads/2019/02/Part2.pdf

3 Refer to endnote no. 1 regarding the availability of the pdf version of this archived article.

4 General George Q Brown, 'Accelerate Change or Lose,' USAF Policy Paper, August 2020, https://www.af.mil/Portals/1/documents/csaf/CSAF_22/CSAF_22_Strategic_Approach_Accelerate_Change_or_Lose_31_Aug_2020.pdf

5 Giulio Douhet, *The Command of the Air* (Montgomery, Alabama: Air University Press, 2019), 27, https://www.airuniversity.af.edu/Portals/10/AUPress/Books/B_0160_DOUHET_THE_COMMAND_OF_THE_AIR.pdf

6 Directorate of Operations (Space), *Basic Doctrine of the Indian Air Force 2012*, Indian Air Force, https://www.scribd.com/doc/109721067/Basic-Doctrine-of-Indian-Air-Force-2012-PDF

7 China consistently refused to give out its casualty figure till February 2021, when it accepted four fatalities.

8 The Directors General of Military Operations of India and Pakistan issued a joint communique on 25 February 2021 declaring that both sides would honour a 'ceasefire' on the LoC and 'maintain the sanctity and ceasefire on the Line of Control'. See Sushant Sareen, 'Why the Recent India–Pakistan Ceasefire Agreement Is Badly Drafted,' The Print, 2 March 2021, https://theprint.in/opinion/why-the-recent-india-pakistan-ceasefire-agreement-is-badly-drafted/613771/

9 At the time of writing, only a partial disengagement of troops has taken place in the Pangong lake area. For more, read Dinakar Peri, 'India, China complete disengagement at Pangong Tso,' *The Hindu*, 19 February 2021, https://www.thehindu.com/news/national/india-china-complete-disengagement-at-pangong-tso/article33877842.ece

10 Laxman Behera and Madhulika Baniwal, 'Bang for Buck: India's Defence Expenditure in Wider Perspective,' MP-IDSA, 10 July 2020, https://idsa.in/specialfeature/india-defence-expenditure-laxman-madhulika-100720

11 Yogesh Joshi and Anit Mukerjee, 'From Denial to Punishment: The Security Dilemma and Changes in India's Military Strategy towards China,' *Asian Security* 15:1 (2019): 25–43, DOI: 10.1080/14799855.2019.1539817

12 MMRCA is the acronym for Medium Multi Role Combat Aircraft. The government wanted to acquire 126 MMRCA for

which the acquisition process started in 2003 but could not be completed till 2018, when the project was shelved. For more on this, read Deba R. Mohanty, 'MMRCA 2.0: Why Defence Procurement Decision Making Is Problematic,' *The Financial Express*, 21 August 2021, https://www.financialexpress.com/defence/mmrca-2-0-why-defence-procurement-decision-making-is-problematic/1286824/

13 Air Marshal B.K. Pandey, 'DRDO to Develop Indigenous AWACS,' *SP's Aviation* 4 (2015), http://www.sps-aviation.com/story/?id=1651

14 Shiv Aroor, 'India Wants Home Grown AWACS to Double as Tanker,' Live First, 28 February 2018, https://www.livefistdefence.com/2018/02/indian-air-force-wants-home-grown-awacs-to-double-as-tanker.html

15 S.K. Gurung, 'India Starts Process for Procuring Six Tanker Aircraft,' *The Economic Times*, 25 January 2018, https://economictimes.indiatimes.com/news/defence/iaf-starts-process-for-procuring-six-tanker-aircraft/articleshow/62654532.cms?from=mdr

16 While there has been no official figure on the number of squadrons required for a two-front scenario, various media reports have pegged the number at 39.5, 40 or even 42. However, 39.5 is the most quoted number.

17 Snehesh Alex Philips, 'IAF Set to Place Orders for 21 MiG-29 Jets from Russia by December to Shore Up Aircraft Strength,' The Print, 6 October 2020, https://theprint.in/defence/iaf-set-to-place-orders-for-21-mig-29-jets-from-russia-by-dec-to-shore-up-aircraft-strength/517907/

18 S.K. Gurung, 'Six Global Companies Respond to India's RFI for 110 Fighter Jets,' *The Economic Times*, 6 July 2018, https://economictimes.indiatimes.com/news/defence/six-global-companies-respond-to-indias-rfi-for-buying-110-fighter-jets/articleshow/64887437.cms?from=mdr

19 See Basic Doctrine of IAF, 26.

20 See Basic Doctrine of IAF, 17.

21 Ajai Shukla, 'IAF to Increase Squadron Strength: 3 More to be Added in 2020,' *Business Standard*, 19 January 2020, https://www.business-standard.com/article/economy-policy/iaf-to-increase-squadron-strength-3-more-to-be-inducted-in-2020-120011801028_1.html

22 Shiv Aroor, 'Looking at Twelve Squadrons of Tejas Mk2: IAF Chief Confirms,' Live First, 12 September 2018, https://www.livefistdefence.com/2018/09/looking-at-12-squadrons-of-lca-tejas-mk-2-iaf-chief-confirms.html

23 Group Captain Joseph Noronha, 'Strength Lies in Numbers: Rebuilding the IAF Fleet,' *Indian Defence Review* 3.4 (Oct–Dec 2018), http://www.indiandefencereview.com/news/strength-lies-in-numbers-rebuilding-the-combat-fleet-of-the-iaf/

24 Shishir Gupta, 'Long-awaited Indigenous Light Combat Aircraft Tejas MkII Targeted by 2022,' *The Hindustan Times*, 23 August 2019, https://www.hindustantimes.com/india-news/indigenous-light-combat-aircraft-targeted-by-2022/story-MGy2MXsapn8H6IDjUNt12H.html

25 Noronha, 'Strength Lies in Numbers.'

26 MP-IDSA (Manohar Parrikar Institute of Defence Analyses), New Delhi, is the new name of what earlier was just IDSA.

27 CIA declassified report titled 'Pakistan-India: Effect of Pakistani AEW Aircraft on the Military Balance,' https://www.cia.gov/library/readingroom/docs/CIA-RDP90T00114R000700310001-7.pdf

28 Sujan Dutta, 'This Is What the Indian Air Force's Fighter Squadron Strength Has Been Reduced To,' The Print, 20 September 2018, https://theprint.in/india/governance/this-is-what-the-indian-air-forces-fighter-squadron-strength-has-been-reduced-to/121323/s

29 To a question from the audience at the 15th Energising Indian Aerospace Industry International Conference 29–30 September 2020 about when the IAF's squadron strength would go back to 42 squadrons, the deputy chief of air staff said: 'It is very difficult to predict ... but we will hit around 37 to 38 [squadrons] taking in to consideration that there are no delays in the LCA variants ... we would in about one decade [be at] 37 [squadrons] but the fleet would be much, much more capable.' See time mark 2:09:45 of video recording of the event available on Youtube at https://www.youtube.com/watch?v=mrlRAQWn2aA

30 Amrita Nayak Dutta, 'Mid-Air Refuellers, UAVs: Bhadauria Explains How the IAF Is Bracing for the New Nature of War,'

The Print, 29 May2020, https://theprint.in/defence/iaf-hunting-for-6-midair-refuellers-more-uavs-as-wars-moving-to-skies-says-chief-bhadauria/431713/

31 Snehesh Alex Philip, 'Modi Government Okays 6 More 'Eyes in the Sky' for IAF, DRDO Project to Cost Rs 11,000 Crores,' The Print, 9 September 2021, https://theprint.in/defence/modi-govt-okays-6-more-eyes-in-the-sky-for-iaf-drdo-project-to-cost-rs-11000-crore/730697

32 Shekhar Gupta, 'What the IAF-PAF Dogfight Reveals,' *The Hindustan Times*, 25 April 2020, https://www.hindustantimes.com/columns/opinion-what-the-iaf-paf-dogfight-reveals/story-dDa4H38Xtq7LPnj6DtkZRN.html

33 Raunak Kunde, 'Sukhoi-30 MKI Starts Getting New Secured Radio and Radio Altimeter,' *Indian Defence Review*, 15 September 2021, https://idrw.org/sukhoi-30mki-starts-getting-new-secured-radio-and-radio-altimeter/

34 For details see global firepower website at https://www.globalfirepower.com/country-military-strength-detail.php?country_id=china

35 Webdesk, 'China Downplays J-20 Stealth Fighter Sighted Near Indian Border,' *The Week*, 18 August 2020, https://www.theweek.in/news/india/2020/08/18/china-downplays-j-20-stealth-fighter-being-sighted-near-india-border.html

36 Liu Zhen, 'China-India Border Dispute: PLA Bombers Pictured Close to Troubled Region,' *South China Morning Post*, 9 September 2020, https://www.scmp.com/news/china/military/article/3100891/china-india-border-dispute-pla-bombers-pictured-close-troubled

37 Douglas Barrie, 'India's Brahmos: An added Target in the Air?' IISS Military Balance Blog, 25 September 2020, https://www.iiss.org/blogs/military-balance/2020/09/india-brahmos-missile#:~:text=The%20air%2Dlaunched%20Brahmos%20is,%2Dattack%20(FGA)%20aircraft.&text=One%20option%20could%20be%20also,as%20AEW%26C%20and%20tanker%20aircraft

38 Mike Yeo, 'China Ramps Up Production of New Airborne Early Warning Aircraft,' *Defense News*, 5 February 2018, https://www.defensenews.com/digital-show-dailies/singapore-airshow/2018/02/05/china-ramps-up-production-of-new-airborne-early-warning-aircraft/

39 See holdings for Pakistan at https://www.globalfirepower.com/country-military-strength-detail.php?country_id=pakistan

40 Press Trust of India, 'Pakistan Buys 25 China Made J-10C Fighter Jets in Response to India's Rafale Aircraft Acquisition,' *The Hindu*, 30 December 2021, https://www.thehindu.com/news/international/pakistan-buys-25-china-made-j-10c-fighter-jets-in-response-to-indias-rafale-aircraft-acquisition/article38068802.ece

41 'IAF Caught Napping: Pakistan Now Operates More AWACS Aircraft than India,' *Indian Defence Review*, https://idrw.org/iaf-caught-napping-pakistan-now-operates-more-awacs-aircraft-than-india/#:~:text=IAF%20caught%20napping%2C%20Pakistan%20now%20operates%20more%20AWACS%20Aircraft%20than%20India,-Published%20April%2020&text=Down%20to%20three%20aircraft%2C%20PAF,2000%20Erieye%20AEW%26C%20to%20Six. Also, see FlightGlobal report, 'Saab Lands Secretive AEW&C Deal,' https://www.flightglobal.com/defence/saab-2000-lands-secretive-aewandc-deal/138431.article

42 'Ukraine to Upgrade Pakistan Air Force 1L-78 Tanker Plane,' *Defense World*, 4 June 2020, https://www.defenseworld.net/news/27134/Ukraine_to_Upgrade_Pakistan_Air_Force_Il_78_Tanker_Plane#.YMBck_kzY2wailable

43 Snehesh Alex Philip, 'ACM Bhadauria Said We're Ready for Two-front War with China-Pakistan, but There Are Deficits,' The Print, 9 October 2020, https://www.defenseworld.net/news/27134/Ukraine_to_Upgrade_Pakistan_Air_Force_Il_78_Tanker_Plane#.YMBck_kzY2w

44 Press Trust of India, 'Pakistan Violates Cease-fire Agreement; Fires along IB in J&K's Samba,' PTI, 3 May 2021 https://indianexpress.com/article/india/pakistan-violates-ceasefire-agreement-fires-along-ib-in-j-ks-samba-7300148/

45 For more on the defence budget for FY2021–22 read Abhishek Bhalla, 'Defence Budget: Only 0.4% Hike in Capital Expenditure as Armed Forces Overshot Last Budget by 23,000 Crores,' *India Today*, 1 February 2021, https://www.indiatoday.in/business/budget-2021/story/defence-budget-only-0-4-hike-in-capital-expenditure-as-armed-forces-overshot-last-budget-by-rs-23-000-crore-1764937-2021-02-01

46 'India's Economic Situation Much Worse than Ever, GDP May Shrink 9.6% this Fiscal: World Bank,' Businesstoday.in, 8 October 2020, https://www.businesstoday.in/current/economy-politics/world-bank-sees-india-gdp-contracting-by-96-fy21-economic-situation-much-worse-than-ever/story/418295.html

47 The Ministry of Finance would inform the Ministry of Defence of these values to plan for the next financial year.

48 For example, the use by the US Air Force of training technicians as brought out in Sgt Daryl Knee, 'Virtual, Augmented Reality May Hold Key to Air Force Training,' U.S. Air Force, 18 January 2019, https://www.af.mil/News/Article-Display/Article/1735247/virtual-augmented-reality-may-hold-key-to-future-air-force-training/. Similarly, for aircrew training, see Valerie Insinna, 'US Air Force's T-38 Trainer Could Soon Dogfight with Augmented Reality Adversaries,' *Defense News*, 20 March 2021, https://www.defensenews.com/air/2021/03/19/the-air-forces-t-38-trainer-could-dogfight-with-augmented-reality-adversaries-soon/

49 In-flight refueling of civilian airliners is next on the horizon. See James Pitman, 'A Century On, Is It Time for In-flight Refueling to Come of Age?' Royal Aeronautical Society, 3 November 2020, https://www.aerosociety.com/news/a-century-on-is-it-time-for-in-flight-refuelling-to-come-of-age/

50 Shaan Shaikh, 'The Air and Missile War in Nagorno Karabakh: Lessons for the Future of Strike and Defense,' *Center for Strategic and International Studies*, 8 December 2020, https://www.csis.org/analysis/air-and-missile-war-nagorno-karabakh-lessons-future-strike-and-defense; Also, see Zachary Kallenborn, 'Seven (initial) Drone Warfare Lessons from Ukraine,' Modern War Institute at West Point, 12 May 2022, https://mwi.usma.edu/seven-initial-drone-warfare-lessons-from-ukraine/

51 ET online, 'India Keeps an Eye on Drone Warfare Even as It Considers Buying the US MQ-9 Reaper,' *The Economic Times*, 13 October 2020, https://economictimes.indiatimes.com/news/defence/india-keeps-an-eye-on-drone-warfare-even-as-it-considers-buying-the-us-mq-9-reaper/harop/harpy-suicide-drones/slideshow/78638042.cms

52 Manu Pubby, 'Government Approves $400 Million Plan to Procure Armed Heron TP Drones from Israel,' *The Economic Times*, 14 July 2018, https://economictimes.indiatimes.

com/news/defence/government-approves-400-million-plan-to-procure-armed-heron-tp-drones-from-israel/articleshow/48906195.cms

53 ANI, 'Armed Forces Push Case for Arming Israeli Drone Fleet with Laser Guided Bombs, Missiles,' *The Economic Times*, 10 August 2020, https://economictimes.indiatimes.com/news/defence/armed-forces-push-case-for-arming-israeli-drone-fleet-with-laser-guided-bombs-missiles/articleshow/77445721.cms

54 'While on Trial for CRPF, Rustom 1 Crashes into a Wall in Jagdalpur,' *Indian Defence Research Wing*, 29 March 2021, https://idrw.org/while-on-trials-for-crpf-rustom-1-crashes-into-a-wall-in-jagdalpur/; Also, see *Business Today*, 'DRDO Unmanned Aerial Vehicle Rustom 2 Crashes in Karnataka,' Businesstoday.in, 17 September 2019, https://www.businesstoday.in/latest/trends/drdo-unmanned-aerial-vehicle-rustom-2-crashes-karnataka/story/379525.html

55 Snehesh Alex Philips, 'Army Showcases Swarm Drones at Army Day Parade,' The Print, 15 January 2021, https://theprint.in/defence/army-showcases-swarm-drones-at-army-day-parade-plans-to-scale-up-capability-soon/586020/

56 Press Trust of India, 'Indian Navy Leases Two Sea Guardian Drones from US to Enhance Surveillance Over IOR,' *The Economic Times*, 26 November 2021, https://economictimes.indiatimes.com/news/defence/indian-navy-leases-two-sea-guardian-drones-from-us-to-enhance-surveillance-over-ior/articleshow/79430125.cms?from=mdr

57 Richard P. Hallion, 'Air and Space Power: Rising and Accelerating,' in John Andreas Olsen, *A History of Air Warfare* (Dulles, Virginia: Potomac Books, 2010), 380.

58 Snehesh Alex Philips, 'IAF to Focus on Bombs and Air-to-Air Missiles for Edge Over Pakistan,' The Print, 28 February 2020, https://theprint.in/defence/iaf-to-focus-on-bombs-air-to-air-missiles-for-edge-over-pakistan/372802/

59 Ashley Tellis, 'India Capable but Constrained,' in Gary J. Schmitt, *A Hard Look at Hard Power: Assessing the Key Capabilities of US Allies and Security Partners, Second Edition* (Carlisle, PA: US Army War College Press, 2020), 138.

60 Richard P. Hallion, 'Air and Space Power,' 378.

61 See the report of the Kargil Review Committee, *From Surprise to Reckoning: The Kargil Review Committee Report* (New Delhi: SAGE, 2000). The fact that the security establishment was caught on the backfoot in eastern Ladakh has been covered in many reports; for example, see Ameya Pratap Singh, 'Intelligence Lessons from Ladakh Stand-off,' *The Indian Express*, 22 December 2020, https://indianexpress.com/article/opinion/columns/india-china-ladakh -lac-army-7115578/

62 Media Center, 'Quad Leaders' Joint Statement: "The Spirit of the Quad",' 12 March 2021, Ministry of External Affairs, Government of India https://www.mea.gov.in/bilateral-documents.htm?dtl/33620/Quad+Leaders+Joint+-Statement+The+Spirit+of+the+Quad

63 For a fascinating exposition of the link between economic change and military conflict, read Paul Kennedy, *The Rise and Fall of the Great Powers* (New York: Harper Collins, 1988), https://cheirif.files.wordpress.com/2015/08/paul-kennedy-the-rise-and-fall-of-the-great-powers-19891.pdf

64 Colin Clark, 'Gen. Hyten on the New American Way of War: All Domain Operations,' *Breaking Defense*, 18 February 2020, https://breakingdefense.com/2020/02/gen-hyten-on-the-new-american-way-of-war-all-domain-operations/

65 Jason Lamb and Jeremy Buyer, 'The Psychological High Ground: The Surprising Key to Accelerating Change,' *War on the Rocks*, 21 September 2020, https://warontherocks.com/2020/09/securing-the-psychological-high-ground-the-surprising-key-to-accelerating-change/

66 Rebecca Grant, 'The Second Offset,' *Air Force Magazine*, July 2016, 32–36, https://www.airforcemag.com/PDF/MagazineArchive/Documents/2016/July%20 2016/0716secondoffset.pdf

67 Rebecca Grant, 'The Second Offset.'

CHAPTER 6 HOW CAN THE INDIAN ARMY ADDRESS THE RESOURCE MODERNISATION LOGJAM?

1 India has fought four major wars in 1947–1948, 1962, 1965, 1971, and a more localised conflict in 1999. The country has also been fighting terrorism and insurgencies since 1955 in the north eastern parts of India, Punjab, Kashmir and a large number of districts in the eastern, central and southern states.

2 *Times of India*, '"Not a Single Bullet Fired in 40 Years": China Welcomes PM Modi's Remarks on Border Dispute,' *The Times of India*, 5 June 2017, https://m.timesofindia.com/india/china-welcomes-pm-modis-remarks-on-sino-india-border/amp_articleshow/58998740.cms

3 Sandeep Unnithan, 'The ChiPak Threat,' *India Today*, 23 October 2010, https://timesofindia.indiatimes.com/india/CCS-nod-for-raising-mountain-strike-corps-along-China-border/articleshow_b2/21132826.cms?mobile=nohiPak

4 John F. Burns, 'India's New Defence Chief Sees Chinese Military Threat,' *The New York Times*, 5 May 1998, https://www.nytimes.com/1998/05/05/world/india-s-new-defense-chief-sees-chinese-military-threat.html

5 Josy Joseph, 'CCS Nod for Raising Mountain Strike Corps along China Border,' *The Times of India*, 18 July 2013, https://timesofindia.indiatimes.com/india/CCS-nod-for-raising-mountain-strike-corps-along-China-border/articleshow_b2/21132826.cms?mobile=no

6 Manoj Joshi, 'Making Sense of the Depsang Incursion,' *The Hindu*, 7 May 2013, https://www.thehindu.com/opinion/op-ed/making-sense-of-the-depsang-incursion/article4689838.ece

7 Josy Joseph, 'CCS Nod for Raising Mountain Strike Corps.'

8 Rajat Pandit, 'India, China set to end 16-day Chumar stand-off by Saturday,' *The Times of India*, 26 September 2014, https://timesofindia.indiatimes.com/india/India-China-set-to-end-16-day-Chumar-stand-off-by-Saturday/articleshow/43467644.cms

9 For a detailed assessment of the Chinese employment of Three Warfares strategy during the Doklam standoff see Vivek Chadha, *Kargil: Past Perfect, Future Uncertain?* (New Delhi: Knowledge World, 2019), 159–176.

10 Dinakar Peri, 'Indian, Chinese Troops Face Off in Eastern Ladakh, Sikkim,' *The Hindu*, 10 May 2020, https://www.thehindu.com/news/national/indian-chinese-troops-face-off-in-eastern-ladakh-sikkim/article31548893.ece

11 Manu Pubby, 'As Sightings of Chinese Submarines Become Frequent, Navy Steps Up Guard in Indian Ocean Region,' *The Economic Times*, 12 July 2018, https://economictimes.

indiatimes.com/news/defence/as-sightings-of-chinese-submarines-become-frequent-navy-steps-up-guard-in-indian-ocean-region/articleshow/48397646.cms?from=mdr

12 See Anil Trigunayat and Paras Ratna, 'Countering China's Charm Offensive in India's Neighbourhood: Strategy Begins at Home,' *Financial Express*, 21 August 2020, https://www.financialexpress.com/defence/countering-chinas-charm-offensive-in-indias-neighbourhood-strategy-begins-at-home/2061541/

13 'The Galwan Valley Crisis Explained through 17 News Reports,' *Hindustan Times*, 22 June 2020, https://www.hindustantimes.com/india-news/the-galwan-valley-face-off-explained-through-17-news-reports/story-UzyJFQdaOEDgJZH2dE1MON.html

14 'Galwan Valley Clash: Modi Government Grants Emergency Financial Powers to Three Services,' *The New Indian Express*, 21 June 2020, https://www.newindianexpress.com/nation/2020/jun/21/galwan-valley-clash-modi-government-grants-emergency-financial-powers-to-three-services-2159547.html

15 Dinakar Peri, 'Budget 2020: Meagre Defence Hike Threatens Military Modernisation,' *The Hindu*, 1 February 2020, https://www.thehindu.com/business/budget/337-lakh-crore-allocated-for-defence-budget/article30712444.ece

16 Pavan Srinath, 'Opinion: Army Is Drowning in Hefty Salaries,' *Hindustan Times*, 2 February 2019, https://www.hindustantimes.com/budget/opinion-army-is-drowning-in-hefty-pensions-and-salaries/story-b9HXPfAXAY1EH8GQ80axSK.html

17 Bharat Karnad, 'Army Will Be without Arms ... If It Doesn't Revert to Five-Year Colour Service,' Security Wise Blog, 22 July 2018, https://bharatkarnad.com/2018/07/22/army-will-be-without-arms-if-it-doesnt-revert-to-five-year-colour-service/

18 Snehesh Alex Philip, 'Veterans Must Know that Rising Defence Pension Bill Needs to Be Tamed for Military's Own Good,' The Print, 6 November 2020, https://theprint.in/opinion/brahmastra/veterans-must-know-that-rising-defence-pension-bill-needs-to-be-tamed-for-militarys-own-good/538189/

19 Laxman Kumar Behera and Vinay Kaushal, 'Defence Pension: A Comparative Study of India, US and UK,' MP-IDSA, 23 April

2020, https://idsa.in/policybrief/defence-pension-india-us-uk-230420

20 Ajai Shukla, 'Air Force Chief Outlines Plan to Solve Shortage of Fighter Squadrons,' *Business Standard*, 5 October 2019, https://www.business-standard.com/article/defence/air-force-chief-outlines-plan-to-solve-shortage-of-fighter-squadrons-119100401549_1.html

21 Pradip R. Sagar, 'Third Aircraft Carrier Absolutely Necessary, Says Navy Chief,' *The Week*, 3 December 2020, https://www.theweek.in/news/india/2020/12/03/third-aircraft-carrier-absolutely-necessary-says-navy-chief.html

22 *Capital Outlay on Defence Services, Procurement Policy and Defence Planning*, Standing Committee on Defence (2017–2018) Forty Second Report, Sixteenth Lok Sabha, March 2020, Para 1.11, http://164.100.47.193/lsscommittee/Defence/16_Defence_42.pdfce_42.pdf

23 *Capital Outlay on Defence Services, Procurement Policy, Defence Planning and Married Accommodation Project*, Standing Committee on Defence (2019–2020) Seventh Report, Seventeenth Lok Sabha, March 2020, 11, http://164.100.47.193/lsscommittee/Defence/17_Defence_7.pdf

24 *Capital Outlay*, 2019–2020.

25 *Capital Outlay*, 2019–2020.

26 *Capital Outlay*, 2019–2020.

27 For a more detailed analysis, see Vikrant Deshpande, *Hybrid Warfare: The Changing Character of Conflict* (New Delhi: Pentagon Press, 2018)

28 Indian Army, Land Warfare Doctrine—2018, Government of India, 2, https://www.indianarmy.nic.in/Site/FormTemplete/frmTempSimple.aspx?MnId=hA7p1YLbFOh5fUss-w4K2PA==&ParentID=vVSuMk049SpFTSaWDyHkNg==

29 Snehesh Alex Philip, 'What is Shekatkar Report, Defence Ministry's First Order of Business After Lockdown,' The Print, 20 April 2020, https://theprint.in/defence/what-is-shekatkar-report-defence-ministrys-first-order-of-business-after-lockdown/405435/

30 General Bipin Rawat in an interview with Sandeep Unnithan, 'Rightsizing Will Strengthen the Army's Capacities, Prepare It for Future Wars: General Bipin Rawat,' *India Today*, 12

January 2019, https://www.indiatoday.in/magazine/cover-story/story/20190121-rightsizing-will-strengthen-the-army-s-capacities-prepare-it-for-future-wars-general-bipin-rawat-1427774-2019-01-12

31 Unstarred Question No. 1795, Lok Sabha, 'Vacancies in Para Military Forces,' Ministry of Home Affairs, Government of India, 2 July 2019, https://www.mha.gov.in/MHA1/Par2017/pdfs/par2019-pdfs/ls-02072019/1795.pdf

32 'Mohsen Fakhrizadeh: Iran Scientist "killed by Remote-Controlled Weapon",' BBC News, 30 November 2020, https://www.bbc.com/news/world-middle-east-55128970

33 Garrett Reim, 'UAVs Could Start Replacing Manned Fighters in Mid-2020: USAF,' FlightGlobal, 28 February 2020, https://www.FlightGlobal.com/military-uavs/uavs-could-start-replacing-manned-fighters-in-mid-2020s-usaf/136978.article#:~:text=UAVs%20could%20start%20replacing%20manned%20fighters%20in%20mid%2D2020%3A%20USAF&text=As%20older%20Lockheed%20Martin%20F,unmanned%20air%20vehicles%20(UAV)

34 Daniel Faggella, 'The Self-Driving Car Timeline–Predictions from the Top 11 Global Automakers,' Emerj, 14 March 2020, https://emerj.com/ai-adoption-timelines/self-driving-car-timeline-themselves-top-11-automakers/

35 See Vivek Chadha, *Even If It Ain't Broke Yet Do Fix It: Enhancing Effectiveness Through Military Change* (New Delhi: Pentagon Press, 2016), 36–40.

CHAPTER 7 VECTORED THRUST: THE FUTURE OF INDIAN AIR POWER

1 For more on hybrid warfare, see Vikrant Deshpande, *Hybrid Warfare: The Changing Character of Conflict* (New Delhi: Pentagon Press, 2018).

2 For details on the concept of TEAM, see Kishore Kumar Khera, *Combat Aviation, Flight Path: 1968–2018* (New Delhi: KW Publishers, 2020), 301–302.

3 Based on the analysis of data in International Institute for Strategic Studies (IISS), *The Military Balance 2020* (London: Routledge, 2020).

4 IISS, *Military Balance 2020*.

5 For more on this aspect, see Vivek Chadha, 'Pakistan's Hybrid War in South Asia: A Case Study of India and Afghanistan,' in Vikrant Deshpande, *Hybrid Warfare*, 37–61.

6 Ben Hubbard, Palko Karasz, and Stanley Reed, 'Two Major Saudi Oil Installations Hit by Drone Strike, and the U.S. Blames Iran,' *The New York Times*, 15 September 2019, https://www.nytimes.com/2019/09/14/world/middleeast/saudi-arabia-refineries-drone-attack.html)

7 'Qasem Soleimani: US Kills Top Iranian General in Baghdad Air Strike,' BBC News, 3 January 2020, https://www.bbc.com/news/world-middle-east-50979463 and 'Mohsen Fakhrizadeh: Iran scientist "killed by remote-controlled weapon"', BBC News, 30 November 2020, https://www.bbc.com/news/world-middle-east-55128970

8 Maj. Gen. S.B. Asthana, 'Strategic Inferences from Armenia–Azerbaijan Conflict 2020, Post Ceasefire,' WION, 5 December 2020, https://www.wionews.com/opinions-blogs/strategic-inferences-from-armenia-azerbaijan-conflict-2020-post-ceasefire-347702

9 Iranian Maj. Gen. Qasem Soleimani was assassinated by the US using a UCAV. However, a similar attempt by the US attack to eliminate leadership target in Yemen failed. In both these case, one successful and one failure, the attacker, the US, had no risk for her personnel. This is unlike a manned mission to kill Osama bin Laden in Attobabad, Pakistan, a decade earlier. There was a risk for the US military personnel in that mission.

10 Dinaker Peri, 'Ladakh Standoff: India, China Finalising Phased Disengagement Plan,' *The Hindu*, 11 November 2020, https://www.thehindu.com/news/national/ladakh-standoff-india-china-finalising-phased-disengagement-plan/article33074294.ece

11 'How Drones Helped Azerbaijan Defeat Armenia, and the Implications for Future Modern Warfare,' The Print, 14 November 2020, https://theprint.in/opinion/how-drones-helped-azerbaijan-defeat-armenia-and-the-implications-for-future-modern-warfare/544668/

12 Manmohan Bahadur, 'An Expert Explains: The Role of the Indian Air Force in Eastern Ladakh,' *The Indian Express*, 3 October 2020, https://indianexpress.com/article/explained/an-expert-explains-iaf-role-in-eastern-ladakh-6618417/

13 Based on the authorisation of 42 combat aircraft squadrons and ancillary units for the Indian Air Force and Indian Navy. Detailed calculations can be read in Kishore Kumar Khera, *Combat Aviation: Flight Path 1968–2018* (New Delhi: KW Publishers, 2020), 247.

14 Based on the planned phase-out of ageing aircraft and induction of new aircraft that are likely to be procured. Detailed calculations are available in Khera, *Combat Aviation*, 266–273.

15 'Defence Ministry Gives Nod to Acquisition Proposals Worth Rs 28,000 Crore,' *Business Today*, 21 December 2020, https://www.businesstoday.in/current/economy-politics/defence-ministry-gives-nod-to-acquisition-proposals-worth-rs-28000-crore/story/425244.html

16 'Rafale Fleet Will Be a Game-Changer for India: Experts,' *The Tribune*, 29 July 2020, https://www.tribuneindia.com/news/nation/rafale-fleet-will-be-a-game-changer-for-india-experts-119541

17 Anurag Sharma, 'Time IAF Upgraded Its Largest Combat Fleet,' IDSA Commentary, 30 September 2020, https://idsa.in/idsacomments/iaf-upgraded-largest-combat-fleet-asharma-300920

18 Press Information Bureau, Government of India Press Release, 'Successful Firing of Brahmos Air Launched Missile from Su-30 MKI Aircraft,' PTI, 17 December 2019, https://pib.gov.in/Pressreleaseshare.aspx?PRID=1596778

19 'Indian Air Force's LCA to Get Astra Missile Firepower, Not Rafale's Meteor,' *The Economics Times*, 21 January 2020, https://economictimes.indiatimes.com/news/defence/air-forces-lca-to-get-astra-firepower-not-rafales-meteor/articleshow/73466978.cms?utm_source=contentofinterest&utm_medium=text&utm_campaign=cppst

20 'BrahMos Missile with Indigenous Systems Flight-tested,' *The Hindu*, 30 September 2020, https://www.thehindu.com/news/national/india-test-fires-brahmos-supersonic-cruise-missile/article32730424.ece

21 Snehesh Alex Phillip, 'India Working on Next "Astra" Missile with 160 Km Range as Mk1 Is Integrated in IAF and Navy,' The Print, 15 December 2020, https://theprint.in/defence/india-

working-on-next-astra-missile-with-160-km-range-as-mk1-is-integrated-in-iaf-navy/566699/

22 Press Information Bureau, Government of India Press Release, 'DRDO Successfully Flight Tests Hypersonic Technology Demonstrator Vehicle,' 7 September 2020, https://www.pib.gov.in/PressReleasePage.aspx?PRID=1651956

23 Sanjeev Verma, 'IAF Lacked ODL during Balakot Strike,' *The Times of India*, 15 December 2019, https://timesofindia.indiatimes.com/city/chandigarh/iaf-lacked-odl-during-balakot-strike-fighter-jets-went-incommunicado/articleshow/72633716.cms

24 Press Information Bureau, Government of India Press Release, 'Quantum Communication between Two DRDO Laboratories,' 9 December 2020, https://pib.gov.in/PressReleasePage.aspx?PRID=1679349

25 Liu Zen, 'China's Latest Quantum Radar Won't Just Track Stealth Bombers, But Ballistic Missiles in Space Too,' *South China Morning Post*, 15 June 2018, https://www.scmp.com/news/china/diplomacy-defence/article/2151086/chinas-latest-quantum-radar-wont-just-track-stealth

26 Chaitanya Mallapur, 'India Tops List of Drone-Importing Nations,' *Business Standard*, 4 May 2015, https://www.business-standard.com/article/specials/india-tops-list-of-drone-importing-nations-115050400136_1.html

27 Rajat Pandit, 'India Leases Top-Notch US Drones for Surveillance Amid Border Row with China,' *The Times of India*, 26 November 2020, https://timesofindia.indiatimes.com/india/india-leases-top-notch-us-drones-for-surveillance-amidst-border-row-with-china/articleshow/79413719.cms

28 'IAF's Mehar Baba Prize, India's First Competition in Defence Sector: All You Need to Know,' *The Indian Express*, 16 October 2018, https://indianexpress.com/article/india/iafs-mehar-baba-prize-indias-first-competition-in-defence-sector-all-you-need-to-know-5404071/

29 'India's First Integrated Defence Communication Network Launched,' *Business Standard*, 30 June 2016, https://www.business-standard.com/article/current-affairs/india-s-first-integrated-defence-communication-network-launched-116063000506_1.html

30 Sujan R. Chinoy, 'CDS Appointment Step Towards Seamless Coordination in Higher Defence Management,' *The Indian Express*, 31 December 2019, https://indianexpress.com/article/opinion/columns/general-bipin-rawat-cds-indian-army-6192092/

CHAPTER 8 BEYOND EQUAL OPPORTUNITIES: WOMEN IN THE ARMED FORCES

1 Ashley J. Tellis. 'India: Capable but Constrained,' in Gary J. Schmitt, *A Hard Look at Hard Power: Assessing the Defense Capabilities of Key US Allies and Security* (Pennsylvania: Strategic Studies Institute, 2020)

2 Sylvia Chant and Caroline Sweetman, 'Fixing Women or Fixing the World? "Smart Economics", Efficiency Approaches, and Gender Equality in Development,' *Gender and Development* 20, no. 3 (2012): 518.

3 Orna Sasson-Levy and Sarit Amram-Katz, 'Gender Integration in Israeli Officer Training: Degendering and Regendering the Military,' *Signs* 33, no. 1 (Autumn 2007), 105–133

4 Sasson-Levy and Amram-Katz, 'Gender Integration,' 105–133.

5 Chris Dougherty, 'Force Development Options for India by 2030' (Washington, D.C.: Center for a New American Security, 2019).

6 Brian Mullen and Carolyn Copper, 'The Relation between Group Cohesiveness and Performance: An Integration,' Psychological Bulletin 115, no. 2 (1994): 210–227.

7 Robert J. McCoun, Elizabeth Kier, and Aaron Belkin, 'Does Social Cohesion Determine Motivation in Combat?: An Old Question with an Old Answer, *Armed Forces and Society* 4, no. 32 (July 2006): 646–654.

8 Leora N. Rosen and Kathryn H. Knudson, 'Cohesion and the Culture of Hypermasculinity in U.S. Army Units, *Armed Forces and Society* 3, no. 29 (March 2003): 325–351.

9 Sahana Dharampuri interview with Paal Krokeide, permanent mission of Norway to the UN, 19 December 2012, Cited in a report titled 'Not Just a Numbers Game: Increasing Women's Participation in UN Peacekeeping,' International Peace Institute, 2013.

10 William H. Sewell, Jr, 'A Theory of Structure: Duality, Agency, and Transformation,' *American Journal of Sociology* 98, no. 1 (1992): 1–29.

11 Sandra Biskupski-Mujanovic, 'Smart Peacekeeping: Deploying Canadian Women for a Better Place,' *International Journal: Canada's Journal of Global Policy Analysis*, 74, no. 3 (September 2019): 405–421.

12 'Army's appeal to J&K Mothers: Prevent Your Sons from Becoming Terrorists,' *India Today*, 9 March 2019, https://www.indiatoday.in/india/story/army-appeal-to-j-k-mothers-prevent-your-sons-from-becoming-terrorists-1473994-2019-03-09

13 D. M. Marvin, 'Occupational Propinquity as a Factor in Marriage Selection,' *Publications of the American Statistical Association* 17, no. 123 (September 1918): 131–150.

14 Ana Swanson, 'These Are the Jobs Where People Are Most Likely to Marry One Another,' *The Washington Post*, 21 September 2015, https://www.washingtonpost.com/news/wonk/wp/2015/09/21/these-are-the-jobs-where-people-are-most-likely-to-marry-each-another/

15 Rebecca A. Adelman, 'Recognizing Military Wives,' in *Figuring Violence: Affective Investments in Perpetual War* (Baltimore, US: Fordham University Press, 2018).

16 Eileen Patten and Kim Parker, 'Women in the U.S. Military: Growing Share, Distinctive Profile,' Pew Research Center, 22 December 2011, https://www.pewresearch.org/wp-content/uploads/sites/3/2011/12/women-in-the-military.pdf

17 Michael T. Koch and Sarah A. Fulton, 'In the Defense of Women: Gender, Office Holding, and National Security Policy in Established Democracies,' *The Journal of Politics* 73, no. 1 (January 2011).

18 Kanwal Sibal, 'The Role of Military Diplomacy In India's Foreign Policy,' *World Affairs* 23, no. 1 (Spring 2019).

19 Ginette Dionne, Philip S. Dale, Michel Boivin, and Robert Plomin, 'Genetic Evidence for Bidirectional Effects of Early Lexical and Grammatical Development,' *Child Development* 74, no. 2 (Mar–Apr 2003): 394–412.

CHAPTER 9 REFORMING INDIAN INTELLIGENCE

1 Ramesh Menon, 'Bhishma Parva,' *The Mahabharata: A Modern Rendering, 2 volumes* (New Delhi: Rupa, 2007).

2 Michael Liebig, 'The Contours of Kautilya's Intelligence Doctrine,' Internal Paper, Department of Political Science, South Asia Institute, Heidelberg University, 2017; Michael Liebeg, 'Endogenous Politico-Cultural Resources: The Relevance of Kautilya's Arthashashtra for Modern India,' Doctoral Dissertation; Michael Liebeg and Subrata Mitra, *Kautilya's Arthashashtra* (Baden Baden: Nomos, 2016).

3 See the report of the Kargil Review Committee, *From Surprise to Reckoning: The Kargil Review Committee Report, 15 December 1999* (New Delhi: SAGE, 2000).

4 Sunil Sainis, 'Intelligence Reforms,' *Bharat Rakshak Monitor* 3, no. 4 (Jan–Feb 2001), http://www.bharat-rakshak.com/MONITOR/ISSUE3-4/sainis.html dtd 22.03.2010

5 Neeraj Chauhan, *Hindustan Times*, 20 September 2020.

6 Bhashyam Kasturi, *Intelligence Services: Analysis, Organisation and Functions* (New Delhi: Lancer, 1995).

7 B.B. Nandy, 'A Tradition of Bungling,' *The Pioneer*, 9 October 2004.

8 IDSA Task Force, *A Case for Intelligence Reforms in India* (New Delhi: Institute for Defence Studies and Analyses, 2012).

9 Saikat Datta, 'Ghosts Who Walk,' *Outlook*, 19 February 2011, http://www.outlookindia.com/printarticle.aspx?270538

10 Ajai Shukla, 'Playing into China's Hands in Ladakh,' *Business Standard*, 7 August 2020.

11 Sumit Ganguly and Frank O'Donell, 'China Is Taking Advantage of India's Intelligence Failures,' *Foreign Policy*, 27 August 2020, https://foreignpolicy.com/2020/08/27/india-china-galwan-intelligence-failure/

12 B. Raman: 'Wanted Secret Agents'; *Outlook*, http://www.outlookidia.com, 19 June 2012.

13 Rana Banerji, 'Legalising Intelligence Gathering,' *The Hindu*, 8 July 2014, https://www.thehindu.com/opinion/op-ed/legalising-intelligence-gathering/article6186885.ece

14 Christopher Andrew, *The Defence of the Realm: The Authorized History of MI 5* (London: Allen Lane/Penguin, 2009) and Keith Jefferey, *MI 6: The History of the Secret Intelligence Service (1909–1949)* (London: Bloomsbury, 2010).

15 Hans Born and Ian Leigh, *Making Intelligence Accountable: Legal Standards and Best Practice for Oversight of Intelligence*

Agencies (Oslo: Publishing House of the Parliament of Norway, 2005).

16 Manoj Joshi and Pushan Das, 'India's Intelligence Agencies in Need of Reform and Oversight,' ORF Issue Brief 98, July 2015, www.orfonline.org

17 Observer Research Foundation, Seminar on Enabling Intelligence in India: Autonomy, Accountability and Oversight, 28 July 2011, http://www.indiastrategic.in/topstories1112_Bill_on_intelligence.htm

18 M. Hamid Ansari, 'Intelligence for the World of Tomorrow,' 19 January 2010, https://mhamidansari.nic.in/speechesinterviews/address-shri-m-hamid-ansari-honble-vice-president-india-fourth-r-n-kao-memorial

19 Vikram Sood, 'Intelligence and Foreign Policy: India and the World in 2050,' in Arvind Gupta and Anil Wadhwa, *India's Foreign Policy: Surviving in a Turbulent World* (New Delhi: SAGE, 2020), 174.

20 'Vohra: Bipartisan National Security Policy imperative,' *The Tribune*, 3 December 2014, https://www.tribuneindia.com/news/archive/features/vohra-bipartisan-national-security-policy-imperative-13663

21 IDSA Task Force, *A Case for Intelligence Reforms*, Chapter 9 (New Delhi: Institute of Defence Studies and Analyses, 2012).

22 Ritu Sarin, 'Govt Gets Its Blueprint for Revamp of Intelligence,' *Indian Express*, 1 June 2007.

23 ET Bureau, 'Counter-terror Centre to be Ready Before '12: P. Chidambaram,' *The Economic Times*, 1 December 2010, https://economictimes.indiatimes.com/news/politics-and-nation/counter-terror-centre-to-be-ready-before-12-p-chidambaram/articleshow/7018909.cms

24 N.N. Vohra, 'Management of National Security: Some Concerns,' India International Centre, Occasional Paper 60, 2014.

25 D.C. Nath, 'Thoughts on Intelligence Reform,' IDSA Round Table, 6 August 2010.

26 IDSA Task Force, *A Case for Intelligence Reforms in India*, Chapter 2.

27 Rana Banerji, 'India's Mixed Success with Foreign Intelligence Agencies,' *Asia Times*, 10 October 2018.

28 David J. Betz and Tim Stevens, *Cyberspace and the State: Towards a Strategy for Cyber-Power* (London: Routledge/ International Institute of Strategic Studies, 2011).

29 Sood, 'Intelligence and Foreign Policy,' 167.

30 Rick Yanuzzi, 'In-Q-Tel: A New Partnership between the CIA and the Private Sector,' *Defence Intelligence Journal* 9, no. 1 (Winter 2000).

31 James Cook, 'Spooks Come in from the Cold with Venture Capital Fund that Keeps UK Security Services One Step Ahead,' *The Sunday Telegraph*, 19 July 2020.

32 Kilian Vieth and Thorsten Wetzling, 'Data-driven Intelligence Oversight :Recommendations for a System Update,' Stiftung Neue Verantworting, November 2019.

33 B.B. Nandy, 'I Spy, No Need for Reform!' *The Statesman*, 29 April 2004.

34 B.B. Nandy, `Bumbling Intelligence,' *The Statesman*, 8 June 2008.

CHAPTER 10 INDIA'S COUNTER-INSURGENCY CRISIS

1 Vijendra Jafa, 'Counterinsurgency Warfare: The Use and Abuse of Military Force,' *Faultlines III* (New Delhi: Institute for Conflict Management-Bulwark), 79–129.

2 See Sumit Ganguly and David P. Fidler, *India and Counterinsurgency: Lessons Learned* (London: Routledge, 2013).

3 For example, see Arjun Subramaniam, *Full Spectrum: India's Wars 1972–2020* (New Delhi: HarperCollins, 2020), 57–59. Subramaniam argues, of civilian fatalities in the 1966 air strikes, that 'locals vaguely insist that there were several without being able to provide any kind of evidence of numbers'. The relocation programme is not mentioned.

4 For a first-hand account of the failure of attempted political negotiations, see K.P.S. Gill, *The Knights of Falsehood* (New Delhi: Har-Anand, 2008).

5 E.N. Rammohan, 'Manipur: A Degenerated Insurgency,' in *Faultlines* XI (New Delhi: Institute for Conflict Management, 2002), 64

6 Navnita Chadha Behera, *State, Identity and Violence: Jammu, Kashmir and Ladakh* (New Delhi: Manohar, 2000), 84.

7 South Asia Terrorism Portal, 'Datasheet-Jammu and Kashmir,' https://www.satp.org/datasheet-terrorist-attack/fatalities/india-jammukashmir (accessed 30 January 2021). Although the SATP's dataset varies marginally from official records, all figures in this essay use this source for the purposes of consistency.

8 World Bank, https://data.worldbank.org/indicator/VC.IHR.PSRC.P5?end=2018&locations=IN-IQ-AF-MX-US&start=2018&view=bar

9 Rekha Chowdhury, 'Turnout, Dominance, Region, Religion: The Big Takeaways of the J&K DDC Polls,' The Wire, 29 December 2020, https://thewire.in/politics/jammu-kashmir-district-development-council-elections

10 Mufti Islah, 'Militant Recruitments Continue in Kashmir, 2020 Spike the Second Highest in Last 10 Years,' News18, 20 November 2020, https://www.news18.com/news/india/militant-recruitments-continue-in-jk-2020-spike-second-highest-in-last-10-years-3103445.html

11 C. Dasgupta, *War and Diplomacy in Kashmir 1947–1948* (New Delhi: SAGE, 2002), 102.

12 L.P. Sen, *Slender Was the Thread* (New Delhi: Orient Longman, 1994), 19.

13 Karan Singh, *Autobiography* (New Delhi: Oxford University Press, 1994), 255.

14 Cited in Behera, *State, Identity and Violence*, 116.

15 A.S. Dulat, *Kashmir: The Vajpayee Years* (New Delhi: HarperCollins, 2017).

16 Roger Trinquier, trans. Daniel Lee, *Modern Warfare: A French View of Counterinsurgency* (London: Pall Mall Press, 1963), 3–4.

17 Alistair Horne, *A Savage War of Peace: Algeria, 1954–1962* (New York: New York Review of Books, 2006).

18 Caroline Elkins, *Imperial Reckoning: The Untold Story of Britain's Gulag in Kenya* (New York: Henry Holt, 2005).

19 Paul Dixon, '"Hearts and Minds"? British Counter-Insurgency from Malaya to Iraq,' *Journal of Strategic Studies* 32:3 (2009): 353–381.

20 Aloke Tikku, 'Anti-Naxal Campaign to Begin in Eleven Places,' *The Hindustan Times*, 24 October 2009, https://www.hindustantimes.com/delhi/anti-naxal-offensive-to-begin-in-eleven-places/story-CoLqpWbutXwp6iNdGuJk6O.html

21 Pranab Dhal Samanta, 'Gadchiroli to be Naxal Free in a Year: Pillai,' *The Indian Express*, 14 February 2010, http://archive.indianexpress.com/news/gadchiroli-to-be-naxalfree-in-a-year-pillai/579506/

22 SATP, 'Datasheet-Chattisgarh,' https://www.satp.org/datasheet-terrorist-attack/fatalities/india-maoistinsurgency-chhattisgarh

23 Manoj Joshi, *The Lost Rebellion: Kashmir in the Nineties* (New Delhi: Penguin, 1999), 23.

24 Praveen Swami, *India, Pakistan and the Secret Jihad* (London: Routledge, 2008).

25 Praveen Swami, 'Kashmir: Fewer Troops, More Peace,' *The Hindu*, 14 January 2014, https://www.thehindu.com/opinion/lead/kashmir-fewer-troops-more-peace/article5597916.ece

26 'Security forces recover more pistols than AK-47s from Jammu and Kashmir terrorists', *The Economic Times*, 9 November 2020, https://economictimes.indiatimes.com/news/defence/security-forces-recover-more-pistols-than-ak-47s-from-jammu-and-kashmir-terrorists/articleshow/79128056.cms?

27 Khalid Shah, 'Kashmir Militancy: Weaponless, but Far from the End,' Observer Research Foundation, 14 December 2020, https://www.orfonline.org/expert-speak/kashmirs-militancy-weapon-less-but-far-from-the-end/

28 For example, see Gargi Verma, 'Chhattisgarh CM Baghel: CRPF Near Maoist Ambush that Killed 17, but Stayed Put,' *The Indian Express*, 14 August 2020 , https://indianexpress.com/article/india/chhattisgarh-cm-baghel-crpf-near-maoist-ambush-that-killed-17-but-stayed-put-6553890/

29 Praveen Swami, 'Pathankot Attack: DNA Tests Do Not Confirm Claim of Two More Terrorists,' *The Indian Express*, 21 May 2016, https://indianexpress.com/article/india/india-news-india/pathankot-attack-probe-forensic-report-dna-indian-air-force-2808022/

30 Bureau of Police Research and Development (BPRD), *Data on Police Organisations (As on January 1, 2018)* (New Delhi: BPR&D, 2019), 31–72.

31 BPRD, *Data on Police Organisations*, 13–28.

32 Kaushik Roy, 'Great Mughals, Warfare and COIN in Afghanistan,' in Scott Gates and Kaushik Roy, *War and State-*

Building in Afghanistan: Historical and Modern Perspectives (London: Bloomsbury, 2015), 52.

AFTERWORD

1 Pew Research Center, 'India has very high levels of religion-related social hostilities', Pew Research Center, 28 June 2018, https://www.pewresearch.org/2018-06-28_religionindia_shi_420px/

2 Conrad Hackett, 'By 2050, India to Have World's Largest Populations of Hindus and Muslims,' Pew Research Center, 21 April 2015, https://www.pewresearch.org/fact-tank/2015/04/21/by-2050-india-to-have-worlds-largest-populations-of-hindus-and-muslims/

3 Arvind Subramanian and Josh Felman, 'India's Stalled Rise: How the State Has Stifled Growth,' *Foreign Affairs*, January–February 2022, https://www.foreignaffairs.com/articles/india/2021-12-14/indias-stalled-rise

ABOUT THE CONTRIBUTORS

Manoj Joshi is a Delhi-based journalist and commentator. He is a distinguished fellow at the Observer Research Foundation, New Delhi, and the author of *Understanding the India–China Border: The Enduring Threat of War in High Himalaya* (London: C. Hurst and New Delhi: HarperCollins, 2022) and *Kashmir: The Lost Rebellion* (New Delhi: Penguin, 1999). He was a member of the Government of India task force on reforming India's national security system as well as the National Security Council Advisory Board.

Praveen Swami is an award-winning Delhi-based journalist. He has been reporting on regional conflicts in South Asia for over two decades now. He is the author of *India, Pakistan and the Secret Jihad* (London: Routledge, 2006) and *The Kargil War* (New Delhi: LeftWord, 1999).

Sanjaya Baru is presently a distinguished fellow at the United Service Institution of India. He was the editor of *The Financial Express* and *Business Standard* and editorial page editor of *Times of India*. Baru was the media advisor to Prime Minister Manmohan Singh and a member of the National Security Advisory Board of India. He was also the director of Geo-economics, Geopolitics and Strategy, International Institute of Strategic Studies, UK. His publications include *Strategic Consequences of*

India's Economic Performance (2006); *The Accidental Prime Minister* (2014); *1991: How Narasimha Rao Made History* (2016) and *India's Power Elite: Class, Caste and a Cultural Revolution* (2021).

Pranay Kotasthane is the chairperson of High-Tech Geopolitics Programme at the Takshashila Institution, an independent centre for public policy research and education. Pranay teaches public policy, international relations and public finance in Takshashila's graduate programmes.

Admiral Arun Prakash retired as India's 20th naval chief and chairman of the Chiefs of Staff in end-2006. He specialised as an aviator, and during his forty-year career, he commanded a fighter squadron, an air station and four warships, including the aircraft carrier INS *Viraat*.

As flag officer, he commanded the Eastern Fleet, the National Defence Academy, the Andaman and Nicobar Joint Command and the Western Naval Command. He also headed the navy's aviation and personnel branches and served as the vice chief.

Admiral Arun Prakash graduated from IAF Test Pilots School, Defence Services Staff College and US Naval War College. He was awarded the Vir Chakra for his gallantry in the 1971 war. As member of the Arun Singh Task Force and Naresh Chandra Committee, he served on the national security reform panel and, post-retirement for two terms, on the National Security Advisory Board.

Lieutenant General D.S. Hooda (retd) is an infantry officer with an army career spanning forty years. During his service, he acquired a vast experience of serving in active counterinsurgency areas of both Jammu and Kashmir and the North East. He retired as the Northern Army commander, during which he was responsible for handling the disputed and troubled India–Pakistan and India–China borders as well as counterterrorist operations in Jammu and Kashmir.

Air Vice Marshal Manmohan Bahadur (retd) was an experimental test pilot and a cat-A flying instructor in the Indian Air Force. Besides operational tenures in Jammu and Kashmir, he was the head of the training team in Defence Services Staff College and Assistant Chief of the Air Staff looking after transport and helicopter operations. On retirement he joined the Centre for Air Power Studies, where he was the additional director general. Air Marshal Bahadur has lectured at military colleges in India and abroad and is a regular op-ed contributor in national dailies.

Colonel Vivek Chadha (retd) served in the Indian Army for twenty-two years before taking up research on defence and security related issues. He is presently a research fellow at the Manohar Parrikar Institute for Defence Studies and Analyses, New Delhi. His recent books include *CDS and Beyond: Integration of the Indian Armed Forces*; *Kargil: Past Perfect, Future Uncertain?* and *Even If It Ain't Broke Yet Do Fix It: Enhancing Effectiveness through Military Change*. He is on the editorial board of the *Journal of Defence Studies*.

Group Captain Kishore Kumar Khera (retd) is an independent analyst and holds a Chair of Excellence at the United Service Institution of India. He served as a fighter pilot in the Indian Air Force for thirty-three years. He was a pioneering member of the Composite Battle Response and Analysis (COBRA) Group and headed the Operational Planning and Analysis Group. He was a research fellow at the Manohar Parrikar Institute for Defence Studies and Analyses, New Delhi. His recent books include *Combat Aviation: Flight Path 1968–2018*; *Modern Non-Lethal Weapons: Concepts, Application, Legal and Moral Perspective*; *Nuclear Weapons: Untangling the Societal Enigma* and *Chinese Military Legal System: An Analysis*.

Nishtha Gautam, a Delhi-based journalist, has written for several Indian and international newspapers on gender and conflict.

INDEX